"A REMARKABLE MASTERPIECE ONE OF THE GREAT BOOKS"

COLIN WILSON
AUTHOR OF *THE OUTSIDER*

"He took big chances smuggling hash from Greece to Egypt, sailing his small boat by back routes, but his risks were successfully tempered by his practicality, his canny sense of psychology, and his close bond with his crew, who revered him as "Abd el Hai."

"Throughout de Monfreid retains the pureness of a shrewd amateur—that is, a man who has a long-range value: his sense of total freedom. . . . The pre-World War I world which ADVENTURES OF A RED SEA SMUGGLER reveals, with its Chinese hermits, Greek priests smugglers, and bedouins, ought to make it a classic."

VILLAGE VOICE

"A remarkable and entertaining book."
THE HARTFORD TIMES

"A romantic and inspiring saga of daring adventure and contraband on the high seas. An underground classic, out-of-print in English for thirty years, which will undoubtedly evoke that familiar enchanted response from the audience who made Castaneda's *Don Juan* Series such a legend."

DAVID DALTON, AUTHOR OF *JANIS, JAMES DEAN,* ETC.

"... Very good autobiography. Closely observed and tightly written. The author shows himself to be a truly remarkable man. . . . He had a genuine burning itch for adventure. But no matter how exotic the events—haggling over the quality of hash as if he knew the first thing about it, living at sea on top of a boatload of rotting sea snails, ingratiating himself with local officials to take the heat off his smuggling gig, bargaining for water on a desert island—his attention never spaces out, but always burns clear and intense.

"There is a moving spiritual seriousness on every page."

ROLLING STONE

"All Monfreid's work has the same curious magic—of the sea, of open spaces, of far horizons, and of his own unusual personality. There is a distinct resemblance to Henry Miller. He feels that his life is an epic. Hemingway said, "Nobody lives his life all the way up to the hilt, except perhaps a bullfighter." But both Miller and Monfried have certainly done their best; and they have the power to convey it in their books. This is why Monfreid is a cult-figure among the young in France— as Miller in America. . . . *Adventures of a Red Sea Smuggler* is among those unusual books that has achieved the status of a classic without effort, rising with natural buoyancy like a cork. . . . Monfried is genuinely an extraordinary human being . . . probably the last of the great adventurers."

COLIN WILSON

"As with Homer's *Ulysses*, Monfreid's Monfreid challenges danger with wit and cunning. . . . For all its flavor of the reveries of a hashish-eater, Monfreid never touched the stuff: he only shipped it to a peasant society that craved stimulants to supplement their poor diets.

"He got his kicks jousting with partner-adversaries and struggling to understand where their notions of honor collided with the equally honored law of nature-survival. Gorgis, his businessman connection and the middleman Stavros hustle Monfreid throughout, yet Monfreid refuses to explain them away simply by throwing glib 'psychological' subtitles, or by labelling them fatcats or backstabbers. 'I liked Stavros and he had declared himself an honorable bandit but money was after all his chief interest. And he was a man subject to temptation. Better not to tempt the devil, I wisely concluded'—lines worthy of any of Sidney Greenstreet's philsophical asides in the *Maltese Falcon*.

"Enough mystery and suspense here for anyone."

BOSTON PHOENIX

"Hot adventure on the high seas, my friends. This is a true and less-than-tragic tale of smuggling 50 years ago. The author wears the proportions of a great legionnaire, pirating and privateering himself into the hearts of the Middle East! Creating legends all over the place! Outwitting customs-men!"

CITY

ADVENTURES OF

A RED SEA SMUGGLER

by

HENRY DE MONFREID

Introduction □ Colin Wilson

Translated by HELEN BUCHANAN BELL

HILLSTONE
A DIVISION OF STONEHILL PUBLISHING
New York

*The publisher wishes to gratefully acknowledge the valuable
assistance given by Mr. Peter Ariowitsch in
the publication of this edition.*

First published in France as
LA CROISIERE DU HACHICH
Published in hardcover in the United States as
HASHISH: THE AUTOBIOGRAPHY OF A RED SEA SMUGGLER
(Stonehill, 1973)

First softcover printing

Cover:
Art Direction, Harris Lewine
Design & illustration, Stan Zagorski

ISBN: 088373-006-5. Library of Congress Catalog Card Number: 73-80672.
Printed in the United States of America.

CONTENTS

ADVENTURES OF A RED SEA SMUGGLER

INTRODUCTION

BY COLIN WILSON

IT WAS IN June 1956, just after the publication of my first book *The Outsider,* that I drove down to north Devon to meet the writer, Negley Farson, for the first time. As the car turned into the short drive that led to his cliff-top house, I saw him sitting outside the front door, a huge bear of a man, stripped to the waist, and with one leg of his flannel trousers rolled up to expose the deep hole in his shin—the result of an air crash in the First World War. There was a touch of the super-human about Negley. He had been one of the world's great foreign correspondents, with that curious instinct for news that had led him to be present at the arrest of Gandhi, and, when the Russian revolution broke out in 1917, to be actually staying in a hotel above the Red Square. He made me think of Maxim Gorki's description of Tolstoy, sitting under the outspread branches of a tree and looking like some pagan nature god. It was my first personal contact with that curious human species we call the *adventurer.*

Regrettably, my only contact with the author of this book has been through our correspondence and, yet, the impression that comes to me through the pages of his autobiographies, is oddly reminiscent of Negley Farson. There is that same love of the strange and the distant, that same touch of the non-human, as if he is some kind of alien on our planet. Negley died in 1960; fourteen years later, de Monfreid still writes and paints at the French village of Ingrandes. But I have the sad suspicion that this great adventurer may be the last of his species—our world is becoming too small for such men.

I must admit that I am fascinated by the psychology of the adventurer. Undoubtedly, there is *something* a little weird about it. Books like Robert Ardrey's *African Genesis* have made us all aware that one of the most basic of all animal urges is the territorial imperative. Ordinary human beings can never feel really comfortable without a home—some small square of territory they can regard as their own. In writing on the subject of criminology, I have noticed how many curiously "inhuman" murders are committed by tramps and other human derelicts without territory. And Robert Ardrey has reinforced the point with that extraordinary story of "Carpenter's monkeys," in which it was found that among a group of rhesus monkeys taken for a long, ship-board voyage (where "territory" is impossible) the mothers would allow their children to die of starvation, and the males allow other males to rape their wives. But, once the group was placed on an island (where they could re-establish their territorial imperatives) the mothers again would die to protect their children, and husbands to protect their wives.

How, then, do we explain the urge that drives exceptional men like Monfreid to spend their lives as wanderers, moving like exiles amidst alien cultures? Monfreid himself is aware of the paradox, as we can see from the following conversation from another of his books, *Pearls, Arms and Hashish:*

"You cannot always stay on the outside," the governor said.
"But perhaps I belong outside," I suggested.
"Impossible!" the governor snorted from the depths of his armchair. "Unless you are a criminal or an anarchist!"

And later, in the same chapter, Monfreid reveals a certain insight into his motivations.

. . . . I found myself repeating as a grown man the same phrase I had uttered so often as a child, my face among the fragrant herbs of the Cape. "Why can't they leave me alone?" To be alone—was it so abnormal, so unnatural a desire? Was my society indispensable to others? Or was it merely, in another form, the same nagging insistence of my relatives and schoolmates—bent on making all men after the same pattern? . . . For thirty years I had sought a compromise. That was over and done with. Between the governor's world and mine there could be none. We did not even speak a common tongue. To me, that other world, its confused objectives, its preoccupations, its stifling proximities, its 'honorable calling' that permitted so many interpretations, seemed purposeless. My world, the clean world of the sea, was to the governor a secret garden, remote, shadowy, poisonous. The individual and the group: must that necessarily mean the individual *against* the group . . . or the group against the individual?

In *Seven Pillars of Wisdom,* T. E. Lawrence describes being taken through a ruined palace on the edge of the desert by the Arabs. The wall of each room had been mixed with a different spice—cinnamon, cloves, etc.—and the Arabs claimed to be able to distinguish these. Finally, they led him to a room with broken windows, in which there was no smell—only the cold, eddyless wind of the desert. "This," said the Arabs, "is the best smell of all." The smell of openness, of freedom. For Lawrence, it was symbolized by the desert, for Monfreid, by the ocean.

Lawrence's love of the desert, however, sprang from rather neurotic personal motivations: the shame of his illegitimacy and his physical masochism. Moreover, for him, the need for adventure seemed to burn itself out after the Armistice of 1918. Monfreid continued to be a wanderer until he was almost seventy; and, in the late 1940s, finally settled down, it seems, only

when modern communications had turned the Mediterranean, that wide ocean he had loved, into a duck-
pond.

When the editor at the Stonehill Publishing Company sent me *Adventures of a Red Sea Smuggler*
(the English edition was originally titled *Hashish:
The Autobiography of a Red Sea Smuggler*) together
with the suggestion that I write an introduction, I
wrote to the London Library and asked them to send
me more of Monfreid's writings.   An enormous parcel
arrived with thirty or so uniform volumes in French.
A few days later, Monfreid, himself—I had written to
him in Paris—sent me his most recent volume, *Le Feu
de Saint-Elme, Ma vie d'aventures* (*Saint Elmo's Fire,
My Life of Adventures*), in answer to my questions as
to what he had done since the original publication of
Adventures of a Red Sea Smuggler (*Hashish*) in 1934.
However, before long I started to experience some misgivings.   Wasn't all this—sixty volumes about "my
life of adventure"—a bit too much of a good thing?   I,
myself, detest travel, and the kind of adventures that
had occupied Monfreid's life from 1910 to 1930 are
my idea of hell.   One year spent in the pursuit of a
certain Captain Ternel and his ship, the *Kaipan*,
seemed surely less of an adventure than a waste of
time.   I found myself wondering whether Monfreid is
not basically a naive egoist with the typical adventurer's flair for self-dramatization (a characteristic also
to be found in T. E. Lawrence and Archibald Belaney,
an Englishman who lived among the American Indians
and whose *Grey Owl* books were famous in the 1930s).
But a dip into *Pearls, Arms and Hashish* immediately
dispelled these feelings.

At one point during the 1920s, an American au-
thoress named Ida Treat had suggested to Monfreid
that he write his own memoirs, but he dismissed the
idea, explaining that he was interested only in the
present. He did, however, agree to cooperate with
Miss Treat by allowing her to transcribe their con-
versations and thus provide the material for such a
book, to be written by her. When *Pearls, Arms and
Hashish* eventually appeared, in 1930, it was funda-
mentally a book *by* Monfreid, with all those charac-
teristics of style that we recognize from his own *Secrets
of the Red Sea* and *Adventures of a Red Sea Smuggler*.
Miss Treat contributed an introduction and an after-
word, but the substance of the book, though written
straightforwardly and without much art, contains the
essence of Monfreid, conveyed by him in the first person.

After a minimal amount of time discussing his boy-
hood by the sea and his unsuccessful career as a dairy
farmer, Monfreid launches into his Arabian adventures. Like all his books, it moves forward swiftly;
yet there are many moments of calm that add a dimen-
sion of depth. I opened it at random, and found the
following passages:

For three days, we made little headway, rolling on a sea
like oil—a heavy swell and only occasional puffs of wind.
All about us, huge jellyfish stirred slowly in the transparent
water; so transparent themselves, they seemed more like
freaks of light than living matter. . . .

In the east, the horizon paled. A chacal barked. Cocks
crowed on the terraces of the town. A white half-moon
shot over the rim of the sea. Slowly it climbed the sky.

At midnight a little land breeze crept down from the mountains in timid gusts, bringing the smell of sheepfolds and
dried grass—the familiar odour of the African bush. . . .

In those waters, dawn brings dead calm. As the sun mounts, the sea lies a blazing mirror of yellow light, its surface ruffled here and there by passing gusts or bands of leaping fish. . . . Towards ten o'clock, the horizon is barred by a dark line that widens and advances, marking the return of the east wind that blows from the open water when the sun is high.

There are no purple passages, as such: the writing is all functional. But these moments suddenly create the sights and smells of Africa, revealing that Monfreid is indeed a poet, whose aim is to reflect a particular vision of the world. This, I think, is the realization that suddenly came to Monfreid himself when he read *Pearls, Arms and Hashish* and henceforth determined to write his own biographies. His vision has something in common with Hemingway's—the feeling that most human beings fail to *see* the world around them, with its alien beauty and its strangeness, because they are too preoccupied with trivial emotions and the craving for security. His adventures are the material of his poetry, the means by which he conveys his vision. There are some poets—the majority perhaps— who try to capture their vision in brief, concentrated moments. But there is another group (to which Monfreid belongs), like Wordsworth or Whitman, whose vision is essentially *expansive;* it is as if they could go on re-evoking their basic images—the hills and lakes of Cumberland, the rivers and open plains of America —forever.

Monfreid is genuinely an extraordinary human being. This is not something he tries to tell us; it simply emerges between the lines. To begin with, there is his curious intuition or second sight. A man who is out of tune with his "true self" is always running into bad luck, as if fate is rapping his knuckles. Monfreid follows some deep instinct, and it usually works. He has developed a version of the "jungle sensitiveness" that, for instance, alerted the tiger hunter, Jim Corbett—author of *Man Eaters of Kumaon*—to the presence of a man-eater lying in wait. When he pays attention to that warning bell inside himself, things go well; when he ignores or overrules it, they go badly.

A typical example of this intuition occurred on one occasion, when Monfreid fell into the hands of the British shortly after delivering a load of contraband, for which an Arab had written him a receipt in his log book. As he stands in the office of a British major, he sees the log book in the open safe. The major stands at the door, talking to another officer.

And suddenly, by a form of presentiment, second sight or whatever you may choose to call it—a phenomenon that I have experienced more than once in desperate circumstances—I was certain, I *knew* that the major would not stir. Stooping down, I crept beneath the table, pushed the safe door ajar, seized the red-covered book, and opened it. The page with the receipt was missing. . . .

Monfreid's second-in-command had destroyed it, and Monfreid knew that. Once again, luck has been on his side. But how did he *know* the major would not turn round? It seems probable that he was using some faculty that most of us possess—perhaps a kind of telepathy—but one that we have little occasion to develop. Monfreid's books are full of episodes such as this. And they seem to suggest that part of his unconscious aim, in escaping into this life of sea and desert, was to re-establish contact with a deeper level of his being that in "civilized" life might have remained permanently undeveloped.

I must underline another point about Monfreid that the skeptic may prefer to overlook. He was undoubtedly a man of extraordinary courage. In an important essay on Hemingway, Edmund Wilson pointed out that Hemingway's real virtues as a writer tend to get overlaid with a noisy emphasis on physical courage, suggesting, in fact, that Hemingway was inclined to boastfulness. He cited the episode at the end of *A Farewell to Arms*, where the hero performs a marathon feat of rowing across a Swiss lake, as an early example of this tendency.

This is a difficult question; for courage *is* an important virtue and, if a writer does possess it, there is no reason to deliberately conceal it. But, with Monfreid, courage is never spotlighted. When he describes sailing from Aden to Bombay in a ship that was little more than a large rowboat, Monfreid does not emphasize the danger; but the perceptive reader infers it. Only occasionally do we become fully aware of the real quality of his courage.

In another episode, Monfreid is arrested by a British coastal patrol and taken to Perim. His own boat, the *Fat el Rahman,* is taken in tow, but he is allowed no communication with his own crew. He is held at the Governor's residence, from which he can see his own boat two miles across the bay. He begins taking early morning swims from the beach below the Residency, to get his hosts accustomed to the idea that he likes to swim. Then, one day, the Governor tells him that he has received orders to release him. Monfreid can go —but not with his boat. Monfreid knows what will happen if he accepts the Governor's invitation. His crew will be told that he deserted them, and that they can buy their release by telling all they know about his gun-running activities. It becomes urgent that he establish contact with them. At three o'clock in the morning, he slips down to the beach and into the sea. Man-eating sharks make phosphorescent trails through the water. Finally, swimming against the current, he reaches his boat, and pulls himself on board under the nose of a sentry. He sleeps under a canvas until morning, when the crew comes on board. He tells Abdi, his mate, what has happened, then slips back into the water to swim back to the Residency. And at eight o'clock he is once again in his room, ready to eat breakfast.

Monfreid seems to have been bitten by some peculiarly virulent form of the freedom bug and some clues to the problem begin to emerge in the accounts of his childhood. His father was half-American, half-French, a painter of the Impressionist school, apparently successful enough to own a house by the sea (in the south of France) and an apartment in Paris. His mother was the daughter of a farming family, whom his father married for her beauty. Her instincts were anything but Bohemian; and, although they loved one another, husband and wife were in continual conflict. Henry says that in all their quarrels, he took the side of his mother, but secretly sympathized with his father. The child spent much of his time with his mother's family, who owned vineyards by the Mediterranean. He seems to have found it rather stifling. His father was an enthusiastic amateur sailor from whom Henry inherited his love of the sea.

At the age of eight, he went to live in Paris for a time; it was "grey, malodorous and airless" and he loathed it. To relieve the monotony, he practiced balancing feats on the edge of their balcony, five floors up. It was at the 1889 Exposition that he saw the Buffalo Bill shows, which excited and impressed him.

It could not have been long after that Archibald Belaney saw those same Wild West shows, and was suddenly possessed by a passionate desire to go to the United States and become an American Indian. In the 1930s he suddenly became famous as the author of the *Grey Owl* books. I mention Belaney because, like Lawrence and Monfreid, he was another of that very small band of born adventurers, men obsessed by the spirit of the wilderness. But the parallel again makes one aware of the good fortune that seems to have accompanied Monfreid for most of his life. Grey Owl, like Lawrence, died tragically—worn out by a lecture tour, and by the strain of pretending to be an Indian. Monfreid, on the other hand, seems to have possessed a streak of French pragmatism and common sense that served to protect him from the less pleasant aspects of the adventurer's fate.

Monfreid's start was slow enough. When he mentioned his intention of becoming a sailor, there was instant and violent opposition from his mother and her family. (His mother and father had separated many years before, so he had lost an ally.) His mother's family considered him an "outsider." They didn't like the way he spent so much time at the beach by himself. They told him he was selfish, like his father. His mother cried. Henry gave way, and became a model student (although he was expelled from one school for his habit of clambering over the roof-tops after dark). It looked as if his life was going to be an unhappy compromise. He flatly refused to become a lawyer or solicitor, but did agree to go into business. There followed ten years or so of false starts and frustrations. He acquired a mistress and two children, and worked as a coffee salesman for three years. Then, for the next five years, he worked as a "laboratory expert" in a dairy firm.

As he approached the age of thirty, Monfreid felt that his life was drifting by. He resented working for others, and tried to set himself up in business as a poultry breeder. Within six months he was bankrupt. He went back to the milk business, but soon contracted Maltese fever from his cattle and had to spend eight months in bed. His mother had died, and he now met an attractive and level-headed young woman named Armgart who fell in love with him and agreed to care for his two children.

Monfreid decided he had had enough of civilization. A friend offered him a job as a bookkeeper in a factory in Abyssinia. The very name, Abyssinia, filled him with excitement. In July, 1910, he sailed from Marseilles to Djibouti in North Africa.

It was still not quite the "new start" he expected. He found the place too Europeanized—it was almost worse than a French provincial town. He was more fascinated by the inland tribes, but this interest soon made his fellow countrymen suspicious. They were there to make a quick fortune—like Rimbaud a decade earlier—and couldn't understand a man who seemed possessed by an obscure urge to "go native." Monfreid was sent to a trading post in the bush, and took a fifteen-year-old Somali mistress who taught him Arabic. It was in 1912 when this girl was killed in a shooting accident (which may even have been murder) that Monfreid suddenly had a feeling of having finally cut loose from his past, of being prepared, at last, to make a real start on a life of adventure.

Yet he was also preparing to embark on a new career as a husband and, as such, it was necessary to find a way to make a living from the sea. The obvious solution seemed to be pearl fishing. He experimented with the artificial cultivation of pearls and then a stroke of luck enabled him to buy his own boat. One night, a Sudanese pearl diver swam out to his hired boat and offered to sell him a pearl—obviously acquired illegally. Monfreid bought it for ten dollars. He sold it for precisely a hundred times that amount. Shortly after that, he had another piece of luck. He bought a "dead" pearl for a hundred and sixty dollars, and then took the risk of chipping off its outer layer to see if it was, in fact, "dead" all the way through. If he had been mistaken, he would have lost his hundred and sixty dollars. As it was, he discovered a live pearl inside, worth over three thousand dollars.

Monfreid also engaged in some spying activity on behalf of the French governor of Djibouti, taking photographs of a partly deserted Turkish colony at Sheik Said. He found himself in trouble with the Turks, had to hurriedly flee from the Turkish town of Moka—where he was virtually arrested—only to find that the same governor was not willing to offer him any kind of support. This was the occasion when he was told that only criminals and anarchists belong 'outside'—and the point at which he decided to become a smuggler of arms.

He was, in his own small way, highly successful in the illicit arms business. It had to be a small way because the trade was then dominated by a big syndicate. Monfreid declined to be intimidated, and felt secure enough to return to France and marry Armgart in 1913. There seemed to be every possibility that, like Rimbaud, he would soon have enough money to return to France and settle down in a white villa by the sea. By now he had become a Moslem; he was liked and trusted by the Arabs. By good luck, cunning, and skill as a sailor, he was becoming a successful arms dealer. Then came the First World War. Monfreid was arrested and held in prison for three months. A man whom he had earlier dismissed for stealing led the authorities to buried cartridges. Monfreid was finally forced to pay a fine—which took every penny he had —and was ordered to leave the country immediately. He sailed back to France, vowing to the coastline of French Somaliland, "I shall return!"

And this is where *Adventures of a Red Sea Smuggler* begins. It will be obvious to the reader that it is not, in the ordinary sense, a self-complete book; his opening sentence assumes that you have read its predecessor, *Secrets of the Red Sea*. But that makes surprisingly little difference. And if it has no real beginning, the tragic death of his stepson in the last chapter certainly gives it a sad and unforgettable finality. This volume is a fragment, but one of those perfectly chosen fragments that gives an accurate picture of the whole to which it belongs.

It was not long after this that there came another turning point in Monfreid's life. On a ship he met the man whom he would later describe as *"un grand diable d'un abbée"* (a great devil of a priest)—Teilhard de Chardin. In Teilhard he found a dedicated scientist and philosopher, a man obsessed by the problem of the meaning of human existence. This was, of course, almost thirty years before the Jesuit became world famous for his attempts to bridge the apparent gap between the Roman Catholic Church and modern science, researches that were not revealed until after his death in 1955 when, the Vatican finally permitted publication of his manuscripts. Teilhard was on his way back from China and for three months, probably in 1929, Monfreid took him on geological expeditions along the Red Sea coast, the two of them becoming close friends.

The friendship was made closer by the opposition of

the Governor of Obock, who told Teilhard that Monfreid was probably using him as a cover for various illegal projects. Teilhard indignantly rejected that idea. He also rejected a governmental escort for his geological expeditions into the mountains, saying that Monfreid would serve as his guide. The Governor placed a detachment of guards around Obock, with orders to make sure that neither the priest nor the "Sea Wolf" left the village. Since Monfreid's boat was moored in the harbour, this presented no real difficulty: they had only to slip out to sea and go ashore further up the coast.

It seems clear that the friendship effected some deep change in the "Sea Wolf." His life had been exciting —but superficial. Monfreid had impressed the Arabs because he possessed many of those qualities that also distinguished Lawrence of Arabia: singleness of purpose, courage, a certain moral inflexibility, and a quality that could be described as "inwardness." Yet he could not be said to possess true "inner *direction*," for these qualities were floating free, held together only by his remarkable personality. Monfreid now became deeply interested in paleontology and the problems concerned with man's evolution. Once again, luck was with him. He had met the right man at the right time. After ten years of smuggling, he had been in danger of becoming a slave to his own legend: Abdel-Hai, man of action and scourge of authority. Teilhard de Chardin seems to have taught him that, to be a true outsider, one has only to live outside the intellectual conventions of our culture—not, necessarily, outside the law.

It must have been also at about this time that Ida Treat came to Djibouti in the course of a Mediterranean cruise. While her ship lay outside the harbour in quarantine, a sailboat passed by. She was struck by the sight of the lean, muscular European at the helm, and by the pretty blond girl who sat beside him—his daughter. The passengers waved to him—evidently he was some kind of celebrity. This, she learned, was the legendary Abd-el-Hai, "the most remarkable figure from Suez to Bombay." "I would be merciless if I could catch him red-handed," an official at the next table snorted irritably. "But my dear fellow," another passenger promptly retorted, "you never will." As she listened to the gossip Miss Treat's appetite was whetted.

A year later, Miss Treat chanced to see Monfreid again, this time in a Paris museum of paleontology in company with "a tall scientist in ecclesiastical black," obviously Teilhard. And so the acquaintance with Teilhard had led Monfreid accidentally to a second turning point in his life. Miss Treat, thoroughly fascinated, told Monfreid she was interested in writing a book about him. Monfreid agreed, and they spent a great deal of the following year together—in Monfreid's house and on his boat—working on the book that became *Pearls, Arms and Hashish*.

Now it is guesswork on my part—but, I believe, a pretty reliable guess—that Monfreid read *Pearls, Arms and Hashish,* thought of all that had been left out, all he had forgotten to say, and decided that he may as well set the record straight with a more detailed autobiography. Besides, it must have struck him that he had no need for an amanuensis; Miss Treat had taken down the story in his own words—up to his *"charras"* episode. The result was *Secrets of the Red Sea, Adventures of a Red Sea Smuggler* and thirty or so other volumes describing his African adventures; after which he wrote a detailed account of his earlier years in eleven volumes, under the title *Towards Adventure*. His most recent volume, *Le Feu de Saint-*

XXVI ADVENTURES OF A RED SEA SMUGGLER

Elme, is an attempt at a one-volume compression of all the previous volumes, and is certainly indispensable reading for all his admirers.

All Monfreid's work has the same curious magic—of the sea, of open spaces, of far horizons, and of his own unusual personality. There is a distinct resemblance to Henry Miller. He feels that his life is an epic. Hemingway said, "Nobody lives his life all the way up to the hilt, except perhaps a bullfighter." But both Miller and Monfreid have certainly done their best; and they have the power to convey it in their books. This is why Monfreid is a cult-figure among the young in France—as Miller is in America. And it would also be true to say, I think, that Monfreid's readers identify with Monfreid himself rather than with any of his particular adventures; that is to say, they are less inclined to feel "I wish I'd done that" than "I wish I was that sort of person." *Adventures of a Red Sea Smuggler* is among those unusual books that has achieved the status of a classic without effort, rising with natural buoyancy like a cork.

Monfreid's adventures with drug-running did not end with the events described in this book. In one of its last chapters he describes his meeting with the Creole Captain Ternel, late of the Anglo–Indian Navy. When the cultivation of marijuana was forbidden in Greece at the end of the war, Monfreid discovered that it was still legal to buy another variety, called *charras,* in India. Ternel, who lived in Bombay, became his agent. This time, the Mediterranean drug syndicate made a more determined effort to force Monfreid out of the business. They bribed Ternel to steal the cargo —six tons of *charras*—and to flee with it on a steamer specially purchased for this purpose. But the syndicate was not actually intending to rob Monfreid; they told him they had his *charras* and would pay him a fair

price. Monfreid dug in his heels. For once, he had
the law on his side. He sent off dozens of cables and
finally tracked the steamer to the Seychelles, where he
succeeded in having the cargo seized by the authorities.
By now his *charras* had doubled in quantity—Ternel
had used Monfreid's permit to buy another six tons.
Monfreid regarded this as the spoils of war, having
spent a year in chasing the pirate. But he still had a
problem: his cables had alerted the whole Mediterranean to the cargo of hashish. It was seized for a
period by the Abyssinian government (at the request
of the British) and threatened with destruction. Monfreid at last succeeded in getting it released by explaining that he intended to send it to Hamburg and to sell
it to a German manufacturer of chemicals; moreover,
he intended to transport it from Aden in a British ship.
And, in due course, the twelve tons of *charras* arrived
at the docks in Hamburg, to be met by police, customs men and representatives of three nations. It was
promptly seized—and discovered to be a mixture of
earth and salt. . . . The "Sea Wolf" again had dem-
onstrated that a fox would also have been an appropriate symbol for his coat of arms.

If I have given the impression that Monfreid's "life
of adventure" ended in 1930, let me hasten to correct
it. It was then that a new stage of his life began—his
writing career—though he was still a long way from
settling down. With the profits from the *charras*, he
was now fairly prosperous. But the emperor, Haile
Selassie, was getting tired of harboring this smuggler,
whose books were spreading his reputation—and his
defiance of authority—all over Europe. He decided
to get rid of Monfreid by the simplest means—assassi-
nation. (It surprises me that no one had tried it before—the drug syndicates of those days were obviously
more scrupulous than they are today.)

One day, Monfreid noticed that a banana tree in his garden had been trimmed in such a way as to afford anyone sitting in it a clear view of his sitting-room window, and of the piano at which he sat every evening. When a gardener—of whom he was suspicious—asked for the evening off to visit a sick relative, Monfreid posted his lieutenant, Abdi, with a rifle pointing at the tree, and then sat by the window, relying on the poor aim of the gardener. A shot suddenly shattered the glass—then there were two more, fired by Abdi. They found the gardener, bleeding, at the foot of the tree. He died as his accomplices carried him off. But Monfreid's goods were seized and he was deported to France.

He was not a man to take this lying down. When the French declined to help him recover his goods, he established contact with Mussolini—an admirer of his books. When Monfreid spoke of his nostalgia for Abyssinia, Mussolini remarked: "I'll be going there. . . . ." The consequence was that when the Italians invaded Ethiopia, Monfreid went along as a foreign correspondent for the newspaper, *Paris-Soir*. (We may feel this was reprehensible; but since Haile Selassie had made an attempt on Monfreid's life and seized his goods, it is understandable that he felt no such misgiving.)

Monfreid was in Harrar when France fell in 1940. An attempt to get back to Djibouti was unsuccessful. In 1941, Haile Selassie, aided by the British, drove out the Italians. Accused of collaborating with the invaders, Monfreid was taken prisoner by the British and deported to a prisoner-of-war camp in Kenya. He was, however, found not guilty and spent the remainder of the war years as manager of an estate—Mawingo —at the foot of Mount Kenya. His companion, Madeleine Villaroge, was allowed to join him there (Armgart had died in Paris before the war). After some years, the two moved to a hut in the forest, and lived for the next three years by hunting. Finally, they returned to France; Monfreid found himself a pleasant 17th century house at Ingrandes, in the valley of the Anglin (he may have been attracted to it by a nearby pond called the Red Sea). Yet even then, in his seventies, he was not ready to settle down. He embarked on a trip to the Indian Ocean in a boat, the *Rodali,* searching for traces of a pirate named Levasseur. In a storm, the compass broke and for two weeks, the world believed Monfreid had finally died at sea, a fitting end for the old "Wolf." But he appeared once more—the parallel with Hemingway is remarkable—to return to Ingrandes and spend his last days painting and writing further volumes of autobiography.

Henry de Monfreid's letters to me, and the inscription in *Le Feu de Saint-Elme,* show a firm hand; it would be impossible to guess from his writing that he is nearly ninety-five. I like to hope that he will live to be at least a hundred; not just because he is probably the last of the great adventurers, but as living proof of Shaw's dictum that neither the brain nor the body will fail when the will is in earnest.

Colin Wilson
APRIL, 1974

ADVENTURES OF A RED SEA SMUGGLER

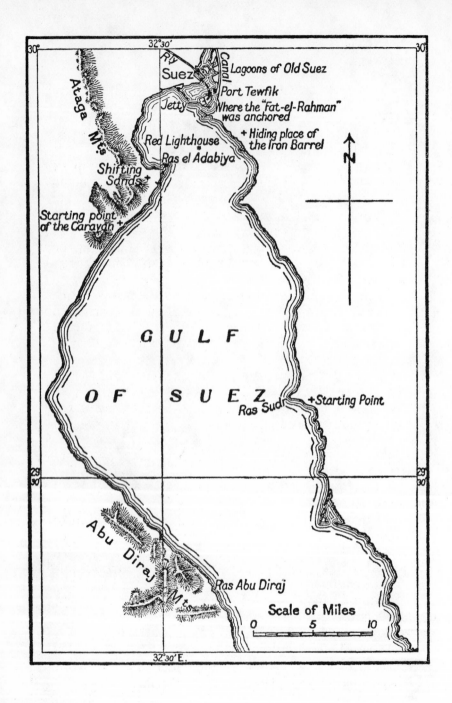

Suez

R^y

Canal

Lagoons of Old Suez

Port Tewfik

Jetty

Where the "Fat-el-Rahman"
was anchored

+ Hiding place of
the Iron Barrel

Red Lighthouse

Ras el Adabiya

Ataga M^{ts}

Shifting
Sands

Starting point
of the Caravan

N

G U L F

O F   S U E Z

Ras Sudr

+Starting Point

Abu Diraj

M^t

Ras Abu Diraj

Scale of Miles

0   5   10

30°

30°

32°30'

29°
30'

29°
30'

32°30' E.

CHAPTER I

MY FRIEND FLOQUET

THE SEASON was now too far advanced to contemplate going to Makalla. Summer had nearly come, and in a few weeks the western monsoon would be beginning to blow, so for the moment I gave up all idea of going to fetch the wood I needed for building my ship. The thought of having to fight my way back against the wind with a cumbersome cargo of planks and beams was anything but tempting.

My dream, though unfulfilled, would remain a source of secret happiness, giving me courage and strength to face life and wrest something from it. For men must always follow a dream, no matter what. If fortune does not favour the old, it is, perhaps, because they can no longer believe in those chimeras, those mirages of the spirit, which the young go for helter-skelter, so sure of being able to reach them that obstacles fall under their unheeding feet, before their existence has been suspected.

At the end of the first volume of my memoirs, I said I would speak at length of the shady means taken by the Government of Djibouti to have me condemned in 1915.

At that time I believed in justice; I had the childlike credulity of a savage. A judge to me was a being of superior essence, far above mere human emotions like hatred or envy, and I could no more have doubted this than I could have doubted my own conscience. But, alas, my illusions soon lay in the dust, and I sank into a quagmire of distress in which I floundered drearily, seeking in vain for one patch of solid ground.

When I read again my log-book written at this period, the bitter words rise from the pages and renew those long-past sufferings.

But why lay forth my misery? What good can it do? Why tear their illusions from those who have been lucky enough to keep them?

My only reason for referring at all to that nightmare of my past is to speak of an incident which resulted from it, and which put me in contact with a man who had belonged to the famous syndicate of dealers in arms from which I had bought my last cargo on credit.

As I recounted in *Secrets of the Red Sea*, the munitions which had been seized on the island of Maskali had been advanced to me by this syndicate. If I had not been a sort of Don Quixote at that time, with my head full of outworn ideas of chivalry, I should have boldly declared the truth, not caring if I did compromise my powerful suppliers, and in that case things might have turned out very differently for me. But I could not resist playing the romantically chivalrous part, and my *beau geste* led to my condemnation.

When I got back to Djibouti and had earned a little money by working as a diver, these honourable tradesmen had not the slightest scruple about taking it from me. What did they risk, since I had been fool enough to exonerate them from all responsibility, taking the entire blame on my own shoulders?

The agent for the firm in whose employment I had originally been, demanded payment for the confiscated arms, and threatened to sue me for the money. All the other members of this honourable syndicate backed him up except one, Monsieur Floquet, who flatly refused to be a party to any such thing. He drew on his head the enmity of the others, for the moral reasons he advanced for not claiming any money from me constituted an eloquent reproach. Finally, the syndicate shied at calling in public opinion, for these people who trample all the virtues underfoot when they can do so with impunity are very sensitive about respectability and their reputations in the eyes of society.

Now when I look back on the events of that time

across fifteen years' experience of men, I wonder a little cynically whether Floquet acted from sheer love of justice, or simply from prudence.

He was a man who had always puzzled me, and the more I saw of him and the better I thought I knew him, the deeper in reality grew the mystery of his soul. At the moment of which I speak I felt for him a deep friendship, which increased as I sensed that he had the same feelings for me.

He was a curious-looking fellow; his colourless eyes, set in a pale face, did not seem to see, and made one uncomfortable as do the eyes of a blind man. He was slender and muscular, and although he was barely forty, his hair was snow-white. He wore it very long and brushed back off his forehead. His voice was as colourless as his eyes; he was generally taciturn, but when a subject interested him, he would suddenly wake up and become very voluble.

His employees quickly established themselves in his business; they were rapidly promoted to confidential positions and left unsupervised. They took unscrupulous advantage of this, seemingly with impunity, until one day for no apparent reason Floquet would fly into a terrible rage and sack the lot. His anger was a nervous reflex like the crazy courage of a coward in arms against his weakness.

One might deduce from this that Floquet was kind and indulgent only from moral weakness, and yet this man was more devoted than a father to my wife and children during my long absences. Nothing can make me forget his infinite goodness to them.

At this time I am sure that Floquet would have laid down his life for me, as I would mine for him. I believed him to be that rare and precious thing in a frivolous and treacherous world, a true friend, incapable of disloyalty, in whom one could have absolute confidence.

Yet at times this mysterious man showed peculiar tendencies, and these fugitive reflections of his hidden soul were terrifying, as are all things which come out of an abyss. For instance, he took pleasure in certain forms of cruelty, and loved to fire at cats sleeping unsuspectingly in shadowy corners. At the siesta hour, when beasts and men were asleep, overpowered by the intolerable heat, one could hear the sharp report of his rifle, then the cry of the wounded animal as it dragged itself away to die. Behind the closed shutters of the veranda Floquet would smile secretly in the dim light, and return silently to his comfortable chair to wait for the next chance.

In direct contrast to this, he was spontaneously and whole-heartedly charitable. He would advance several months' pay to an employee who was hopelessly tubercular, and pay his passage home to France so that he could go and die in peace beside his old mother. Nothing forced him to this generosity, neither public opinion nor mine, for he carefully concealed such good actions.

He would take up the defence of an obscure native, some miserable coolie whose fate could not affect him personally in the least. He would move heaven and earth to help him, even going so far as to brave the Governor's anger on his behalf. What could one make of these contradictions? It was difficult to reconcile the kindness he showed to me and to many others with these disquieting traits in his nature. I was forced to explain it to myself by a lack of balance, a sort of hysteria, and I forced myself to see only great and noble qualities in him. Here was a fine fellow who did good by stealth, while posing before the world as a creature without heart. My friendship deepened to affection, and for ten years I believed he repaid me in kind.

An unexpected spurt of activity in the sea-snail trade gave me the chance to be of service to Floquet. He proposed that I should go to Massawa with my *boutre*, the *Fat-el-Rahman*, and fish for them on his behalf. We made a partnership, to which I contributed my work and the small capital I had left. He provided the bulk of the capital, and undertook the sale in Europe, through a well-known broker in Le Havre who was his customer and friend.

I had just let my other two *boutres*, which were smaller than the *Fat-el-Rahman*, to the Government as coastguard ships. My adopted son Lucien was employed by the Government as clerk in the surveying department. My wife and my daughter Gisèle, now six years old, were living at Obock. They would come with me as far as Massawa, where I intended to put them on board an Italian liner bound for Europe, for my wife was worn out by the torrid climate of the coast, and even more so by the constant state of worry to which my wandering life condemned her.

CHAPTER II

A PRISONER'S SMILE

As soon as we had left Obock and rounded the Ras Bir, the heavy swell from the Indian Ocean plunged my family into the agonies of hopeless sea-sickness. We had to tack for three days to get through the strait of Bab-el-Mandeb, through which swept the north winds, particularly violent at this time of year.

The currents are stemmed only for a few short hours at high tide. The rest of the time, all the waters accumulated by the south-east winter winds rush down in a furious stream into the Ocean.

It is necessary to sail close to the coasts in order to benefit by the cross-currents and eddies; this kind of navigation is very dangerous. It can only be practised by very small ships, and even for them it is often fatal.

One can never be sure how such a struggle will end; one always enters upon it with apprehension, each time one swears never again, and each time as soon as one has come safely through, all is forgotten in the joy of victory. I kept on with this exhausting navigation for twelve hours, then made my way into the inner channels of the archipelago of Assab in order to have a day's calm. Thanks to this rest, my passengers recovered a little, and were able to eat.

The *Fat-el-Rahman* had no cabins; we lived on the narrow benches of the after-deck. At night we slept on the deck itself, rolled in blankets, and by day we rigged up an old bit of sail-cloth to shelter us from the sun.

You can understand that it was not exactly comfortable for a woman, so, in order to give my wife a rest, I decided to put in at Assab, the most southerly port of Eritrea.

The Italian who was Resident there, Doctor Lanzoni, welcomed us with touching cordiality. He was a fat

6

man with a broad face covered with pimples, and his
nose was so voluminous and violet that it looked like
a potato or a very fat bud about to burst into leaf. But
as is often the case with men who have thick lips, fleshy
noses and high complexions, he had something which
made one forget his ugliness after a few minutes.
These unkind gifts of nature often go with cheery and
good-humoured dispositions, and though my daughter
had been terrified at first by this vast and noisy animal,
she was soon playing familiarly with him. He put
himself to a lot of trouble to entertain us, and showed
us round his domain.

We went to see the convicts of the penitentiary at
work, this being the only amusement available. It was
a prison for natives, like the one the French used to
have at Obock. The men were chained by the leg in
pairs, and dirty and often blood-stained rags protected
their ankles from the heavy iron rings. One of each
pair carried the middle of the chain in his hand, so
that they could walk more easily.

These fettered men were working on the construction
of a road. They worked slowly; indeed, all their movements were slow because of their chains. Even the
black Tigrean soldiers who acted as warders seemed to
have caught the infection, for they too dragged themselves about.

'What crimes have these negroes committed?' I asked.

'Oh, nothing serious in most cases, but the law is
very severe. The smallest theft is punished by several
years' imprisonment. However, if they have more than
three years to serve, they generally die before the end of
their sentence, even though they are treated humanely.

'The real criminals, the assassins, are condemned to
solitary confinement for life, for, as you know, Italy
has abolished the death penalty. In these cases, we
allow relatives to bring them food, so that they rarely
survive for long.'

'How do you mean?'

'Well, when they are Dankalis, their families bring

them poison. They prefer that way out. Some Residents tried to stop this by forbidding all visits, but this made no real difference, for with the complicity of native warders they managed in the long run to get hold of poison. So really, it is better to put no obstacles in their way.'

I watched the dreary detachment coming back from work and entering the courtyard by the single vaulted door pierced in the blank and melancholy wall.

One always feels a sort of embarrassment before human beings in captivity, a kind of shame at brandishing one's freedom before their wistful eyes.

They asked us for cigarettes. I hadn't any, but Lanzoni handed me several packets and, suddenly hailing a warder, went some distance off, so that he could pretend not to see that rules were being broken, for these poor devils are forbidden tobacco. I hastily flung over the packets of cigarettes, knowing they would be shared out, for prisoners feel a bond of brotherhood in their common misfortune.

It is only in the hell of a convict prison, when men have given up all hope of being able to exploit, enslave and oppress others for their own enrichment, that their thoughts turn to brotherhood, which then seems to them the sole remedy for their distress, for in giving little they receive much.

Suddenly, one of these creatures dressed in the grey uniform, on which a number in large black figures replaced all that had previously differentiated him from his fellows, turned round. The face on which despair had set its seal brightened into a smile, showing two rows of dazzlingly white teeth.

Where had I seen this face before? I couldn't put a name to it, but I was convinced I had already met this man somewhere.

He was about to speak, but the warder slashed him with his whip to make him get back into the ranks, and I saw him no more.

I went back to my ship haunted by this vision of

distress. I must have recalled to this captive the time when he was a free man, and even now as he slept in the promiscuous heap in the airless cell, he was smiling at memories of liberty.

During the night, my attention was attracted by hails from the shore. A human form was crouching on the sand, waiting. My curiosity was aroused, and I sent the *pirogue* to fetch the visitor. It was a Dankali woman, the wife of one of the prisoners. I could only see her vaguely through the darkness. From time to time, the starlight flickered for a moment on a purely cut profile or a pair of wild, dark eyes. She seemed to be very young, barely twenty.

Her husband had been in prison for a year. She kept prowling round the penitentiary like the female of a wild beast caught in a snare, which cannot keep away from the spot where her mate was captured. She cherished the hope that her man would be able to escape, and until he could, she came every day to bring him goat's milk from her mountain herd.

This evening an askari had told her that the prisoner wished her to speak to me.

'What is your husband's name?' I asked.

'Youssouf Heibou; he is an Abyssinian. His chain-companion is a Dankali from Tajura, who knows you. He saw you when you threw the cigarettes, and tried to speak to you. So Youssouf thought that perhaps you could . . .'

'Could what? Help them to escape?'

She nodded silently.

'That is madness,' I replied, deeply moved by this naïve clinging to an impossible hope.

'If you have something which cuts iron, he could get away. He has been asking me for that this long time, but where could I get such a tool?'

The vision of this man in prison, the haunting memory of his sad smile, the solemnity of the night in these lava solitudes with the sea sleeping under the surf, this untamed woman so true to her female instincts, all seemed to me to partake of a greatness in comparison with which human contingencies ceased to matter.

So I gave the woman the blade of a metal-saw.

Noiselessly she vanished into the darkness, without a word of thanks. Little did I know that she took my destiny with her. My action was to set free a venomous reptile, whose treacherous bite was destined to cost me dear.

In order to make my story clear, I shall sum up briefly the facts that I learned some time after.

The man who had smiled at me, the chain-companion of this Youssouf Heibou, was one of the two Dankali sailors whom Gabré had abducted by force on board the *boutre* with his eight companions whom he wished to save from slavery (this story is told in *Aventures de Mer*). After the adventures already recounted and the drowning of the unfortunate victims, they had been picked up by the Italian patroller along with the crew of the *boutre* which had been scuttled. Thanks to the care they had taken to lower the sails before the search-light should fall on them, their ship had not been clearly seen and her hull, as she sank beneath the water, had easily been mistaken for a *pirogue*. However, some of the officers had declared that it wasn't one. The whole business seemed dubious, because of the presence of this Dankali from Tajura, a well-known slave-market, among Zaranigs, who are just as well-known as slave-traders.

An inquiry was set on foot at Massawa, but the accused had had plenty of time to settle on their story, so they declared with firm unanimity that their ship had been wrecked on the Sintyan reef.

A commission was sent, and sure enough, the wreck which Gabré had sunk there when he was captured was found. Readers will remember that two days after this shipwreck I had taken off the ledger and the ship's papers. The discovery of this document which indicated that there were eight passengers on board would have ruined the guilty men, for when they were picked up they were still horrified at the odious crime they had just committed, and dared not speak of their victims as passengers who had been drowned in the wreck, so they had declared that every one had been saved. I had unwittingly destroyed the proof that they were lying. This circumstance fitted in with their story, for there was nothing to show that the boat found on the Sintyan reef was not theirs.

A verdict of 'Not proven' was returned, and the entire Arab crew immediately hastened from the country, their consciences not being sufficiently clear to allow them to remain there in peace.

As for the two Dankalis, they stayed to get another ship. They had only been lookers-on at this drama, which seemed ordinary enough to them, and in their simplicity, since they had done nothing wrong, they imagined they had nothing to fear.

But alas, human justice is not so subtle, but strikes blindly. Some days after the verdict had been given, the authorities at Massawa were informed that an over-turned ship had been cast up by the sea on the beach at Beilul. The remains of two corpses were mixed up in the wreckage, and it could be seen that their hands were fettered.

This discovery led to a reopening of the enquiry, and the two unlucky sailors, who were still at Massawa, were immediately arrested. Skilfully questioned, they contradicted themselves, admitted part of the truth, then took refuge in obstinate denials of things which had been fully proved, as all negroes do.

They were condemned to ten years' hard labour and sent to Assab.

One died a month later, and the other became the chain-companion of Youssouf or Joseph Heibou, whose wife had come to see me this evening on the beach at Assab. This Dankali sailor knew me because he had seen me several times at Djibouti, and it was his poor smile which was to give the signal for the drama which fate had timed to begin with the escape of his companion, whom I did not know.

This Youssouf Heibou was a Tigrean whose spying activities had landed him in prison. As usual, he had been a pupil of the mission school. It is most discouraging to note how often the only result of the undeniably self-sacrificing efforts of the missionaries is to produce odious Tartuffes endowed with all the vices. This is not the fault of the missionaries; it is due to the mentality of these primitive races. They cannot understand the practical virtues of the Christian religion, and the cult of dissimulation is all they learn from it.

Joseph, once in possession of my saw-blade, had only to wait his chance. His chain-companion readily agreed to try his luck with him. The chain had to be cut during working hours, for at night it was removed, and there were always warders on the look-out at this moment.

The weeks passed, but they passed almost joyously, gilded by the hope of freedom which made all hardships easy to bear.

One day, Joseph and his companion happened to be at the end of a team of workers engaged in digging a trench. A warder supervised them from a bank where he was sitting drowsing, overcome by the heat. Joseph realized that his hour had come. In a few minutes he had sawn through the padlock. His legs were now free, but his unfortunate companion still had the whole length of the chain attached to his right leg. In vain he implored Heibou to cut open his padlock too, the Tigrean thought of nothing but his own freedom.

Paying no attention to the prayers of his comrade, he fled between the rocks; then when he reached the shelter of a clump of mimosas he wheeled sharply round, and sped like an arrow towards the mountains. The unhappy Dankali, abandoned, could not resist trying to make a bid for liberty. He held his chain in his hand, so as to be able to run, but the noise he made woke the warder up. The latter, dazed with sleep, did not immediately realize what had happened. The convicts were working with unusual ardour, even forgetting the songs which generally accompanied their labour. This feverish and silent activity astonished him, but he had still no suspicion of what had happened. Mechanically, he counted the workers. There were two missing.

'They went over there,' said one of the convicts, pointing in an opposite direction, 'no doubt to relieve themselves.'

In a second, a shrill blast from the warder's whistle had galvanized into life the little troop of armed soldiers which guarded the convicts. Off they went in pursuit of the fugitives across the chaos of rocks and mimosa. From time to time, a red tarboosh could be seen bobbing on the heights, then all disappeared into the mountains. The minutes dragged painfully by. Then a distant shot was heard, followed by three others, and the heavy silence fell again.

The convicts waited.

At last, the troop could be seen afar off, heading for home. Two of the soldiers were carrying a limp burden. It was the luckless Dankali, whose back had been broken by a bullet. Hindered in his progress by his chain, he had been seen. The pursuers rushed after him. In spite of the twenty-five pounds of iron he was dragging after him, he had maintained his start, for he was running for his life. A deep ravine barred his way, and in his desperation he threw himself from the perpendicular wall and rolled down, carrying blocks of stone with him as he fell. By a miracle he arrived alive at the foot. This time, he had a very long start, for nobody dared to follow him in his crazy leap. But from the top of the cliff the soldiers fired at him as he ran out from cover over the sands of the river-bed. The first three shots missed him, but the fourth killed him on the spot.

Heibou had got safely away. He had known what

he was doing when he had left his unlucky comrade hampered by his chain. He had calculated that the capture of the Dankali would occupy the soldiers long enough to let him get clear away, and that is exactly what happened.

So that was what my saw had been used for. I had given it out of pity for a heartrending smile, it had cost the unhappy wretch his life and saved a low scoundrel. This was the beginning of a sinister affair; but the time has not come yet to relate it—we must follow the chain of events.

CHAPTER III

THE TROCAS FISHERS

I INSTALLED a collapsible hut near Massawa, on the Ras Madour, at the foot of the great lighthouse, and there I left my wife and my daughter Gisèle. In this way I could see them sometimes during the trocas-fishing expedition, which would last for about four months.

The life of the trocas fishers is spent in the horrible stench of these big sea snails rotting in the hold. Of all filthy odours, this one is easily first, being almost unimaginably foul.

We should take two or three months to fill the boat, which had no deck, so we had to live right on top of the putrefying mass. We ate, drank and slept there, and we finished up by becoming absolutely insensible to the smell. Tiny black flies were hatched out in clouds from this putrefaction, and surrounded the ship like a living veil. No wind was violent enough to drive them away, and only during the night did we have a respite from them. These horrible little creatures got into our ears, noses and mouths. If we tried to drive them away, we only squashed them, for they stuck like glue and did not fly away. They fell into all our food, and we ate them by the hundred. At first we spat them out with disgust, but soon we got tired of struggling against this tenacious plague, so we just swallowed them resignedly, and finally got so used to them that we no longer noticed them, just as we no longer smelt the vile stench.

A ship laden with trocas can be scented six miles away if one passes to windward of her, and when the crew go ashore, in spite of the most minute and careful washing, their hair, skin and clothing hold the smell for several days.

These trocas fishers do not consort with the divers, who despise them as the skilled workman despises the navvy, and consider their work rough and lacking in art. Generally they are Dankalis from the coast, very simple and primitive men, who are capable of doing the most repugnant work without the slightest feeling of disgust.

The work seems fairly easy. All that is necessary is to be able to stay for many hours immersed in the warm waters that bathe the madreporic banks.

The regions most fruitful for sea-snail fishing are situated to the north of Suakin and stretch to the other side of Jidda. There you find vast solitudes where cargo boats never venture. The coast of Arabia, forty or fifty miles away, is deserted and waterless, and only frequented by smugglers or pirates, who follow the inner channel between the reefs and the coast in order to avoid the everlasting north wind which comes down from Egypt and dies away in the middle of the Red Sea.

The ship which is fishing for trocas is anchored among the big reefs which spread over the surface of the water like great tables, separated from each other by winding straits. In the summer months the sea-level is about two feet lower than in winter; therefore, summer, when the men can get a footing on the reefs, is the trocas-fishing season. Even under the best conditions they are generally in water up to their waists and often up to their armpits. They advance slowly, pushing before them a box with one side made of glass, which they place against the surface of the water in order to get a better view of the bottom. Whenever they see a trocas, they have to plunge their entire body under water in order to seize it; they are always white with salt, for the burning wind and the sun dry in a few seconds the salt water left on their skins.

The reef is a complicated world teeming with intense life. Its surface is covered with holes hidden under trap-doors of brittle coral which give way under your bare feet and take the skin all off your legs. The bottom of the black openings is alive with venomous sea-urchins, which at the slightest contact strike out with their slender tentacles. Venomous fishes, whose bites are often mortal, sleep in the warm water. The most terrible variety hides under the rocks and cannot be distinguished from the seaweed. Others, motionless in the crystalline, sun-bathed water, undulate their many-coloured fins like the airy feathers of marvellous birds. The fishers sing loudly and churn up the water in order to put these dangerous inhabitants of the coral forest to flight. When the tide is high, all the fishers return to their ships, the only refuge in these solitudes out of sight of land.

A sail stretched over a few spars serves them as a tent, and there the poor fellows lie, enjoying their rest and listening to the monotonous music of the tamboura, indifferent to the sticky flies, the sizzling heat rising from the surface of the water, and the stench they are breathing. They slowly savour a cupful of a decoction made from coffee-bark, which is always brackish because of the stagnant water in the wooden barrels. But the peppery taste of the ginger flavouring gives them the illusion of a delicious drink.

The rashes on their skins smart from the salt, so they rub them with chewed tobacco. They all have these rashes, which are caused by contact with a kind of colourless jelly-fish, which is invisible in the water, and the touch of which sets up a very painful irritation like that produced by nettles, which turns into a pruriginous rash. Nearly all of them have phagedenic wounds on their legs. This tropical disease gradually eats away the flesh right in to the bone, and to these indolent wounds they apply thin plates of lead or brass.

In spite of myself I thought of life on the galleys when I saw in what a miserable state these men lived. All of them were gay, however, believing they were there of their own free will. It didn't occur to them that their poverty compelled them to do this work, under penalty of dying of hunger, and nobody had ever told them they were to be pitied. They were blissfully unaware that life contained luxuries which were more indispensable to Europeans than necessities, so without care or regret they enjoyed this passing hour of rest. What a sublime lesson for a civilized man capable of realizing what he has become.

At this season, prolonged periods of calm brood over these inland seas. The surface of the water is like a uniformly dull mirror, on which the flat reefs can no longer be distinguished. The horizon melts into the sky; one is in unlimited space, in immeasurable emptiness.

I had been living for nearly two months among all these *boutres*. Five of them were fishing for me, but there were more than fifty scattered among the reefs, so far from each other as to be practically out of sight. I had got attached to all these poor fellows, who often came and asked me for a *daoua* (remedy) for a sick comrade.

Djobert, of whom I spoke when I was describing the wreck of the *Ibn-el-Bahr* in *Aventures de Mer*, was on a big *boutre* moored a cable's length from us. Some of the men I had in my crew at the time of the wreck were with him. They were fishing for trocas and *sadafs* (pearl oysters) at the same time. As usual they had a swarm of urchins five or six years of age with them, but this time there was a veritable infant among them, barely two years old. He was the son of Ramadan, whose wife had died just before the ship set sail. He had no time to take a fresh wife, so the simplest thing to do was to bring the baby along. And he got on excellently among all these rough fellows, who are so infinitely gentle with little children.

One night, the mooring-rope of Djobert's *boutre* was broken by an unexpected gust of wind, and they were obliged to hoist the sail as best they could in the darkness, and hastily seek another anchorage before the sea should get rough. The tiny creature had been asleep on the folded sail, clutching the ship's cat in his arms. During this abrupt manœuvre, in the darkness and scurry, both of them were thrown overboard without any one noticing. The sleeping child went down to the bottom without uttering a cry, but the cat rose to the surface, mewing desperately. One of the men took pity on it and dived to save it. It was then the men bethought them of the baby, the cat's inseparable companion, and they realized what had happened. After half an hour's searching, the small, unconscious body was brought back. They thought he was dead, but I arrived in time to save him by means of artificial respiration.

This proves once again that there should always be a cat on board a ship, and that it is not without reason that it is looked upon as a mascot.

CHAPTER IV

MR. KI

AN UNNAMED island rises out of this reef-strewn wilderness. It is really one of the madreporic tables on which the sand has chosen to accumulate. Why on this one rather than on another? Probably it is a question of currents, for this islet is at the edge of the reefs, and lies open to the sea. In winter it is invisible, so little does it rise above the surface of the water. In summer, when the level of the water sinks, it forms a sort of horseshoe twenty yards wide and fifty long. There is nothing on it, not a blade of grass or the scrubbiest bush, yet from April to September two Chinese live there.

The divers had more than once spoken to me of these 'Chinas' who traded in trepangs, so when in the rosy light of dawn I made out their hut on the edge of the water, I felt curious and decided to go and have a closer look at these two yellow men lost in the countries of the black races.

Nothing was stirring on the island as I ran my *pirogue* up on the beach, save armies of hermit crabs which retreated in serried ranks making noises like castanets.

The hut was made of mats, and was much smaller than it had appeared outlined against the sky. On the beach was an enormous cauldron set on a brick hearth, a heap of firewood, a pile of sacks under an old tarpaulin, and on the sand, drying in the sun, rows of small objects neatly set out. These were the trepangs.

Naturally, a smell of rotten fish hovered over everything. Our shouts caused some greyish bundles to stir, and several Somalis, drunk with sleep and rubbing their eyes, crawled out from beneath the empty sacks.

While we were exchanging the traditional *nabatba* (Somali greeting), the mat which acted as door to the hut was pushed aside, and a fleshless yellow head of indefinite age was thrust out cautiously. A bare second it stared, then wrinkled up in a smile, and the entire man, head and body, emerged from the hut and came towards us. Only his face was Chinese, for he was clad in a loin-cloth, and his skin was burnt as black as any negro's.

After hesitating remarks in various languages, like a musician tuning his instrument, he finally found the correct note and addressed me in French, before I had uttered a single word which might have revealed my nationality.

Mr. Ki, with exquisite courtesy, begged me to enter his modest dwelling, as ceremoniously as if it had been a palace. His companion had just wakened up. He looked younger; he was probably Mr. Ki's son or else his servant. He greeted us with that Chinese smile which renders the face absolutely inscrutable and devoid of all expression. It is an impenetrable armour, a wall of defence behind which the Chinaman can see without being seen, through the narrow slits of his eyes.

Mr. Ki told me he had been coming there for several years. In September he left for China with his cargo of trepangs. He had a fleet of twenty ships fishing for him on the neighbouring reefs, and he spent his days and weeks waiting for the return of the fishermen. His occupation of preparing future swallow's nest left him plenty of leisure, so to give himself something to do he sold a lot of odds and ends, of trifling value in themselves, but which were greatly prized by the crews of the trocas-fishing *boutres*. He sold matches by the dozen, for example, on condition that the empty boxes were returned to him, and incense, cigarettes in packets of four, fish-hooks and string.

Mr. Ki slept on a mat, and in a corner was an empty petrol tin, converted into a tiny chapel for a little ebony Buddha. Beneath it glimmered the small flame of an opium lamp under its brownish glass chimney. I looked at it with a smile, and Mr. Ki answered me with another smile, but a living, expressive one this time, as the mask fell for a moment from his face. This Chinaman could have spoken by smiles only. He said:

'So long as I have that, I am at home anywhere, and everywhere I am happy. Do you smoke?'

'Yes, sometimes; I have no prejudice against opium.'

Mr. Ki smiled again. This smile meant:

'You think you smoke, poor barbarian, but all you do is to profane a marvellous thing meant only for those who follow the teachings of Buddha.'

And probably Mr. Ki was right.

Then we had tea, a special blend which he brought from China for his private and particular use, whose subtle aroma did not desecrate this sanctuary where Buddha kept watch.

I mused over the immense gulf which separates us from this race, with its so ancient civilization. I had before me the two ends of the chain—on the one hand the primitive Dankalis, finding pleasure in a mouthful of *kecher* and a chew of tobacco, and on the other hand this subtle Chinaman, living half naked on a sandy islet, and drawing exquisite satisfaction from his mental reactions alone.

I felt like an animal about half-way between them, capable more or less of understanding both of them, but incapable of imitating either.

Fishing for trepangs is carried on on sandy bottoms with about fifteen feet of water, in much the same way as *sadaf* fishing, that is to say, from *houris*. Divers scrutinize the bottom through a *mourailla* (box with one side of glass).

Trepangs are holothuries about six or eight inches long and as thick as a child's wrist. They resemble soft, fat, round worms, brownish in colour. When they are kneaded gently with the fingers, they get hard and swell out, finally stiffening in a sort of spasm and sending out a jet of water at one end. Immediately after this, they become flabby again.

This curious way of expressing itself has caused this

creature to be dubbed Zob-el-Bahr by the Arabs. This virile name is most suggestive. The Chinese, perhaps because of this strange behaviour, believe that the trepang has aphrodisiac properties. They consume great quantities of them, perhaps from choice, but more likely from necessity, for every respectable Chinaman has numerous wives, and he makes it a point of honour to fulfil his duties in a fitting manner.

As soon as the trepangs are fished, they are buried in the sand for four or five days. There they lose the qualities to which they owe their name. Good-bye for ever to these noble swellings; when they are dug up, they are withered and contracted and permanently flabby.

They are then plunged into boiling water and cooked for about half an hour. Then they are cooled in sea-water, cut in two longwise, and dried in the sun. In this form they look rather like horn knife-handles.

Mr. Ki also bought the pectoral fins of sharks, from which, on cooking, a stringy substance rather like vermicelli is extracted. This is an aphrodisiac too, and if not more efficacious than the trepangs it is at least much more expensive. This is a special food for aged mandarins.

There are many other things in the Oriental seas which are supposed to be aphrodisiac; an atmosphere of the Arabian nights still hangs about them. Despising love, the races of these countries care only for the act of reproduction, and they live to render it constant homage. It is easy to understand, in these conditions, that there comes a moment when it is necessary to give nature some support. In Europe we content ourselves with spiritual affection, platonic love, and so on, when virility fails.

I have never tasted these strange foods to see if they deserved their reputation, but one thing I have noted, and that is that the flesh of the shark most definitely has aphrodisiac properties. When the crew, condemned to the chastity of a long voyage, eats shark, either fresh or dried, the poor cabin-boy has often to stand the consequences. This seems quite normal to the Arabs and Somalis, and nobody thinks of being shocked or even amused. . . . One more difference between them and us Europeans.

So Mr. Ki on his forgotten islet worked for the greater happiness of thousands of his fellow-countrymen. Perhaps that was a satisfaction to him as he dreamed beside his secret little lamp, while the smoke of his drug bore him off to realms of bliss where access is forbidden to barbarians.

CHAPTER V

THE FLIES FROM SINAI

I REJOINED my wife and daughter in the temporary shelter which I had set up at Ras Madour under the great lighthouse facing the sea.

The next business was to send off the three hundred tons of trocas I had collected. Although these sea snails had been emptied and cleaned, the horrible smell of carrion which has caused trocas to be classed as evil-smelling merchandise still rose from the bundles. The Compagnie de Navigation refused to take them on the packet *Roma* due to pass in three days, because the Duke of A—— was on board on his way home from a cruise to Mogadiccio. This annoyed me, for the trocas market was rising, and I was ready to make any sacrifice in order to get them off as soon as possible.

The *Roma* was a small vessel, only three or four thousand tons burthen, very spick and span and elegant —almost a yacht. The holds were empty and I was determined that they should take my goods.

I went to see the second in command, and held a long conversation with him about the evil reputation of trocas. A gift of seemly proportions easily persuaded him that my bundles were so well sewn up that no smell could come through. Besides, the holds had stout doors, and were in the stern, so the Duke would notice nothing. I got a first-class passage for my wife and daughter. Later, they told me the details of this voyage, of which they preserved happy memories. But my trocas gave rise to a comical incident once the *Roma* was out at sea.

At first, all went well—nobody felt any odour; but after the ship passed Suez, strange clouds of small flies of unknown species invaded the liner and made the passengers' lives a burden. The Duke asked the captain for an explanation. He consulted his officers, but nobody could tell him whence they came. Then the second, fearing that the ducal curiosity might prove inconvenient if not satisfied in some way, told a story of how the same thing had happened to him once before as he passed through these regions on a small cargo boat of which he was at that time captain. The flies, he stated, were of an extremely rare species, brought by a special wind from the mountains of Sinai. Shades of Moses!

The duke was quite satisfied with this explanation, in view of the sacredness of the mountains involved, and in the end he did as the poor fishers do: since he couldn't stop the nuisance, he just put up with it.

CHAPTER VI

BUSINESS IS BUSINESS

WHEN I GOT back to Djibouti, I found Floquet very busy on the beach at Boulaos, digging out of the sand immense heaps of trocas which had been abandoned there some time before by an unlucky speculator. This poor devil had put all his own money and that of several others into the purchase of enormous stocks, which he was to hold until the price went up. But he waited too long; prices fell, and he ruined himself and was put in prison by his creditors when he returned to Europe. Later on, the unfortunate fellow blew his brains out, and his trocas were left where they were, on the beach at Boulaos. The sand drifted over them, the years passed by, and they were forgotten.

When Floquet saw that after so many years of inactivity there was a fresh demand for trocas in the market, he exulted. Nobody fished them any more, so there would be a scarcity. He proposed to the representatives of the dead man's family to buy these old shells which, he said, were only good for making lime. Secretly he hoped that the mother-of-pearl, buried away from the sun, had remained in good condition, and sure enough, he found three hundred tons of trocas perfectly preserved, which he was able to send off as freshly gathered.

He sold them at an enormous price. The suicide's speculation had turned out all right after all, but another reaped the benefit, and his children in their poverty never guessed that they had sold their fortune for a song.

This is only a very commonplace incident in that jungle of treachery and ugliness known as 'business'. Floquet, according to its laws, was quite justified in acting as he did. I should probably have done the same if I had been in his place. I might have had a little trouble with my conscience, when I thought of those four children living in poverty, and I might have thought of sending them some compensation. Half of the profits really belonged to them . . . then I should have reflected that a quarter would be ample . . . and in the end I should have kept the lot. Only, in the bottom of my heart there would have remained a drop of bitterness which would have poisoned the rest of my life. Lucky are those who can act in such a way that they will not afterwards despise themselves, and who can live satisfied to receive admiration for virtues they do not possess. These are the only people who should go into business—they will get on all right; but the others should abstain, for they will be victims in one way or another, either of the jungle or of their consciences.

For these only the pursuit of science or the arts is possible, unless they simply till the soil, which is one form of the struggle with nature. But most of them form part of the vast herd of human creatures resigned, envious, or rebellious, who don't realize the great happiness they possess in having no wrongs on their consciences and being able to look every man straight in the face.

At this time I did not utter these fine sentiments to myself, for everything in me was subconscious; I acted on impulses which I did not seek to analyse, and only much later did I formulate the motives which had directed my life.

At the moment, I was lost in admiration at Floquet's cleverness, and was delighted at the magnificent deal he had pulled off.

The price of trocas was still rising. Those I had shipped from Massawa on the *Roma* must have reached their destination long ago, and I insisted that Floquet should sell at once.

'Don't be alarmed,' he said, 'my agent is a prudent and clever fellow, you can be sure that all that is needful has been done, and we shall soon be getting the statements.'

I kept in touch with the quotations for trocas by almost daily telegrams; suddenly the prices began to fall.

'Are our goods sold?' I asked Floquet.

'Sure to be,' he answered, 'for they have been at Le Havre for over three weeks.'

Two days later, the market crashed, and from seven thousand francs a ton trocas fell to fifteen hundred.

Still no statements from Le Havre.

At last, by the following mail, they arrived. Floquet, colourless as usual, announced to me in his listless voice that our cargo had been sold the day after the crash. He stood up to the blow without wincing, like a good sport. Sold at this rate, he lost two hundred thousand francs on our cargo. As for me, I lost all the capital I had engaged in the enterprise.

I could not admit that such a catastrophe was possible. Why had this famous agent waited for three weeks, in spite of orders to sell at once, and then sold the day after the fall in prices? I hinted that there was something not square about this, but Floquet protested vehemently. Besides, the agent gave most detailed and solid explanations, as they always do in such cases. He had sold the merchandise as soon as it arrived, but as he had been told to sell 'in the best conditions', he had thought he was doing right in fixing the payment thirty days later 'at market price', so sure was he of the rise. And indeed, the demand increased steadily, and no fishing expedition had yet been organized.

Yes . . . but . . . the three hundred tons of trocas from Boulaos which Floquet had thrown on the market and which were supposed to be fresh goods had stampeded the speculators; there had been a panic and the fall had been terrific.

A week later the prices rose again, and the man who had bought our trocas cleared over a million francs.

Floquet took all this with disconcerting calm, which I admired unreservedly at this moment. All the same, I wanted to set out for Le Havre to lodge a complaint, or start an enquiry. Floquet did all he could to dissuade me, and finally informed me curtly that he would not be a party to any such course of action.

Just think, attack so powerful a man! He had the Legion of Honour, was President of the Chamber of Commerce, had an immense fortune, the finest house in Le Havre, rich properties and shootings, a magnificent Hispano and a marvellous collection of pictures. He enjoyed the esteem and consideration of the entire town, and his word was law in the Chamber of Commerce. He was the respectable man, the business man of stainless reputation, the accomplished gentleman, and if they did not raise a statue to his memory when he died, the town would certainly one day give his name to a street which was tired of bearing that of Pasteur or Joan of Arc.

The idea that I had been swindled flitted for a moment through my head, but my friendship for Floquet was too great, and my confidence in him too absolute not to banish it at once. I hastily brushed aside such a horrible thought. We are always a little cowardly in facing ideas that will trouble our hearts; we shrink before moral suffering as we do before the surgeon's knife which will cure our ill. We prefer the torture of doubt to the ghastly pain of certainty.

But all the same, this deal left me sick and disgusted for ever with business men and their methods, these pitiless games in which those who know the rules can ruin with impunity the poor innocents who believe in the value of justice, honour, integrity and conscience.

It had been a good lesson to me, and it would be the last. Henceforth, I should conduct my affairs alone, far from the beaten tracks in which the practised hands had set snares.

I certainly believe that there may be honest men in business, but as swindlers so skilfully disguise themselves as honest men, I am afraid of making mistakes. So I prefer to leave the whole business alone, like a basket of mushrooms of doubtful purity.

CHAPTER VII

PORT VENDRES

I was still in this frame of mind when one evening I sat listening to my friend Chabaud telling me about his life as a midshipman on board a vessel belonging to the Chargeurs Réunis. He spoke about the hashish smuggling in Egypt. It was a State institution, it appeared, jealously hidden and kept secret, but with agents everywhere, high up in the police, in the customs service, even in the diplomatic service. Like a flash it occurred to me that here was a new field of action into which I could plunge as navigators of old plunged into unknown seas in the happy days when the globe was not yet all explored. I would smuggle hashish under the nose of this trust. I didn't know the first thing about it; however, that might be a trump card in my hand, for my ignorance would keep me from being afraid. I didn't even know exactly what hashish was; everything would have to be learnt and done; it meant adventure and discovery. I knew only two things—that it was grown in Greece, and sold very dear in Egypt. That doesn't seem much on which to build an enterprise, but it was enough. If I had had all the information one might have thought indispensable, I should probably never have dared to plunge into this adventure. But these two bare facts left me all my courage.

Logically, I should have to begin with buying; the rest would come later. There was no use worrying about possible difficulties to come; they always loom very large and terrible in the distance, but when one arrives at the foot of a wall, there is always some foothold which enables one to climb it.

I remembered the little Greek steamers I had so often seen at Port Vendres, bringing locust-beans to the firm of Santraille. They probably still went there, and might be very useful in giving me the information I required. So I booked a deck-passage on a steamer leaving Djibouti, and twelve days later I reached the pretty seaport in the Eastern Pyrenees, encircled by russet mountains covered with thyme and rosemary.

It was spring; a little snow still lingered on the tops of the Alberes, and a little wind, fresh and pure as crystal, swept down between the cork-oaks, laden with all the aromatic odours which once smelt can never be forgotten, the perfume of Spain and Corsica. Coming as I did from the torrid heat of Aden, where the hot monsoon brought nothing but the iodized smell of seaweed, I breathed in this lavender-scented coolness as if it were new life.

Up on the heights the two towers, the Madeloque and the Massane, watched over the plains of Catalonia as they had done when the armies of the Cardinal were besieging Perpignan. They were only phantoms now, ghosts of the past, still obstinately standing up to the buffets of the tramontana, towering above the high-lying moors with their carpet of sweet-smelling plants. At the narrow quay, an old steamer was unloading locust-beans. A few yards away was the empty terrace of the Café de Commerce, with its two scrubby orange trees in battered tubs and its round metal-bound marble tables. Carts with huge parti-coloured wheels bumped over the cobbles, and over everything was that stale smell of dust, characteristic of ports where it never rains.

I went on board the rusty steamer, over a narrow plank as elastic as a spring-board. A fat man in shirt-sleeves was sitting aft in the shade of a tar-stained awning. He was eating a salad of cod and raw onions, and in front of him was an enormous, pink-fleshed water-lemon. He was the captain. He washed down his salad with great gulps of black wine out of a skin, and when he saw me coming he wiped his mouth with the back of his hand. He glowered sullenly, stuck his pipe insolently in his mouth, and sent forth a jet of saliva which nearly fell on my feet, just to show me how welcome I was. After several attempts on my part at conversation in various languages, this master after God deigned to send me to hell in a jargon which bore some faint resemblance to Italian. It would have been madness to attempt to extract the smallest piece of information about the delicate questions which interested me from this coarse brute.

As I went back over the springy plank I saw a man, dressed just as shabbily as the rest of the people on this elegant vessel, but wearing a celluloid collar, yellow and clouded as a clay pipe, but still a collar. This individual waited politely until I had crossed the slender gangway, keeping my balance by movements worthy of a tight-rope dancer. When I reached the shore end of the plank I mechanically uttered some vague words of greeting. He replied in French. I was saved; this was the man I was looking for. He was the chief engineer, for the old tub boasted a chief engineer.

It was useless to start any conversation where we were, with avalanches of locust-beans showering down on us from the badly fastened sacks which were being swung ashore by the crane. Though I must say that this dirty little man received them on his beribboned straw hat with an indifference born of long habit. I led him off to the deserted Café de Commerce, where I woke the echoes with my shouts. Finally a white apron loomed up out of the shadows and a bald and pallid waiter brought us the traditional can of beer.

My new acquaintance was a little man with an oily face, protuberant eyes, and a flat nose; he reminded me irresistibly of a friendly bull-dog. Without beating about the bush, I asked him what I wanted to know. I spoke as naturally as if I were asking the price of locust-beans, and he did not seem the least bit surprised, but spoke about hashish as if it were the most everyday merchandise.

'My name is Spiro Smirneo; my family lives in the

Piraeus. I shall give you a letter for my wife, and she will introduce you to my cousin Papamanoli, who is a priest. He will take you to relatives in Tripolis who grow and deal in hashish on a very large scale.

'You can trust him, he is an honourable man, as pure as gold,' and he made an expressive gesture as if he were holding an imaginary scale for weighing precious metals between two fingers.

There was no use hanging back; I decided to trust this fellow, follow his indications blindly, and walk straight into the unknown.

CHAPTER VIII

THE VOYAGE TO THE PIRAEUS

NEXT DAY I embarked at Marseilles on the Messageries' packet *Le Calédonien*, which was leaving for the Near East. I went steerage, my finances not permitting anything better for the moment.

These lines are very different from those of China or Madagascar. The fourth class was invaded by repatriated Russians, Bulgars and other dagoes, each one dirtier than the rest. The men were shaggy and bearded, dressed in clothes of indefinite colour, all shining with grease. They looked more or less like the beggars one sees under the porches of provincial churches. You can just imagine the state of their linen, for whenever they shook themselves or simply moved, vermin fell from the folds of their garments.

I couldn't see myself sleeping between decks among this evil-smelling throng, so I went to see the head steward of the third class. I found him in a great state of agitation, not knowing which way to turn. At the last moment, twenty-two Russian women and an incalculable number of children of all ages had been thrust upon him. These were the families of the men in the fourth class. They were Russian peasant women with sunburnt faces and kerchiefs tied over their heads, as uncouth and primitive as the Somali Bedouins, and completely bewildered by the stir on board.

I offered my services as extra steward, and was thankfully taken on. I laid the tables, sorted the silver, and acted as waiter. In return for this I ate with the chief steward the same food as the first-class passengers, slept on a table in the dining-room, and had a share in all the little extras the staff consider their due. By the third day, I had completely mastered my duties; it really looked as if I had missed my vocation.

Fabre was an old head steward who had been tossed about on all the seas of the East, both Near and Far. He was a very decent fellow, and had acquired a mellow philosophy through contact with all the passengers he had rubbed up against. During their voyages, men thrown together by chance indulge in a sort of moral nudism, and lay bare many strange things which they carefully hide in their ordinary lives. Fabre was very amusing on his favourite topic, the frightful trouble caused by that cumbersome, unpacked, dirty and exacting merchandise—passengers.

We called at Malta, a curious town where there is nothing but churches, and the only sound of life is the ringing of church bells. The whole place reminded me of the strange towns one often sees in the nightmares of delirium.

As soon as the ship anchored, a regular battle began between the boatmen for possession of the passengers. These unhappy creatures were hustled hither and thither, and finally one, waving his arms like a marionette unhinged, lost his balance and fell back into a boat. It immediately bore him off with a cry of triumph, and the defeated boatman revenged himself by carrying off his luggage in a different direction. All this took place amid a hail of oaths in Maltese, with many suggestive Arab words intermingled.

The young priests in the second class, freshly hatched out of the seminary, turned vividly pink, and the good nuns covered their faces with their veils and fled under the mocking gaze of an old bearded missionary, who wasn't to be upset by such trifles.

I did not go ashore, for getting back to the ship was too much of a problem. Some passengers had to pay a veritable ransom before they could return. Two French sailors, who had got mixed up with churches when looking for a building of quite another character, solved the matter very simply by throwing their grasping boatmen into the sea. A few strokes with the oars, and they were alongside, and as a tug was just leaving they tied the little boat to it, to the accompaniment of indignant shrieks from the owner as he floundered in the water.

This morning we entered the gulf of Athens. It is an intensely blue lake, surrounded by faintly blue mountains, dotted with rose and green patches, with here and there a white blob like a daisy in a meadow. These were houses and villages, and very picturesque they looked in the rays of the rising sun.

At last we reached the Piraeus, standing against a background of red-gold mountains. In the clear morning light the red roofs stood out vividly against the blue of the sky, and the soft, warm air smelt of lavender and pine-woods.

The fact that this was Greece, land of heroes and demi-gods, lent a glamour born of antique memories to the landscape. I went as far forward as possible, so as not to see the odious modernity of the ship, and smell the coal smoke that trailed in our wake. All I saw was the stem cutting through this blue silk carpet, throwing up curls of white foam, as the triremes of ancient days must have done through this same clear water.

CHAPTER IX

PAPAMANOLI

As soon as I landed I was besieged by an army of small shoe-blacks; I really believe the children here must be born with a shoe-shining outfit. The only way to get peace is to wear canvas shoes.

The carriages for hire were most peculiar, rather like the moth-eaten equipages one sometimes sees even to-day in the Faubourg St. Germain, taking for an airing some very old marquise who disdains such modern inventions as motor-cars. These landaus and victorias at the Piraeus were in the last stages of dilapidation, like the evening clothes hanging in second-hand clothes shops. The coachmen were dressed according to their fancy; most of them were in shirt-sleeves, and wore an immense red woollen sash which they used as a general store-cupboard. Into it they stowed their lunch, when the exigencies of business obliged them to interrupt the eating of it. I should have preferred to see a pair of immense pistols or a wicked-looking cutlass in them, for these men had the faces of brigands of grand opera. They were badly shaved, like peasants on Sundays, and many of them wore old opera hats or toppers with curling brims.

At last I found one who could read and make out the address which the obliging engineer of Port Vendres had given me. He took me to the house of Madame Spiro Smirneo, which was in an outlying suburb.

It was a very trim-looking dwelling, with a door-bell which one pulled. I was received with noisy exclamations of surprise and joy, as if I were an old friend not seen for ages.

Madame Smirneo was a good-looking woman of thirty, as tall and plump and fresh as her husband was little and shrivelled and oily as a black olive. She

pushed me into a green rep arm-chair, and for half
an hour I stayed stunned, while she shouted remarks
at me in Greek, with a vivacity and amiability rather
lost on me, since I didn't understand a single word
she was saying.

At last Papamanoli, who had been hastily summoned,
arrived all out of breath. He was a 'pope', a big, fine-
looking fellow with a wonderful beard, and his towering
head-dress and flowing robes added to his impressive
appearance. He mopped his streaming forehead with
a coquettish pink silk handkerchief, and sleeked back
his hair, which he wore in a neat 'bun'. He had a
splendid head, like that of an Assyrian monarch on an
ancient coin, and his magnificent grey eyes shaded by
long lashes were so eloquent that he hardly needed to
speak. But I was still confronted with the same difficulty: I spoke no Greek and he spoke nothing else. We
had to wait for an interpreter.

Madame Spiro fluttered around, very proud of her
distinguished cousin. She suddenly bethought herself
of her duties as hostess and trotted off at the double,
returning with a tray covered with dishes of rose-petal
jam. This frightfully sweet stuff is eaten by the
spoonful accompanied by numerous glasses of water to
stave off the inevitable sickness as long as possible.

The arrival of the interpreter put an end to our
polite becking and bowing. He looked like a smart
young man from the Home and Colonial and he spoke
Italian. I plunged into exact explanations of what I
had come to do.

The hashish was grown in Tripolis in Morea; nothing
could be simpler, they assured me, than to go and buy
from the growers whatever quantity was desired. It
was a railway journey of about eight hours, and we
arranged to leave next morning at 5 a.m. I spent the
rest of the afternoon settling about the transport of my
goods, so as to save time when they should arrive.

When I spoke about a cargo of hashish as casually as
I might about a cargo of potatoes, the agent of the

Messageries Maritimes was completely taken aback,
but once he had got over the first shock he consulted
his books of reference, and telephoned to the customs.
Then he informed me that I could only ship this
merchandise if I had a permit from the Greek customs,
which would be given me on deposit of a guarantee of
ten francs per kilogram. Theoretically, this deposit
would be refunded when I presented my customs bill
at my port of consignment, but even if I had such a
certificate, I should have to get my money refunded by
the Greek Government. That, I had been told, was
a tough job. In any case, if I had to pay such a
guarantee, I was completely in the soup, for I hadn't
the money.

At sight of my downcast face, Papamanoli smiled
indulgently. He had known from the beginning that
all my attempts to conduct the business would end in
failure. He now took in hand himself to arrange
matters.

We went down to the harbour, and there on the quay
was a certain café, the headquarters of those who
specialized in arranging for the transport of difficult
cargoes. I was amused to note that the majestic,
flowing robes of my guide did not seem to cause the
slightest stir among the dockers and riff-raff of the port;
most of them, indeed, saluted with respect. I wondered
if this would be the case in the Vieux Port if I were
accompanied by an abbé.

We entered the bar in question. It was full of sailors
who had or had not ships, and of all kinds of seafarers,
including many captains of the little coasting steamers
which ploughed the waters of the archipelago in all
directions. They were sitting about in little groups,
drinking coffee and plotting their little schemes, for all
the smuggling and dodges to cheat the maritime
authorities were thought out in this place, and for love
of smuggling, the Greeks are the first nation in the
world, bar none. If I had come in alone, I should
have been looked on with the greatest suspicion, but

as I was with Papamanoli everything was all right. He
shook hands all round with the familiarity of one who
is in a daily haunt, and even the landlord came and
greeted him with marked deference.

From his towering height he gazed round over everybody's head. Finally he seemed to find the person he
was looking for and, waving his vast sleeves in greeting,
he started to wedge himself through the crowd towards
a distant table in a dark corner, at which three men were
seated.

I found myself before a lean and swarthy individual
with a hooked nose from which seemed to sprout an
incredibly black moustache. Never in my life had I
seen so scraggy a human being; he was a veritable
mummy, seeming to have no flesh at all, but only
parchment-like skin stretched directly over his prominent bones. This was the man we were looking for,
this was the *kirios* Caravan, whose very name seemed
to predestine him for the career he had chosen. He
agreed to take charge of my goods as soon as they
arrived at the Piraeus, and transport them on a Greek
steamer which was then in the roads, ready to start
for Marseilles. Naturally, the captain was a friend of
his, which would greatly simplify the formalities, and
the transport of the hashish from the station to the
boat could easily be undertaken at the modest rate of
a drachma per kilo. Caravan spoke Italian, so I could
make arrangements without an interpreter. I tried to
assume an easy air as if I were a hardened smuggler
who found himself quite at home in this strange company. If they could only have guessed that I had never
even set eyes on hashish!

I covertly observed the two men who had been with
Caravan when we came in. They had the sunburnt
appearance of sailors or mountaineers, and were dressed
in the same nondescript way as all the workers on the
quays. A man dressed in this way did not attract the
eye—there were too many others exactly like him; but
it was to my interest to act the detective, and not let

a single detail escape me. The two men for their part
had run a rapid and experienced eye over me, like
men accustomed to judge swiftly and not forget. As
soon as Papamanoli began to speak, they ignored me
entirely, and carelessly got up and strolled towards the
quay, where a customs officer was walking up and down.

Was I a pigeon about to be plucked? I wondered.
Was this Papamanoli a rascal? No, I didn't think so.
I had staked my all on this venture, and the least hesitation would be fatal. I decided to go through to the
bitter end. After all, in such an enterprise there would
always be risks, so I might as well get used to it.

Papamanoli now led me through the rich quarters of
the town towards the cathedral, which was his church.
I could see that he was very well known, and the
numerous deferent greetings addressed to him reassured me, confirming the good impression he had
made on me from the first. Under the vast porch of
the cathedral many ladies, no doubt belonging to his
flock, came and devoutly kissed his hands, gazing at
him adoringly the while. But he seemed to take very
little interest in either his church or his congregation
for the moment; he appeared to be waiting for some
one. Presently, a lady advanced to greet him with
such smiling enthusiasm that I thought she was going
to embrace him. But as soon as he caught sight of
her, his amiable smile faded, and a cold and dignified
hauteur stopped her effusions like a stone wall. She
blushed and seemed a little confused. This was
Madame Catherine Dritza, the wife of the First President of the Tribunal. She spoke French fluently, and
Papamanoli begged her to be our interpreter. She
was a pretty woman of about thirty, dressed with the
quiet elegance of a woman of good social standing.

We had only a few yards to go to her house. It was
a vast mansion with fretted balconies, and the great
bronze knocker on the courtyard gate woke echoes
under the vaults. The door was opened by a dainty
soubrette, and we entered a hall decorated with hunting

trophies. Through it we passed into a provincial-
looking drawing-room cluttered with inferior oil-
paintings, clocks under glass globes, rubbishy knick-
knacks and paper flowers. Papamanoli seemed quite
at home and went first through all the doorways, but
Madame Dritza seemed to find this quite natural.

Once more flower jams were produced, made from
lilies, roses, violets, etc.

I immediately took advantage of the presence of this
amiable interpreter to attack the rather delicate question of commission, which I had not dared to mention
to the dignified priest. I broached the matter very
tentatively, but without the slightest embarrassment
Papamanoli put things on a business footing, as calmly
as if his sacred office included a commercial department. I was much relieved, and as the lady too found
it all quite natural, everything was settled in a very
few minutes, and the conversation drifted to the town
gossip.

How that woman talked! I thought she would never
stop, and I imagined that her husband must be a
taciturn old magistrate, who never got a word in edge-
wise with his voluble young wife. I had only twenty
minutes of it, but I was absolutely dazed, and rendered
incapable of coherent thought. I did manage, however,
to throw one phrase into the gushing stream of her
eloquence, knowing that after that she would do the
rest.

'I have just seen a very strange man,' I said, 'a sort
of desiccated mummy, the mummy of Don Quixote,
perhaps.'

'Ah yes,' interrupted Madame Dritza, 'you mean
Caravan? What a very odd destiny he has had.'

And off she went into a long story, speaking in
French, but throwing a sentence in Greek now and
then at Papamanoli out of politeness. He smiled and
gave his head an occasional shake, looking like a well-
nourished Christ as he stroked his beard, waiting
patiently for her to finish.

It was a most extraordinary story, I had to admit. Caravan, while still a handsome youth, had been accidentally shut up in the Sultan's harem, and so cherished and caressed by the Sultan's hundred and fifty wives that he was permanently and prematurely exhausted. I have recounted elsewhere his prodigious adventure, which is worthy of the pen of Boccaccio.

We went back to dinner at Madame Smirneo's. They dined late, after nine o'clock, as is the Greek custom. It was a very gay meal, under the hanging petrol-lamp; the hostess had done marvels in order to give me a good impression of Greek culinary art. A young man who spoke French had been invited, along with several members of the family, in order to honour my presence with a numerous company. Papamanoli, of course, presided, once more appearing quite at home. It is true that he was a cousin of the hostess.

While we were at dinner, a telegram was handed to the priest. There was a sinister silence while he read the little blue paper, but he smiled to indicate that it contained no bad news, before passing it over to Madame Smirneo. Then they exchanged glances of satisfaction, and he put it calmly in his pocket. I attached not the slightest importance to this very ordinary incident.

It was agreed that the priest should remain for the night, since we had to be off at five next morning. Madame Smirneo seemed quite thrilled at the honour as she got out fine linen sheets from the lavender-scented closet.

I found all these people most kind and friendly, and their simple, cordial manners made me feel as if I had known them for years. They were a pleasant change from the Greeks I had hitherto met—very dubious and unattractive specimens. It is rather a shame that as a general rule one only meets very low-down Greeks abroad, for this has cast a world-wide discredit on this people which at home is sober, hard-working, charitable and hospitable as in the days of old.

My room was exquisitely clean, with its red-lacquered floor and white starched curtains, and a dim light perpetually burning before the gold icon. On the table by my bed I found saucers of the inevitable flower jams, complete with spoons. Really, it was an obsession.

At dawn the whole house was astir. I was called and went into the kitchen, where I found Papamanoli in shirt-sleeves busy grinding the coffee, while his cousin, a coloured scarf charmingly arranged on her pretty head, was blowing up a crackling wood fire. which was sending out showers of sparks.

CHAPTER X

THE JOURNEY TO STENO

WE SET off in the greyness of early morning for the station. At last I should know exactly to what district we were going, for I had not understood a word of the explanations given me the day before in the dining-room. The station was situated in a part of the town which was still asleep, and it looked more like a tram station than a railway station. A sort of little toy train of five or six carriages was already waiting, its doors invitingly open. The engine was puffing about on its own in little sidings, as if gathering strength to begin the journey. Each compartment had one very narrow window in the door, and that was all. These old-fashioned wagons reminded me of the third-class carriages on the train to Perpignan in which I had travelled when I was a child.

A bell was rung to warn any belated travellers to hurry, and the station-master ran out to cast a last glance up the deserted street before playing a little tune on his trumpet. The guard blew his whistle, to which the engine replied by a low groan, and off went the train. It strolled familiarly about the streets of the Piraeus for a little while; friends exchanged greet-ings, women threw parcels to the engine-driver, who also acted as carrier, then it reached the outskirts of the town and rushed wildly off at fifteen miles an hour.

What an enchanting experience is this journey from the Piraeus to Athens at sunrise. The train ran through orchards of pomegranates, and lemon and orange groves. Everywhere there were roses, fields and forests of roses. In the distance the Acropolis stood on its mountain all gilded with the rising sun, and pensive ruins here and there added poesy to the scene. Then suddenly all this vanished, as the train burrowed

47

into the station of Athens, which smelt of smoke, coal-tar and fish.

After half an hour's pause to meditate on the advantages of civilization, off we went again. The line immediately curved westwards round the sides of the blue and rose mountains we had seen the day before from the sea, rising from the golden carpet of flowers. Here and there were pale yellow or pink houses with flat, tiled roofs, standing among olive groves and vine-yards. Great, dark cypresses stood up very still in the clear air. Then we reached a belt of red-trunked pine trees, which filled the air with their resinous perfume, and ever as we climbed the sea spread wider behind us.

Suddenly, as we reached a ridge, the whole gulf of Athens stretched out before us, surrounded by chains of high mountains; the sea was so blue that it looked violet against the ochre of the hill-sides. At certain points the railway hung directly over the sea, and through the crystal-clear water we could see the rocks and rose-coloured seaweeds, fading into the blue depths as the eye travelled farther from the shore.

These solitary beaches are barely skimmed by the waves of this ever-tranquil sea, which seems to spread itself languidly on the sand to sleep. No breaker ever comes to disturb the peace of these shores, which are sheltered by the nearby islands from the deep-sea swell, and in some places the olive trees grow so near the water that their foliage is reflected in it.

Our little train had got up speed, and for two hours we had been running at eighteen miles an hour through this fairy-like landscape, without stopping even at the rare stations which linked up the little villages with their gold-roofed houses to civilization.

About ten o'clock we crossed the canal of Corinth, cut perpendicularly through three hundred feet of rock, sheer down as if it had been sawn. A shabby tramp steamer was trailing along in the bottom of this groove, filling it with black smoke. Once over the metal bridge, we were in the peninsula of Morea, and

soon entered the station of Corinth. We could not
see anything of the famous city; after a few rapid
glimpses of the blue gulf between gloomy houses which
turned their back on the railway line, we plunged anew
into the mountains.

From the foot of a valley hemmed in with hills, the
little train climbed through a winding ravine up over
the rounded shoulders of the hills to a great, wild moor.
Not a single village was to be seen, or indeed any trace
of human habitation. A vegetation of stunted bushes
and rock plants grew as best it could among the chalky
boulders, and covered the spurs of the mountains with
a mantle of heath. Here and there we saw small
enclosures, surrounded by dry-stone dykes, in which
had been planted scrubby vines. Old olive trees with
black and twisted trunks stretched at their feet a
carpet of blue shade on which their owner, tired of
digging the ungrateful earth, could come and drowse
under the silvery foliage in the hot hours of noon,
lulled by the song of the crickets.

Then came herds of goats, stampeding wildly to
escape from this panting train which had dared to
disturb the quiet peace of the heights. The little
shepherd boys in their pleated kilts and betasselled
shoes ran up from all sides to intercept the passage of
the train which was slowly zigzagging up the mountain.
They had no difficulty in keeping pace with it, and ran
alongside, asking for newspapers. The passengers,
amused, threw out the papers bought that morning in
Athens or the Piraeus, and in this way every day the
most distant villages got news of the outside world.
There were very few stations here, and even these few
were far from the hamlets buried in the mountains.
There were no roads, properly speaking, only mule-
tracks, and very stony at that.

During the halts we drank dry white wine with a
resinous tang. It was called *crachi retzina* and cost
only a sou the glass. It was delicious once one got
accustomed to the bitter flavour.

And now the train began to rush down towards Argos and Myli, at the end of the Gulf of Nauplia where Agamemnon once lived. It was now only a wide and smiling valley, with nothing to recall its heroic past, which, indeed, may be pure invention. Herds of cattle grazed indolently among the lush grass. The gulf opened out widely to the sea, from which the triremes had set out for the Trojan war.

The train had now descended to the sea-level, and begun to climb again, but this time into really high mountains. The afternoon sun beat down mercilessly, bringing out an intolerable heat from the welter of rocks. There were flowering brooms and lentisks; then as we got higher, forests of stunted pines twisted into strange shapes, and seas and seas of lavender.

One last zigzag up the face of a blue granite wall, and we were at the top, looking down over the picturesque masses of mountains, whose tops were gilded by the setting sun, while the valleys were filled with purple shadow, and the capes and inlets of the coast stood out sharply against an immense sea which merged into space.

An abrupt change of direction, and there before us stretched the high plateaux covered with green crops, with in the distance a range of snow-capped mountains stained rose by the setting sun. We had reached our destination, which was Steno, about six miles on this side of Tripolis.

A man approached, kissed Papamanoli and then me, and led us to a pretty jaunting-car, drawn by a frisky pony covered with tassels and tiny bells. He was Petros Karamanos. He had a keen, frank face, tanned by the mountain air, and was powerfully built, though without any suggestion of heaviness. He looked like a country gentleman; his calm and assured manner, the authority of his gaze, his simple dress, all bespoke the rich man, owning the soil he trod. He spoke no language but Greek.

The sun was just disappearing behind the mountains in the west, and the air, which had already been very light and fresh, became cold, for we were more than three thousand feet above sea-level. Everywhere were fields of green wheat, apple and cherry orchards. I wondered where grew the magic plant from which hashish, bringer of dreams, was made.

I thought of an old fairy-tale of a little boy sent by a good fairy to look for a magic flower which grew on the inaccessible summit of a distant mountain. Off he had set like me, guided and upheld by faith alone. I wondered if I had really arrived in the place where my magic flower grew, and if I was now to reap the reward of my faith in Destiny.

CHAPTER XI

THE FARM

AFTER AN hour's drive, we reached the foot of a hill covered with heather and flowering broom. A farm with tiled roofs was set against it, facing the rising sun and overlooking the plains covered with orchards and wheat fields. The buildings were of granite, and seemed very ancient. They were as massively constructed as a fortress, with vaulted entrances, and the great flags which paved the courtyard had been worn away by the contact of countless generations of feet.

It was the hour when yokes of oxen returned slowly from their work in the fields, and flocks of black sheep came pouring in at the great outer gate, running in disorder towards the sheepfolds, the ewes with distended udders answering the plaintive bleatings of the hungry lambs. A warm smell of hay and the breath of kine came out to meet the chill of the falling night.

Bare-footed servant girls looked at me curiously. They wore their hair in the local fashion in a sort of coronet on top of their little heads, a fashion marvellously becoming to their clear-cut profiles. Perhaps in the recesses of these wild mountains the antique race has kept its purity, for I noticed that many of the women had the straight noses of the goddesses of old. A hairy groom, dressed as I imagined a companion of Ulysses in the Cyclops' cave might have been dressed, came to take our pony, greeting his master with the humble respect of the serf for his overlord.

Madame Petros appeared on the veranda, which had a beautiful wrought-iron railing. She greeted me with a speech of welcome, punctuated by little ripples of laughter at my obvious bewilderment, which was due to my ignorance of Greek. I was just beginning to feel ridiculous, when an imposing equipage entered the courtyard. Imagine a sort of victoria, such as is still used for marriages in some remote parts of France, but very old and dilapidated, with rattling iron wheels. Two enormous dapple-grey dray horses had dragged this nightmare of a vehicle over the bridle-paths from Tripolis; it was a marvel to me that it still held together. From this ancient but stout carriage descended a swarthy little woman. She was only about twenty, but already had the air of an old maid. This was Petros' niece, who lived in town, moved in polite society and most important of all, spoke French; she had been summoned to act as interpreter.

She began by apologizing for being late and not coming to the station with her carriage to fetch me. She was anything but beautiful, her monkey-like face distorted by nervous twitchings, but the poor girl was so pleasant and amiable that I was thankful indeed for her presence, which brought me, so to speak, out of the darkness into the light of comprehension.

The inside of the house surprised me. It was richly and tastefully decorated, and the ancient walls housed some very fine modern furniture.

Petros went off immediately to fetch a sample of his hashish. I wondered how I was to give an intelligent opinion on it, and not betray the fact that it was the first I had ever seen. I didn't even know how the quality was indicated. I was afraid of making a fool of myself and revealing my ignorance, for after that I could be sure that all the poor stuff which had been unsaleable would be joyfully palmed off on me. I fell back on a method which is often useful. So far as possible, I would be silent. Petros came in with a fragment of brownish matter in his hand. He immediately gave me the clue to how to test the value of his merchandise, by proceeding to sniff it, and hold it up for me to sniff. Then he took a piece and rolled it between his fingers into a slender cone, to which he put a match. It burned with a tiny and rather smoky flame, and when he hastily extinguished it, a heavily perfumed white smoke rose from it. In my turn I took a piece and went through exactly the same manœuvres, only, having noticed how quickly he put out the flame, I on the contrary let it burn. Then in silence, with a cold and rather disdainful air, I held it out to him. He interpreted my silence according to his fears, and instantly exclaimed:

'Oh, but don't be afraid, I have better stuff than this. Only I thought this might perhaps interest you; it is much cheaper.'

I replied with dignity:

'I have not come such a long way to buy cheap stuff. Please show me your best at once.'

He vanished, and returned in a moment with a piece of the same matter, but less brittle and of a greenish hue. He went through the same gestures, but this time the flame was long and very smoky, and he complacently let it burn. That, thought I, is probably the sign of really good quality. Now I knew how to buy hashish. I declared myself satisfied, and we settled on the quantity I was to buy, four hundred *okes* (six hundred kilograms), at the price of twenty francs the *oke*.

'Now,' said he, 'we'll go and fetch the goods from the warehouse where they are stored.'

A servant girl brought us little wax torches, and two hefty workmen armed with huge cudgels accompanied us. Petros opened a vaulted door, behind which a stone staircase led down into the cellars. A musty smell of damp rose from this underground passage, and almost at once we came to a crypt hewn out of the living rock. In this vault, which was circular in form, sacks were piled up; this was the hashish crop of the current year. The two workmen picked out the number of sacks which corresponded to the weight I had ordered, put them in the middle of the floor, then fell upon them with their sticks, in order to break up the contents and reduce them to dust.

We must have formed a strange group. First there

was Papamanoli, the priest, in his flowing black robes, and beside him Petros, holding in his hand a piece of white paper, into which he put a sample from each sack. Each of us held aloft a little wax taper in order to give light to the men who were beating so furiously on the bulging sacks. Our shadows danced fantastically along the vaulted roof, and the bats, panic-stricken and blinded by the light, bumped their horrid, soft bodies against us, making the flames of our candles flicker. I shall never forget this scene, though the others seemed quite unconscious of its picturesque quality. Petros poured the different samples from his paper into a little bag, which he gave me as indicating the average quality of my hashish. The sacks were then carried into a barn, so that the icy cold of the night should prevent the powdered hashish from coagulating afresh.

I went off to my room, escorted by the ugly little niece and one of the handsome young servant girls carrying water, towels and everything needful for the comfort of a guest. I wished my ugly little interpreter at the devil so that I should be left alone with the comely handmaiden, for I felt the need for ethnographical documentation, and the opportunity seemed excellent, but alas. . . .

The hand-woven linen sheets were icy cold, and I could not get them warmed. All the happenings of the day kept going round and round in my head, and the hashish I had breathed in in the crypt had set my imagination afire. I tossed and turned, and finally got up. My room was next to vast attics, certainly the servants' quarters could not be far off. I could always have a look. So off I went groping my way through the darkness, knocking my head against great strings of onions hanging from the beams, and bumping into dusty objects, until suddenly beneath my feet I saw a ray of light, and voices came up from the floor below. I lay down and placed my eye against this crack in the old flooring, and I saw a rustic room with whitewashed

walls, about which two men were moving. They were
Papamanoli and Petros. Papamanoli was undressing
and preparing for bed, while Petros was standing, a
candle in one hand, reading a blue paper which looked
like a telegram. After he had read it, he handed it to
the priest, who instantly held it to the candle flame, let
it burn down to his fingers, and stamped out the ashes
underfoot. A gesture made towards my room showed
me that the two men were speaking about me, and made
me think that this was perhaps the telegram which the
priest had received the evening before while we were
dining at the house of his cousin, Madame Smirneo.

. . . . .

Next morning I was awakened by a humming
activity which filled the house like the murmur of a
beehive. In the barn into which we had carried the
sacks, a crowd of workers were going to and fro
through a thick dust.

In the middle of the room was a sort of table consisting of a very fine metal sieve set up on four legs.
On it the hashish was being thrown in spadefuls. A
big sheet was wrapped round the outside of the table
legs to prevent the fine powder which fell from the
sieve from blowing away. Women with their heads
swathed in handkerchiefs were spreading out and
sifting the powder. After this, men shovelled it into
an enormous iron basin in order that it should be well
mixed.

Madame Petros was sitting before a sewing-machine,
feverishly running up little white linen bags. These
she passed to a woman who stamped an elephant on
them with a rubber stamp. She in turn passed them
to a third woman who filled them, weighed them with
great care, and finally tied them up. They were then
put in neat piles into a great press. When there were a
certain number between the steel plates, a muscular
workman tightened the vice and the sacks flattened
out slowly until they were like square pancakes four

centimetres thick. These pancakes were hard as wax; this is the form in which hashish is exported, and the elephant was Petros' trade-mark. From time to time he himself lent a hand to the brawny fellow who was working the press. I looked at the latter with interest. He was very tall; I could not see his face, as his head was covered with a towel with small eye-holes bored in it, but his eyes seemed vaguely familiar, and suddenly I realized that they were the eyes of Papamanoli. At this moment, having finished, he laughingly removed his improvised cowl, freeing his luxuriant beard and his hair, which had been rolled on top of his head. This priest seemed to take everything as a matter of course, and nobody seemed surprised to see him helping at a busy moment.

This hashish powder had gradually excited the men and women working with it, and they began to sing at the tops of their voices, and joke and laugh like mad things over nothing. I took part in this crazy gaiety like the rest, and even the plain little niece from Tripolis grew quite flirtatious. Fortunately, the work was soon completed, or I don't know how it would all have ended. Outside, a plumber soldered the zinc linings of the packing-cases in which the hashish pancakes were to be packed.

While the work was being finished, the women servants had been setting up a table in the shade of a great walnut-tree in front of the barn. They had put on their Sunday dresses as if it were a holiday, and soon masters and servants sat down together, patriarchal fashion, to eat. It was a Pantagruellian repast. There was a sheep roasted whole, and innumerable chickens, trout, etc. It made me think of the prodigious meals of the Middle Ages of which the old chroniclers tell us. But there was nothing of an orgy about it; those simple people had remained too close to nature to be anything but modest and decent.

For those who are interested I shall describe briefly how the hashish comes to the state in which I had first seen it, powdered and stored in sacks in the cellar. The fields in which the hemp grows are carefully weeded and all the male plants are pulled out. The female plants which remain cannot therefore bear seeds, and the result is that the leaves become fully charged with a resinous matter. The secretion of this sticky substance is farther increased by breaking off the tops of the plants as they grow. When the first leaves, that is to say the lowest ones, turn yellow, the plants are carefully cut down about four inches from the ground, so as not to soil them with earth or sand. Then the crop is dried in the shade and stacked in barns. Some growers only keep the leaves, for the stems are of no value whatever. On very cold winter days when there is a keen frost and the waxen matter secreted by the leaves has become brittle as resin, the dried plants are broken up by rubbing them between two sheets of canvas. This gives a dust made up of broken leaves and the resin which is the active part of hashish. This resin gives the powder the property of forming a sort of cake when pressed, and of softening when heated.

All the farms in this district prepared hashish; it was their chief industry. Each estate had its brand, quoted on the market, and there were good and bad years, exactly as for wines.

My eight cases were now soldered and nailed up ready for transport. They represented all my worldly wealth. After a sketchy dinner, for you may suppose no one was hungry after the midday feast, I retired to sleep the sleep of the just. Hardly was I in my room, however, when I developed an intense thirst. There was no drinking-water to be seen, so I went down to the dining-room in search of some. When I reached the glass door, I saw Petros sitting at his desk, with Papamanoli standing beside him. They were probably writing out a telegram, for several telegraph forms were scattered over the table. I entered without warning, and immediately Petros instinctively pushed a piece of

blotting-paper over what he had written. So it was
something he wanted to keep secret, at least from me.
I pretended not to have noticed anything, took the
water-bottle, said good night and retired.

What did all this mean? I marshalled the facts:

1. A telegram had been received by Papamanoli at
the Piraeus two days before.

2. He had shown it to Petros.

3. To-day they were sending a reply (for Petros'
unconscious gesture showed that what he was writing
concerned me).

I stayed awake half the night, wondering what it
was all about. I felt alternately optimistic and pessimistic, and had great difficulty in controlling my
imagination.

Next morning I was up at dawn. The household
was still asleep except for two bare-footed servant girls
who were lighting a wood fire in the enormous kitchen
chimney. I walked into the dining-room, and went
straight up to the desk at which Petros had been writing.
It was not locked, and amid the litter of papers I found
the clean blotting-paper with which he had covered
the freshly written telegram. Most of the letters were
there, backwards of course, but as it was in Greek I
could not understand the message. I tore off the sheet
and slipped it into my pocket. Later I should see.
I had some difficulty in believing that such kindly,
hospitable people were playing a trick on me, and I did
not feel very happy in acting in this underhand way,
but I had to look out for myself. After all, I was in
their power, and what did I really know about them?
It was already something to have been put on my
guard. With a little luck, everything would soon be
made clear. Often victory or defeat depends on a
straw. But when one is in the position in which I
found myself, one is working in the darkness, guided
only by impulses, instincts and feelings, and one has
to be doubly vigilant, and not despise the smallest
indication.

At seven o'clock we went off to the station, this time in the sumptuous victoria of the ugly niece. The whole family kissed me good-bye, the niece with a dark blush showing through her oily skin. I promised to come back with my wife and children to spend a whole summer, and so on, but I was thankful when the departure of the train put an end to these embarrassing demonstrations. I was once more alone with Papamanoli, but I now knew about thirty words of Greek, so we could carry on a rudimentary conversation, helped out by nods and becks and wreathed smiles. The van in which my cases had been put had been fastened to the tail of our little train, and each time we stopped in a big station Papamanoli mounted guard to see that in the manœuvring it was not unhooked and left behind. At the station of Athens, we were told that it was against the regulations for a goods wagon to be attached like that to a passenger train. Papamanoli vanished into the railway company's offices, and after much argument and a delay of twenty minutes, we were allowed to go on.

When we reached the Piraeus, the *kirios* Caravan was waiting on the platform, thinner than ever. I gave him the *fortatiki*, the receipt for my eight cases, and he disappeared into the crowd. We went out into the station yard to await events. Two barrows had been left just opposite the door of the Rapid Transport, and ten minutes later, porters were piling the cases onto them. Off they went to the quay, which was barely fifty yards away. A boat was right in under the wall, and with a silent rapidity eloquent of long practice, the cases were lowered into it, and with a few strokes of the oars the boat vanished behind an adjacent steamer.

All this had occupied exactly enough time to allow the officer to stroll to the other end of the quay. He had stopped a hundred yards farther up, and, his back still turned to us, was chatting to some of the men I had seen in the café during our first interview with Caravan. When he turned round, everything was over.

I had no doubt that this accommodating customs officer knew on which side his bread was buttered.

At nine o'clock that evening, I had in my pocket the bill of lading for my goods shipped on board the *Aris*, bound for Marseilles, and an insurance policy into the bargain. The manifest bore the description 'hemp flowers'. After all, that was a good enough definition, and the customs at Marseilles knew perfectly well that it meant hashish. The shipping of drugs was authorized at Marseilles and at Djibouti, so there was no need to dissimulate the nature of the merchandise. But this euphemism had been tacitly adopted, so as not to attract the attention of people stupidly hampered by prejudices, and who might interfere with this profitable trafficking. This designation had been in use for a long time. Probably when they started, certain Nosey Parkers had got themselves into trouble by being over zealous in verifying the nature of the goods. Those who succeeded them, realizing that any attacks of conscience would only result in their losing their jobs, passed the 'hemp flowers' as such, without any further investigation, and this commerce became an accepted routine.

I took a passage on board *Le Calédonien* on which I had come. I expected to be at Marseilles before the *Aris*, which had to call in at several ports on the way. The head steward in the third class once more gave me a job. Papamanoli came on board with me, and before leaving gave me the address of a friend at Port Said. He insisted on the importance of seeing him and arranging with him for the disposal of my hashish in Egypt. I got the impression that there were grave reasons for this insistence, but that the priest felt it was not for him to explain. I felt strongly tempted to tell him the story of the blotting-paper, and ask him straight out the meaning of all these telegrams, but I checked the impulse. All the same, I continued to believe in his integrity. I felt that there was a mystery into which he could not, would not, or dared not initiate me, but I felt just as strongly that it was impossible for these people who had received me so frankly and kindly to have arranged to play me some dirty trick.

Two days after the ship left harbour, when the passengers began to make tentative efforts at conversation with each other, I got to know a Greek who spoke French fluently. I copied out the words which were printed backwards on the blotting-paper, and asked him to translate them for me. This did not give me the key to the mystery as I had hoped, except that I learned that the message was addressed to Cairo. Here is the translation:

'. . . Cairo . . .
Deal concluded . . . Caravan . . . shipping Marseilles . . . by . . . maritime . . . we do not know. . . .'

CHAPTER XII

MY FIRST CONTACT WITH EGYPT

As I LANDED at Marseilles I had the pleasure of seeing the *Aris* come into port. I immediately concluded the necessary formalities for the transhipment of my goods onto a Messageries' ship. I met with some difficulty, for this article had never been shipped openly and regularly in such large quantities. The employees at the offices were nonplussed and consulted Monsieur Restoul himself. He received me with an air of offended dignity, and treated me with cold suspicion, but in the end he was forced to admit that I was quite in order with the customs. He only insisted that the designation 'hemp flowers' should be kept, so that the awful word 'hashish' need not be pronounced in the offices of the most virtuous of companies. Besides, that would avoid putting temptation in the way of the crew, for they were infinitely less virtuous, and fully aware of the money to be made out of hashish smuggling. To make assurance doubly sure, I got permission to have my eight cases put in the hold for valuables, of which only the commander had a key. Then I booked a passage on the same boat.

We called at Port Said, where we had to remain a whole day in order to coal. I lost no time in going ashore and looking for the man who had been recommended by Papamanoli. On the wharf, just outside the customs house, stood an athletic Sudanese, who searched us all thoroughly, even examining the thickness of the soles of our shoes. I went straight to the address given. It was a sort of eating-house, with dusty cakes and greasy delicacies exposed in glass cases. A European wearing an apron dozed behind a counter. I showed him the address and he seemed to start broad awake, staring at me in astonishment, as if

I were a phantom. Then, fishing out a sleepy Arab from behind a screen, he sent him to fetch the man I had asked for, one Alexandros Colloucouvaros. To while away the time of waiting, he brought me a cup of Turkish coffee, but I didn't say a word; it seemed more prudent not to. In a quarter of an hour my man arrived, all out of breath. He apologized for not having come to see me on board.

'So you knew I was on the *Chili*?'

'Not exactly, but my cousin wrote that you were coming to see me, and I supposed you would come by her. I expect you have . . . brought something?'

'No, absolutely nothing, at least for the moment.'

'Oh, all right, all right. . . . I just thought. . . . But let us go for a drive.'

The rickety old carriage with its doddering horse and tarboosh-crowned coachman was admirably adapted for a private conversation. We went along a road which wound through the Arab quarters of the town, a part of Port Said unknown to tourists. Sometimes, as we passed the end of a narrow street swarming with natives, we got a whiff of the now familiar odour which I had first smelt when Petros burnt his sample. Hashish is smoked in all the Arab cafés, by the native policemen as well as by the coolies from the docks. The proprietor has only to pay a small back-hander, and discreetly denounce one of his suppliers now and then; in return he is left alone.

We stopped before a café which was very crowded, but where most of the customers seemed to take nothing but a glass of water. They sat in little groups; some of them seemed to be discussing business, while others watched the world go by in silent depression, having nothing better to do. Only on some tables were cups of Turkish coffee, but on all were narghiles which were kept stoked up by native waiters. Such cafés are to be found in every Egyptian town frequented by Greeks; they serve as Labour Exchanges for all sorts of mysterious transactions. If you want to do business with a Greek, it is here you must look for him, for the Greeks of Egypt live in the cafés from midday to midnight.

We went in and sat down at a table. My companion uttered familiar greetings all round, then asked for a narghile. He seemed to fall into a brown study as he sat there inhaling the smoke and fingering his amber-beaded rosary. He blended into his surroundings, becoming exactly like all the other people there, while I was acutely uncomfortable, with the agonizing self-consciousness of some one trying very unsuccessfully to appear at his ease. Of course there was not the slightest smell of hashish here, any more than in an Arab *boui-boui*. If any one had even had the bad taste to pronounce the forbidden word, I believe that they would all have turned into pillars of salt. All the same, every single one of them got his living from trafficking in hashish, either as a retail seller, or as a small-scale smuggler who haunted the liners; they expended prodigious quantities of complicated ideas in order to obtain a very modest result. In a word, they were people who were too lazy, cowardly or sensual to do a regular job of work, preferring to live in this precarious fashion. One good deal brought them enough to live a lotus-eating life for several weeks on the terrace of their favourite café, taking no thought for the morrow.

Alexandros seemed to me to be this type of man. All the same, if I had been told to come to him, and if he had any connexion with those busy active people I had seen in Greece, he must be worth more than those outcasts of society who exhibited their laziness and uselessness before my eyes. I was much amused at the contemptuous way he spoke of them, for he resembled them as one pea resembles another. He warned me of the danger of confiding the smallest deal to any of them, for they were all police spies, when it was worth their while. In a word, I mustn't speak of my affairs to anybody except himself, and he would put me in touch with serious buyers. It was agreed that we should meet at Suez when I came back with my cargo on the 18th August. I showed a certain nerve in fixing this date, for how could I tell how long it would take me to come up the twelve hundred and sixty miles of the Red Sea against the north-west winds in a twelve-ton sailing ship?

The liner had resumed her voyage towards the south, and steamed slowly between the deserted banks of the canal. At the end of my table at meals sat a badly-dressed fellow; taciturn and gloomy as if he were a new passenger who knew nobody. He must have come on at Port Said, for I had never seen him before, yet he did not look like a passenger either, for he always had his suit-case beside him. He was the electrician who was to take charge of the spotlight in the bows of the ship. I began speaking to this depressed-looking creature, and he answered me readily enough with his mouth full, cutting his bread with a pocket-knife the while. He was an old Italian, rather like Victor Emmanuel in the face, and he had been 'doing the canal' the last fifteen years. It is always interesting to talk to old people, and I was sure I could learn many things from him. After dinner I gave him a cigar, and invited him to have a drink with me. When the atmosphere was sufficiently warm and friendly I sent a cloud of smoke towards the ceiling and said, falsely casual:

'What is hashish worth at the moment?'

He started violently and looked wildly round, but calmed down when he saw there was nobody near us. His eyes sparkled; he supposed I was in the business, for if I had been a police spy he would have known me.

'That depends on the quality,' he replied.

And he began a long dissertation on this subject, his tongue loosened by a succession of drinks. In one hour I had learned that everybody in the canal,

electricians, pilots, and so on, did a little clandestine
trading in hashish on the side. The method was
simple and always the same. An oiled packet was
thrown from a liner at an agreed point, and picked up
by somebody in the know, generally the captain of a
dredger. It was then passed on to one or other of the
rapscallion Greeks I had seen in the cafés. The pro-
jectors are also useful for this sort of business, and
there are a thousand other little tricks known to all
smugglers in all countries in the world. But smuggling
went on also on the high seas. This was on a much
bigger scale, and the coastguards or the lighthouse-
keepers were in on it fifty-fifty. The rotundities of the
great sea-buoys marking the neighbourhood of the
roads cried out for employment, and the coasting
captains, customers of Caravan and his fellows, had
not been long in finding a use for them. The Greek
ship arriving from the Piraeus has only to stop at night
at the buoy chosen beforehand. Half-way up the
conical wall there is a little oval door, closing what is
called the man-hole. This door is generally bolted
and screwed down, but this particular one is held by
carefully-greased screw-nuts which can be unscrewed
in a twinkling. Two hundred and fifty or three
hundred kilograms of hashish can then be put in this
floating warehouse, and nothing indicates its presence.
When the ship has deposited her precious cargo, she
can enter the harbour with a clear conscience.

The next morning would happen to be the day when
certain buoys were brought into the dockyard to be
examined and overhauled. This one, you may be sure,
would be included. It would be taken in tow and
trailed majestically across the harbour. The waves
churned by up its passage caused boats crowded with
customs officers to dance on the water. It would be
taken to the dockyard where metal parts were repaired,
and there in private its precious contents would be
removed. I began to understand why the buoys round
about Port Said were continually being repainted. All

these stories of smuggling interested me from one point of view only, inasmuch as they showed that all the hashish smuggled into Egypt came in from the north. So I had had a good idea in planning to bring it in from the south, for this had never been done.

CHAPTER XIII

THE DEATH OF LIEUTENANT VOIRON

ALTHOUGH I HAD nothing to fear legally, I began to be assailed by qualms, as the ship neared Djibouti, that there would be some hitch in transhipping my cases. As soon as I landed I went to see the manager of the customs and explained my difficulty. I told him that this 'hemp blossom' might as well be called hashish, for that was what it was.

'Yes, I know,' he replied. 'You have the right to tranship this merchandise. I am not here as a moral censor, but simply to see that the regulations are carried out. All the same, if this hashish was to be smuggled into the colony and consumed here, I could not take the responsibility of letting such a cargo pass.'

'As far as that goes,' I replied, 'I give my word of honour that not a single ounce of it will remain in Somaliland.'

'All right, make your declaration, and you will be given an escort as far as the frontier, but once you are out of French waters, you can only re-enter them at your own risks.'

I left the chief's office with a light heart, leaving all my worries behind me. Of all the ships I had had, only the faithful *Fat-el-Rahman* was left. She was a stout vessel who had weathered more than one storm, and I backed her with confidence to fight through the thirteen hundred miles against the wind which were in store for us. It was now the beginning of June, the hottest and most disagreeable month because of the damp, and the most dangerous because of the sudden tempests produced by the accumulation of storm-clouds in the mountains. I had the entire ship overhauled and the rigging renewed, since the nature of our cargo would prevent us from putting in at any port during this long voyage. I increased the number of my crew to twelve, in case of illness or other unexpected trouble. Abdi, Mohammed Moussa, Ali Omar, Aden, Salah and Firan, now grown-up, formed half of it; the other six were Dankalis I had had with me on previous voyages. The eight cases were stowed in the bottom of the hold; I had passed the customs and complied with all the other formalities we were ready to start. The first half of my scheme had been carried through successfully.

The hot, moist night seemed to be crushing the sea under its heavy torpor. The deck and tackle were dripping with dew, a sticky, salt-saturated dew. The men fell limply on the deck with sprawling limbs, and slept naked where they lay. They looked like a heap of corpses, so utterly still were the twisted bodies. The air was like steam. I lay, just as exhausted, on the quarter-deck, but was unable to close an eye. The physical anguish induced by this stifling climate was partly responsible for this, but it was chiefly the thought of the adventure before me that kept me awake. I reflected that I had not had very much difficulty in arriving at the point of having six hundred kilos of hashish in my hold, and that all the danger and difficulty were yet to come. And yet on that day at Port Vendres when I had crossed the narrow plank to go on board the little Greek steamer, if any one had told me that in so short a time I should be on board the *Fat-el-Rahman* with these eight cases safely stowed in the hold, I should have been in the seventh heaven. Instead of which I was more worried than ever. I dared not congratulate myself; I felt that any demonstrations of joy on my part might irritate the powers of evil. I dared not be happy, for all my life I have had to pay with sorrow for every bit of happiness I have known. That is a fundamental law of the destiny of men, but happy are those who do not know it. To take thought for the morrow is to renounce all joy, for it is to foresee misfortune. One can plan the happiness of others, never one's own.

Shortly before dawn, a warm breeze rose from the west; this was the *saba*, the local wind corresponding to the great south-west monsoon in the Indian Ocean. It starts in the depths of the Gulf of Tajura, and throws itself with extreme violence over the Gulf of Aden as far as Cape Gardafui. Greenish shivers ran through the phosphorescence of the sleeping sea under the caress of this burning wind. It was time to be off if we wanted to be out of the roads before the sea got too stormy. As the first pulls on the halyard tackle were awaking creaking groans from the badly oiled pulleys, a man hailed us from the jetty. He was a native soldier in uniform, and I thought it was for some tiresome, last-minute formality, so I sent the *pirogue* ashore to see what he wanted. He returned in it.

'What do you want? Have you a paper for me?' I asked.

'No; I simply want to go as far as Obock with you.'

He was a Somali of about twenty-five, so ugly that it hurt to look at him. In addition, he had strange, unseeing eyes like those of a madman, which gave one the creeps. I was on the point of having him sent back ashore, or more simply of having him thrown overboard, since all Somalis swim like fishes, when it occurred to me that by taking him I might be rendering a service to the captain of the military post at Obock, with whom I wanted to keep on good terms. He immediately collapsed in a corner and remained motionless. I was too busy directing the manœuvres to give him another thought until we were just entering the roads of Obock. I had decided to remain there two days, to finish the overhauling of my vessel, and make a complete new set of sails.

The post of Obock was commanded by a Captain Benoit. He was an insignificant little fellow, barely forty, but fat and pursy. He might have been a country lawyer or a tax-collector, or even a station-master. He always looked as if he had put on his uniform for a fancy-dress ball. I don't remember his wife very well. She had the reputation of being a lady with an abnormally large heart, but that is probably a calumny, in any case it is not very interesting.

Two lieutenants completed the staff. One was a certain Aublin, who had risen from the ranks like so many others during the war. He was a man of humble origin, simple and very proud of his rank, and as fond of showing off as a child. A good fellow, all the same, who would not have harmed a fly, and who would really have been more at home pushing a coster's barrow than following a martial destiny. After three years in the trenches, he had been thankful when the formation of this Somali battalion by Lieutenant Depuis gave him a nice cushy job at Obock, far from shot and shell.

The other was Lieutenant Voiron. Tall, well-built and good-looking, he was obviously a man of birth and breeding. Everything about him proclaimed it, yet there was something lacking, all the same. One felt he had not received the education suitable for a man of his class. He had enlisted in the colonial army at the age of nineteen. Violent, enthusiastic and madly courageous, he had not found an outlet in a tame garrison life for these dangerous qualities. As a result, wine and women had already worked ravages, both moral and physical, but he was still an attractive fellow; one felt an instinctive liking for him. One sensed the struggle that went on in this nature which had so much that was fine and even noble in it, but which was too weak to resist the evil influences of the circumstances in which he found himself.

I remember a visit he paid us in our house at Obock.
Knowing that my wife was there, he had put on his
dress uniform. Aublin, who accompanied him, was in
shirt-sleeves and perspiring profusely. He sniggered
at what he called the ridiculous affectation of his comrade. Our house was very simply arranged, but that
did not prevent us from receiving our guests with due
honour. It was pathetic to watch how Voiron reacted
to an atmosphere of refinement and culture. He
seemed to recover instinctively the manners of the
class in which he had been born. We discussed literature and art, and evoked memories of France. The
poor boy was literally transfigured, and showed a side
of his mind which, from fear of ridicule, he had kept
hidden from the rough, uneducated men with whom he
had chosen to cast in his lot. During this time Aublin,
on all fours on the carpet, played bears with my little
daughter.

Then we drank a Pernod, real pre-war stuff I had
brought from Massawa—the absinthe which for so long
reigned supreme in the distant outposts of our colonies.
Under its influence, the unfortunate Voiron changed
completely. All the coarseness of fifteen years in
barracks among vulgar brutes submerged what we had
just seen of delicacy and refinement in his soul. He
became simply a common N.C.O. with the goggly eyes
of a drunkard. It was one of the saddest things I have
ever seen. Aublin did not change. He got a little
redder in the face, that was all. He slapped Voiron
jovially on the back, shouting gaily:

'Ah, Charlie, old man, that's the stuff. A good
Pernod soon makes life rosy.'

Then, turning to me he added:

'He's like that when he has the blues, plays the
aristo, but a stiff peg soon puts him all right. He's
a good pal, is Charlie, not a stuck-up bone in his
body.'

I felt an immense pity for this poor fellow, destined
to go under. I looked at his slim hand with its crested

signet-ring; it seemed to implore an impossible help. Too late, too late.

When I reached Obock I learned that twenty-five Somalis had escaped from the boat which was taking them to France, and had been captured on Italian territory. Captain Benoit had received orders to go and fetch them. He was not at all happy at the thought of this perilous expedition. No doubt it was easy for fifty armed men to escort twenty-five poor devils worn out with fatigue and hunger. But the fifty men were Somalis like the prisoners, and that meant that two Europeans, an officer and an N.C.O., would be isolated with seventy-five negroes in the middle of a desert where everything reminded them that this was where they were born, while the white men were only intruders.

The day before that fixed for the departure, the captain had a severe bout of fever and was compelled to go to bed. Voiron joyfully agreed to take charge of the expedition. Sergeant Montsacré volunteered to accompany him. They were to leave at three o'clock next morning. Captain Benoit would keep with him a sufficient number of men to guard the post. The men were selected with infinite care; all those belonging to the same tribe as the fugitives were rejected, so as to lessen the danger of a revolt on the way. Voiron decided to take only twenty-five men with him, and he said that half of that would have been enough. He and Montsacré were old pals: they had gone through the war together; each knew that he could count on the other to death and beyond, and that was the principal thing.

The camels with the water supply left that evening, so as to be at the halt when the troop should arrive. In the afternoon Voiron came to see me, wildly gay at the idea of escaping at last from the monotony of this post, in which the prudence of Captain Benoit kept them so closely shut up. I gave him some tips about the water-holes and so on. When he was taking his leave, he said:

'Thank you for bringing back Ahmed Fara, my gazelle hunter. We wouldn't have bothered about his deserting, if the mess-table had not suffered severely from his absence.'

'Well, of course,' I said, suddenly remembering the surly guard we had taken on at Djibouti. 'I had forgotten all about him, he tucked himself away into such little space. Any one might have thought he was dumb, too. My sailors tried in vain to get him to eat with them, and not a single word would he utter. Finally they left him alone, concluding he was crazy.'

'Yes, he's an odd fellow, a very odd fellow, but a good sort for all that. He must be worried if he has learnt that his brother has deserted, and that is maybe why he is so queer. But it's a business to know what these devils of niggers are thinking.'

'Oh, they think much as we do; but if I were you I should steer clear of your gazelle hunter. He doesn't inspire confidence at all. Beware of men who are small, ugly, and taciturn.'

'Oh, I don't pay much attention. Anyhow, I am leaving him here, though he would fain be included in the expedition, and says he came back from Djibouti specially for that.'

'You are maybe wrong not to take him then. You may be sure that if he wants to go and take his brother prisoner, it is not with the idea of helping him, but for some reason that neither you nor I could understand. It is always dangerous to oppose a fixed idea in the head of one of those savages whose brutal and simple logic hits like a sledge-hammer. I tell you that yesterday he gave me the impression of a man off his mental balance.'

'Oh, if he has gone potty, I'll clap him into the guard-room. That will calm him. Well, I must be off. Farewell for ever, or so long—I don't know which it will be, and I don't care a tinker's curse.'

His eyes held a strange expression, a look of defiance

to Destiny. Once he had gone I regretted my words.
Why had I told him it would be prudent to humour
the taciturn Somali? By what right had I given him
such advice and inspired him with such fears? I re-
proached myself with vanity, with having wanted to
show off my superior understanding of the soul of the
natives, a damned stupid thing to do. And yet, when
I thought it over, I realized I was unjust to myself,
that it was something infinitely deeper, some warning
from the depths of my subconscious which had forced
me to speak. I would say that I had had a presentiment, only it is so easy to be wise after the event.
All the same, I had felt a sort of physical anguish as
I shook hands with Voiron. Very likely it was he
himself, going as he was to his doom, who transferred
this uncomfortable feeling to me. He had felt death
hovering over him when he had jokingly said 'Farewell
for ever'.

In the middle of the night I was awakened by the
firing of three shots. They came from the Residency,
about half a mile away. I distinctly saw a lantern
waving about on the esplanade where the soldiers
generally drilled. It was just time for the expedition
to start, and I thought that some one was firing off
shots from sheer exuberance. The men had probably
been celebrating their departure by a drink or two,
and young soldiers in a god-forsaken post in the bush
generally express their joy rather noisily. That a
tragedy was being enacted never entered my head.
Soon the dawn broke, a dawn like thousands of
others. Everything seemed very calm when I went
out on the terrace to take my shower. Then I saw
Aublin come running into my courtyard, wild-eyed
and breathless.

'Voiron has been murdered,' he cried as soon as he
caught sight of me. 'This morning when they were
about to start one of the guards deliberately fired three
shots into him . . . he is dead. . . . I came to ask if
you could take his body to Djibouti at once.'

I asked for details. One of the guards who were to remain at Obock, whose brother, as it happened, was among the deserters, had come up to Voiron when he was inspecting his detachment just before the start. The fellow begged and implored to be taken with them. He wore his field kit, and was armed, all ready, with his rifle in his hand. The reader has already guessed that it was Ahmed Fara, the Somali I had brought with me the day before. Voiron refused his request, and threatened to have him put in prison if he continued to bother him.

'But I want to see my brother . . .'

'You will see him when we come back, as I have already told you.'

'No; I want to come with you; I am not a woman to be left to guard the house.'

'Will you go back into barracks and take off all that impedimenta?' shouted Voiron, suddenly flying into the unbalanced rage of the alcoholic.

At this the Somali lost his head, and in a sudden fit of madness fired on his officer. The shot hit Voiron in the belly, and he fell, with a shout for help.

'I was standing at the door of the Residency,' continued Aublin; 'it was a very dark night and I could see nothing. But when I heard the shot and Voiron's voice crying for help, I broke into a cold sweat. I went in, flew upstairs, and leaning from a first-floor window, shrieked "Coming, old top", and at that very moment two other shots rang out.

' "There's going to be trouble, Aublin, me lad," I said to myself, for I thought that the Somalis had mutinied. Then I heard Montsacré bellowing, "Come on, you sons of bitches, get out of your bloody beds."

'And he treated us to a blistering volley. I say "us", for the captain was there too, only his wife had locked the door and forbidden him to stir. Eventually, however, the captain went out in his night-shirt to see what had happened. Voiron, already badly hurt by the first bullet, had been finished off by the other two, one of which had broken his back. Montsacré, who had been at the other end of the line, had made one flying leap to save him, but got to him just in time to lay out the foul murderer with a blow from his rifle-butt. The whole business had taken about eighty seconds, and the entire armed detachment stood there open-mouthed and motionless, stunned by the suddenness of it all. It is true that it was too dark for them to see what was happening.'

While Aublin was telling this story, we were making our way to the Residency. Voiron had been laid on an *angareb* (native bed made of interlaced strips of leather). Death had put its seal of serenity on the handsome, pale face, set in severe lines, and under the folds of the flag which served as shroud, the body of this poor soldier, this outcast who had so bitterly felt his decadence, lay rigid as the effigy of a knight on a marble tomb, such as one sees in old cathedrals. Perhaps Voiron had something of the soul of those old heroes, but what would a Bayard or a Roland have done in the 22nd Colonial Regiment in this twentieth century? He would probably have risen to be a sergeant-major . . . and nothing more. Each age fashions its men.

In spite of myself I felt my emotion rising as I looked at this dead man. For the flag thrown over him, this emblem of our distant country, seemed like a mourning veil thrown on her child by our common mother. For a moment we were all brothers in face of our dead. I tried desperately to keep back my tears and not make a fool of myself. Aublin was sobbing like a child.

Voiron's corpse was carried on board my boat. I had accepted this funereal mission without thinking, but I now remembered that I had the eight cases of hashish in my hold and that the customs officer had warned me not to re-enter French waters, once I had left Djibouti. I told Captain Benoit about this, and it was agreed that to avoid any complications he would say that he had commandeered my *boutre*. The coffin was on the after-deck. The murderer, who had now re-covered consciousness, lay in the bottom of the hold, his face swollen and bloody, staring sullenly before him like a captive beast. Why had he committed this crime? He had wrapped himself in an obstinate silence, and nobody would ever know what thoughts were passing through his rudimentary brain. We had to keep thinking of what he had done in order not to feel desperately sorry for him, for he was in a terrible state. The other Somalis, who had adored Voiron, had nearly lynched him.

Captain Benoit was in full dress uniform, pompous and important, with his face composed to a seemly gloom. As he disembarked on the quay at Djibouti amid the dignitaries who had been notified by telegram, he was quite the hero of the day. He told his little story with much mournful head-shaking and many dramatic gestures. Just think how useful all this would be for promotion.

The funeral was heart-breakingly sad from sheer ridiculousness. A carriage had been turned into a hearse for the occasion, and most grotesque it looked, drawn by two skinny mules. It bumped prosaically over the ruts in the road, and the somnolent Arab who acted as coachman changed his plug to the other cheek, contemptuously shooting forth a jet of brown saliva across the cords of the pall. After all, it was only a *roumi*, an unbeliever, being thrust into the ground. The procession stopped at the European cemetery, and the coolies unloaded the coffin exactly as if it had been a case of merchandise being unshipped on the quay. Some one uttered a hypocritical speech, then the procession broke up and left the cemetery in the pleasant disorder of people glad to be through with a tedious duty.

I thought how hideous death was in these circum-stances. This cemetery with its high walls and scrubby little monuments was such a contrast with the serene melancholy of the tombs I had often glimpsed at sea as I passed near desert islands, with the wild sea wind whistling round them, and the heads of the saw-fish planted before them gleaming in the sun.

Thanks to the declaration of Captain Benoit that he had been obliged to commandeer my ship as there was no other, I had no trouble with the customs, but as soon as I had played to a finish my role of amateur funeral mute, I set sail, afraid that after all the authorities might change their minds about letting me go off with my hashish.

This unexpected return to Djibouti had been of some use. When I arrived I was told that Monsieur Poilut, a shipping agent, had been wailing about me in all the cafés. He could not think it right for hashish to be transported other than clandestinely. It was so well known to the crews of his company's ships that hashish smuggling was a profitable business. He declared that my cargo ought to have been confiscated, spirited away, destroyed. Ah, if only his friend Pascal had been there, you would have seen how he snapped his fingers at the law. Just think . . . six hundred kilos of hashish, nearly a thousand pounds of clear profit. It was a shame and disgrace to let this penniless adventurer de Monfreid make such a fortune. It was only an eccentric like Frangeul who would fail to understand that, and who would persist in carrying out the regulations without trying to get round them. The law in the colony, he said, should be elastic and supple. Justice should be like a strong arm always ready to back up the Governor. These were fundamental principles and it was criminal to forget it.

Monsieur Poilut was an old servant of his company. I don't mean old in years, for he was a Creole who boasted of eternal youth. But he belonged to the heroic days when lieutenants of the Royal Navy commanded the company's liners, haughty and supercilious

creatures who did not deign to be aware of anything that went on lower than the bridge. In those
happy times there was a constellation of pursers of a
race now, alas, extinct, but whose memory will live for
ever. The private trading in which the crew was
allowed to indulge had become a regular and carefully
organized traffic. The most profitable deals were
carried through under the cloak of the sale of Japanese
tea-services, glass-ware, canaries, and aspidistras for
landladies. The facts that the Far Eastern and Indian
Ocean liners called in at Egyptian ports, and that
they docked at Marseilles beside ships from the Near
East, were marvellously helpful to sundry small tran-
shipments and to the smuggling of hashish. The deck,
restaurant, and engine-room staffs had the monopoly
of this smuggling. The pursers put on smoked glasses
and suddenly lost all sense of smell, and everything was
for the best in the best of all possible companies. So
really it was hardly surprising if Monsieur Poilut
grumbled a little at the way I was upsetting such hoary
customs. I was very glad that my unexpected return
had permitted me to learn about the hue and cry that
he was starting after me. The echoes might get as far
as Egypt and might make a devil of a lot of trouble
for me. It behoved me to be on my guard, and
especially to try to avert suspicion.

The only thing that might save me was the extreme
improbability of any one's making the long voyage from
Djibouti to Suez in such a small sailing-ship. Then,
too, Monsieur Poilut declared that this open an-
nouncing of my intentions was just a bluff to provide
an alibi, and that I was really engaged on very different
business in a very different place. Other people might
be taken in, but he was too old a fox to be deceived
by such tricks.

I had the luck to meet young Ali Coubeche on the
quay. It was he who supplied the company's liners
with meat and vegetables. Naturally, then, he was
on very friendly terms with all the pursers. With

Monsieur Poilut his friendship was specially warm, not to say tropical, so I had only to give him to understand that my ship and cargo were really going in quite a different direction to be quite sure that Monsieur Poilut would be informed of it that very evening.

CHAPTER XIV

THE TURTLE FISHER

I SET SAIL just before nightfall, and thanks to exceptionally good weather out at sea, did not put in at Obock. A fair south-west wind brought me rapidly in sight of the Swaba islands at sunrise. This is a chain of six volcanic islets which were probably thrown up by the same commotion as opened up the Red Sea in the Quaternary period. Two of these islets are about three hundred feet above sea-level and golden-brown in colour. In the strait between them, the current makes formidable eddies, which in places break and swirl in dangerous fashion. This strait is a perpetual battle-field, where the fishes devour each other in the struggle for life.

As we approached, schools of tiny fish pursued by carnivorous monsters bounded out of the water with the unanimous rhythm of a troop of ballet-dancers, as if moved by a single spring. Flocks of birds hovering in the air pounced on them with a deafening screaming and beating of wings, and the clamour re-echoed from the steep cliffs of the island on either side. Hundreds of little holes were hollowed in the rocky walls, making them look like gigantic sponges. In these holes the sea-birds build their nests. You can see them at the entrance to their dwellings, generally the males, which bring fish to feed the young, or the female sitting on her eggs. If you fire a shot into the air, it re-echoes like a thunderclap, and a cloud of white birds emerge from these cells like a swarm of bees.

I risked passing through the whirlpool in this strait in the hope of catching some fish. The wind was favourable enough to allow me to do this and still be able to control the currents and steer without danger at a good distance from the rocks. One of the islands, part of the crater of a former volcano, was crescent-shaped, and I knew that wrecks were often thrown up on the little sheltered beach in the curve. Everybody knows the passionate interest sailors take in wrecks.

As I rounded the point and came in sight of the little bay, I saw a naked man running towards us over the sand, waving his loin-cloth. There was only a slight breeze and the sea was very calm, so I was able to approach and anchor without danger in the greenish water, through which gleamed the sandy bottom. The man was a Dankali from Obock, a turtle fisher. His companion, who had gone off in a small boat to fetch water and provisions, had not reappeared, and for ten days he had been there alone, living on raw crabs, and passing whole days immersed in the water in order to stave off the tortures of thirst. The raw crabs were precious for the same reason, for the liquid they contain is much less salty than sea-water. Their serum, like that of all animals, whether they live on land or in water, has a relatively feeble saline content, which never varies. It is comprehensible, therefore, that its assimilation retards the dehydration of the human organism, which is death from thirst. But the unfortunate fellow was reduced to skin and bone; he was terrible to look at with his prominent cheek-bones and hollow eyes, and what he intended to be a joyous smile looked like the grimace of a death's head. As soon as he climbed on board, we had to restrain him from hurting himself by drinking too much water. He realized the danger, and had the courage to drink only a mouthful or two. Then we had boiling hot tea prepared for him. His name was Youssouf. If he had not told us he was twenty-five years old, we should never have been able to assign an age to him, so drawn with starvation was his face. He had come to the island with his brother to fish for turtles.

When they are about to lay their eggs, the sea turtles land on this island at full moon when the tides are highest, for they know that as no other animal comes here, they will not be disturbed. If they see the smallest trace in the sand, they go off again to seek a more secure retreat. The sand must be absolutely virgin, giving proof of complete solitude, before this prudent animal will venture to lay its eggs in it. The fisher therefore takes great care to walk only where the sea will efface his footprints. He goes and lies under a rock, in the black shadow thrown by the moon, and for whole nights he lies motionless and silent, watching the water rise gradually higher on the sand.

No sound can be heard but the regular breaking of the waves on those barren rocks. Who could guess, in this solitude, that a man was watching and waiting for his prey? The stars slowly wheel round the sky, and the moon rises ever higher. The bay is soon flooded with its light, and the sand gleams dazzling white against the black basalt of the rocks. Then a dark form emerges from a fringe of foam, and is left gleaming like a wet stone on the beach. The following wave foams over it, then retires, leaving it a little higher on the sand. Soon it is entirely out of the water, and is seen to be an enormous turtle. Her tiny head moves restlessly from side to side as she inspects her surroundings, then heavily, helping herself along with her flippers, she drags herself to a sandbank above the high-water mark. Silently she scoops out a place, and soon her shell sinks down until it is hardly visible. Then she remains motionless, merged into the sand. If one did not know she was there, one could never find her, but the silent watcher has never taken his eyes off her. He does not stir; the turtle must be allowed to lay her eggs. This takes about an hour. When she has finished, she shakes herself, covers up the eggs with sand and makes for the sea, going backwards so that she can efface the traces of her nocturnal visit with her flippers. At this moment the fisher rushes from his hiding-place and, seizing the turtle, turns her suddenly over on her back. Generally, they come in large numbers, and they have to be turned over very quickly, for once they are alarmed, they manage to drag themselves at a fair speed towards the sea, aided by the steepness of the shore. They are left to lay because the fisherman wants their eggs. They are a precious food, for the yolk, after suitable treatment, becomes hard and will keep indefinitely.

Youssouf went and fetched the fruits of his two months' fishing, a little bag of tortoise-shell taken from a score of turtles captured on moonlit nights. I was immediately struck by the expression on this man's face. There was something aloof and noble in it, and when he spoke, his words revealed a mind of exceptional quality. He had the far-seeing look of a man who contemplates things which are hidden from the herd.

I followed him to the little grotto where he had slept and where he had hidden his little fortune. In it were only his sack of tortoise-shell, an old wooden dish, and some empty tins which had contained the precious water. The cave was fairly big. The light penetrated but dimly into it, and for a few minutes I could not make out a thing. The entrance was cluttered up with innumerable bits of rag, either white or bleached by the weather, hung on reeds that were stuck into fissures in the rock. Each of them was knotted in the same way, and contained a little aromatic wood (*boukour*). They were offerings to the divinity which still haunted this place, as it had done in pagan times, for all Mohammed could do. Farther in, little heaps of ashes on flat stones showed where perfumed resins had been burnt. All the fishers who had passed through this island had thus left evidence of their secret adherence to their primitive religion, which still lingers in their minds.

I found a strange charm in these ancient rites, and I took care not to touch any of those small offerings, which yet had a certain grandeur, for they expressed all the weakness, fear, and anxiety of man in face of the elements. This cavern was a very strange place, and must have struck awe into the simple souls of the solitary men who had come there. The walls were of dead madrepores in tree or fan forms, in the midst of which were scattered giant fossil shells. All this rock had once been vividly alive. It had possessed that mysterious spark which had been transmitted to me also, and which even at that moment was animating me.

I imagined a half-naked Dankali fisherman leaving his *pirogue* on the beach and kneeling there, watching the faint blue smoke rise from a pinch of incense in his primitive perfuming-pan. He would see all round him genii listening to his prayers, and his fears would leave him, since he was no longer alone. As for me, alas, I was a barbarian, and could see nothing but life petrified and extinguished for ever. I had lost that wonderful faculty for seeing a god in every mystery of nature.

Youssouf told us that about twelve days before, one night while he and his brother Mhamed were waiting for the turtles, they had heard voices on the sea. Soon after, several men could be seen swimming towards their island. When they landed, they saw that they were Somalis, and they immediately supposed they had been wrecked. The unfortunate men were utterly exhausted, and some of them, once they had touched the shore, remained unconscious on the sand, worn out by their supreme effort. They were not very terrible, seeing the state they were in, and inspired pity rather than fear. There were ten of them. They told a vague story of shipwreck. Eight of them had not yet come ashore, but it was in vain that their comrades halloed into the night; their hails remained unanswered. The missing men had probably been carried away by the current which had to be crossed before the island could be reached.

Youssouf and his brother had given all the provisions they had to these famished men, and next day Mhamed had embarked them in his big *pirogue* to transport them to the mainland. He reckoned that he would be back

with water and stores in two days at most, for the
Somalis had managed to save their money by carrying
it in their belts, and had promised to buy food at the
post of Angar to replace the provisions the two fishers
had given them. So Youssouf had been left alone on
the island with ten litres of water. He would get food
from the sea, and even if he had to fast for a couple
of days, that wouldn't worry him at all. But during
the day, while he was looking for fish among the rocks
at low tide, he had found a corpse jammed in a ragged
crevice. The head had already been eaten, as is nearly
always the case when the body has not been devoured
by the sharks. The man was naked save for a girdle
round the loins. Hermit crabs swarmed over it, eating
the flesh which was already decomposed. Youssouf
had dragged the corpse ashore to give it a burial fit for
one of the faithful, and had buried it in the sand, head
turned towards the Prophet's tomb. The leather girdle
contained ten gold coins and a vague pulp which could
still be recognized as having once been banknotes of
the Bank of Djibouti. On his wrist, the dead man had
a small aluminium medal. The Dankali showed it to
me; it was a soldier's identity disc, with his name and
regimental number.

I had no longer any doubt that those so-called
shipwrecked mariners were deserters. Very likely they
were the men who had been arrested in Eritrea, whom
the unfortunate Voiron had been setting out to fetch
from Raheita the day he was murdered. I explained
this to Youssouf, and he became very thoughtful, and
asked me if I would take him to some point on the
Dankali coast. What I had just told him had made
him very uneasy about his brother's fate, and he wanted
to set out immediately to find out what had become of
him. The only possible explanation of his long absence
was that he had met with a violent death. Somalis
have generally very little scruple about flinging an
inconvenient Dankali overboard. The man who had
saved their lives might talk when they arrived at the

French post of Angar, and suspicions might be aroused. The deserters knew that a reward had been offered for their capture, and they had probably decided to get rid of their benefactor so that he would not yield to the temptation of betraying them. They had therefore paid their debt of gratitude by sending him immediately to the paradise of the faithful.

I set sail with Youssouf and his few belongings on board, and some hours later I anchored at the little beach of the bay north of Syan. The first thing we saw on the sand was the wreck of a *pirogue*. Youssouf immediately recognized it as his brother's. It had undoubtedly been deliberately destroyed, for beside it we found the great stone with which its bottom had been stove in. It had been there for several days, for there were no traces in the sand, and the khamsin had already covered it with a powdery dust. Youssouf gazed silently at this evidence of the disaster which had overtaken him. He had now no illusions about his brother's fate. Poor Mhamed's corpse, or rather his bleached bones, for that is all that is left of a man in this country very soon after his death, were lying in some deserted corner, mute witness of the imprudence of trying to help one's fellow-creatures. Youssouf went off without a word towards his destiny. I watched his tall form as it grew smaller, then was swallowed up in the African bush, bristling with terrible thorns, hostile and savage as a wild beast at bay.

CHAPTER XV

THE KHAMSIN

BY A LUCKY chance, for which we could hardly have hoped at this season, a fair south-west wind began to blow, before which we ran easily through the strait and right up to the north of the Bay of Beilul. But at this summer season, which is the most dangerous of all in the Red Sea, you can never be sure of the weather. It can change completely in less than an hour.

I saw great storm clouds massing on the mountains of Djebel Asmara, to the north, on the African side, and on our right to the eastward another storm was brewing behind the ragged peaks of Yemen. Gigantic flashes of lightning tore through the black cloud banks, but so far away that we heard not the faintest clap of thunder. The south-east wind, which had brought us so quickly and easily to where we were, faltered and dropped. I reckoned we had now arrived in the middle of the barometric depression caused by these storms. The ship settled down motionless on a leaden sea. An unechoing silence enveloped us under the immense vault of black clouds, and flocks of sea-birds passed swiftly, almost skimming the water, all going the same way, towards the Hanish Islands, in terrified flight before a threatening danger.

The sun was now hidden behind the heaped-up banks of cloud in the north-west. The rounded black masses were edged by loops and swirls of flame. The sky grew red as the reflection from a furnace, and dark bands rayed out from the west like dizzy arches projected towards the zenith to span the world. What was going to happen? Bitterly now I regretted the time I had wasted taking Voiron's body to Djibouti, as but for that I should now be far to the north. What specially worried me was that I had never navigated a ship through these regions in summer. I knew plenty of shelters—I had visited them often enough—but they were only of use in winter when the south-east wind prevails. But it was now July, and I was like a rat in a trap, surrounded as I was by storms. Who could tell from which point the wind would begin to blow? All I knew was that it would blow a hurricane. As night drew on, both sides of the horizon grew clearer, for now uninterruptedly a lurid light played across the entire mass of the clouds, while at intervals jagged flashes of lightning slashed them in all directions. At last the wind rose, hot and baleful.

'*Ouari, ouari*,' cried my men. (The khamsin, the khamsin).

We set our sails to receive it. Immediately it became violent, as if it had been roused to fury by encountering our miserable little bark. How well I understand these ancient legends which personify the winds. Any one who lives with this capricious element as a sailor does, and tries to tame and domesticate it, realizes how exactly these fictions describe his experiences. Every wind has for him a distinct character, a physiognomy; he knows it in the same way as he knows his comrades, his friends or his enemies. This khamsin, or *ouari*, as the natives call it, is a taciturn wind. He runs sullenly under a dust-obscured sky, and his rage breaks forth suddenly against the unlucky ship which lies cowering in his path, under bare poles in her efforts to escape his notice.

Soon we were in a perfect cloud of sand, or of dust rather, this dust which is so fine that it gets into everything. The sea, surprised in its dead calm, took a minute to realize what was happening. The foam ran over its surface like snowflakes driven by the tempest, and already the spray pattered on the deck. But soon it woke up and, shuddering, shook free its mighty waves, which smashed against our hull, while the swell increased every second. Darkness fell, and we were

blindly driven westwards. The whole question was
now how long this would last. Tiny as was our storm-
sail, under which we were fleeing before the tempest,
we were running at least seven or eight knots, and this
speed was necessary if we did not want to be swallowed
up by the pursuing waves. At this rate we should
reach the coast in less than five hours, and with our
prow hard on the reef, we should have no alternative
but to tack and try to outwit our enemy. This being
so, it might be just as well not to let this convenient
but dangerous flight go on too long.

The wind seemed to be making tentative efforts to
turn to the north, which led me to suppose that the
return of the prevailing north-west wind was imminent.
This changing of direction meant the shocking together
of two swells, never a very pleasant thing for a small
boat. Before this tiresome complication should begin,
I wanted to take advantage of the winds, which were
still westerly, to get as far north as possible, and try to
reach the shelter of the Hanish chain. With this
fifteen-mile-long mountain barrier between me and the
wind, I could tack in calm water until daylight. By
guesswork, since I had now no means of taking our
bearings, I steered in the direction I thought the right
one. Overhead a few stars were now shining, but the
dust-storm very low on the water prevented us from
seeing more than half a mile around us. The sea was
very rough, with short, choppy waves. In less than a
quarter of an hour we were white with salt from the
seas which broke continually over us, and which the
burning wind evaporated in a twinkling.

The *ouari* or khamsin has the reputation of breaking
masts and yards. It is this well-known truth which
makes the natives say that it is a heavy wind. If the
mast or yard resists, then the ship turns over, and such
shipwrecks take place in large numbers every year.
The fact is quite accurate, but there is a more scientific
explanation than the appetite for destruction of this
desert wind. It is simply that the dry and burning heat

of the wind makes the wood less pliable and more brittle. So it was with anxiety that I watched the yard bending every time the vessel pitched, and I expected every second to hear a sinister crack from the rigging. This noise of snapping wood is so dreaded by navigators in these parts that when the cabin-boy is preparing wood to heat his oven, every time he breaks a branch, he cries out '*Hatab*' (firewood), as otherwise this sound would cause a start of alarm.

At last the dust-storm cleared, and to starboard I could see the black cones of the Hanish Islands before us. The wind drew forward more and more, but I could still keep the helm in the right direction. The north-west wind was now master of the situation, and had soon swept away the dust, but it also brought along the storm clouds which had accumulated on the Asmara Mountains, and soon the sky was heavily overcast, and it was as dark as if we were in a cellar. The Hanish Islands were now to port. In spite of their nearness, we could only just make out their summits through the dimness. We were less than a mile from them, for we were sailing in their shelter. The sea here was practically calm, although the wind was just as violent. We passed through zones of such extraordinarily phosphorescent water that we seemed to be sailing through liquid phosphorus. In the gloom the sails were lit up by livid reflections, and from time to time our faces gleamed, death-like and sinister as the faces of ghosts. This phosphorescence was strong enough to dazzle us, and prevent us from seeing anything of the big island to port, or the cluster of rocky islets to starboard and to windward. We were in a sort of channel about a mile wide. In the darkness our only guide to the shore on either side was the phosphorescence as the waves broke on it.

Besides the very real danger of such a situation and the terrible anxiety it carried with it, there was an element of moral disarray, just to complete our discomfiture. The weird and infernal nature of the scene, joined to physical fatigue and lack of sleep, would have prevented the strongest brain from functioning normally, and we were all in a sort of crazy state in which we could no longer distinguish clearly between the real and the unreal. I don't know what my thoughts were during these moments; I was in a sort of half-delirious, nightmarish state, a sort of fantastic madness; perhaps I was simply afraid.

Suddenly the wind dropped dead and the sail abruptly sagged. Instinctively I realized we must be in those dangerous eddies produced by the gusts of wind in the mountains which overhung us. We had gone too near the coast. In the brief silence of this unexpected lull, which had fallen on us like a threat, we could hear all round us the sea growling on invisible reefs. Then a sort of whistling ran over the water, increasing in volume as it approached at a dizzy speed, and a gust of wind smacked the ship on the stern. It was so sudden that the yard snapped clean through the middle, and it was lucky that it did, for otherwise the ship would have turned over. The immediate danger of our situation banished all the bogies and evil spirits which were dancing through our imaginations. The sail had to be saved. And only with God's help would we come safely through, with this half-torn canvas wrenching and sweeping everything away into the darkness with its loose cordages.

The sudden gust of wind which had torn away the sail lasted only a minute; it passed like an avalanche, and was succeeded by another dead calm. During this brief lull we managed to bring to the deck the forward part of the lateen yard which still held to the halyard. And now we were under bare poles, with nothing to fear from a fresh gust of wind, but drifting towards this accursed cluster of islets which I knew to lie half a mile to windward.

I could see quite plainly the phosphorescent bar where the sea broke on the rocks. It was a long group, very low on the water, and the current was bearing us towards the middle of it. Should we have time to rig up a jury sail so that we could steer round the islets? I knew they were linked together by jagged rocks just under the water, and that there was no hope of passing between any two of them. I kept the ship across the wind to stave off the end as long as possible, and left to my men the preparation of a sail. They were expert at these emergency riggings which so often have to be made on *boutres*, and at such a moment an order not clearly understood might have delayed them for several seconds, and every second was precious. The minutes seemed like hours, but at last I saw the white triangle of a jib going up. It was as if a radiant sun had risen in this infernal night. At once I felt the ship steady herself against the wind, and begin at long last to make headway.

But now the fiery serpent which was coiling round the rocks was a bare three cables' lengths off. We almost touched it, heading in a parallel direction. It was all I could do with this sail and the wind on the beam, and slowly we drifted nearer. Would this island never end? It seemed a hundred miles long. At last I heaved a sigh of relief; we had reached the point. Just as I was about to bear away in order to round it, I saw the water foaming round a jagged spike which prolonged it half a cable's length. This time it was the end of everything; we could not pass. My mouth was parched and burning, and my cheeks hurt with the force with which I kept my teeth clenched, as if the contraction of all my muscles could stop this awful drifting which was leading us into the jaws of death. Suddenly the wind drew forward, the vessel cast off, and we made straight for the rocks. All the crew felt that their last moment had come, and from the deck where they were gathered I heard the clamour of resignation before the inevitable: '*La illa illalah, la illa illalah.*' How often I had heard it when a dead man was being borne to his grave. But this abrupt drawing forward of the wind had been caused by an eddy, and it immediately attacked us from the other side, guiding our prow into the centre of the strait. Just in the nick of time. God did not want our lives, it would seem. Our hour was not yet.

CHAPTER XVI

BIG GUNS IN ACTION

THEN FOLLOWED a week of painful navigation against head winds, which, however, varied sufficiently in direction to allow of advantageous tacking. As far as possible I hugged the coast, for out at sea there was a very heavy swell, with a strong and unchanging northwest wind. The channel south of Massawa between the mainland and the Dahlak archipelago was much calmer, and there I had the advantage of the changes in wind thanks to the nearness of the continent, and also of the gusts of the khamsin, which blew nearly every evening, coming from deserts still burning from the heat of the sun. In the end I got accustomed to this capricious wind, and endured it for the one virtue it possessed in my eyes, that of blowing from the west. There is often something useful to be learnt from the most disagreeable things as from the worst of men. I passed Massawa without calling in, though I would fain have passed a few hours with my friend Jacques Schouchana, who would be there at this time of year. However, the nature of my cargo might have exposed me to unwelcome curiosity.

After Massawa, right along the northern channel I skirted a low, monotonous coast which rose gradually towards the interior of the country, covered with scrubby, thorny mimosas, tufts of dry grass, and everywhere with stones. I was so short of firewood that I had been reduced to a diet of dates and biscuits, so I was on the look-out for a point where I could put in to gather even a few twigs, and I went northwards in short tacks, so as never to be far from the coast. The coastal reef stretched unbroken, without the smallest opening where one might anchor, even for an hour. The coral slabs which border the shores of these warm

97

seas stretch out for more than a quarter of a mile, and make it quite impossible for the smallest ship to put in, for at their edge the water is too deep to give hold for an anchor.

I saw a small *boutre* coming from the north running before the wind. She followed the line of foam which marked the edge of the reef so closely as almost to touch it. Then suddenly she tacked, went in among the breakers, made straight for land, and anchored right inshore. She had passed through an opening in the reefs which I should never have seen if this miraculous chance had not guided me. It seemed the simplest thing in the world to use this *boutre* as pilot and follow her into the anchorage. But when I reached the opening, it looked so narrow and I knew so little about it that I suddenly changed my mind, and with a twist of the helm I stood out to sea again. This decision had been so swift and unhesitating that afterwards I concluded it had been imposed upon me by my subconscious will. I decided to leave my ship lying-to, in charge of Mhamed Moussa, and go ashore in the *pirogue* with Abdi and Kadigeta in case it was necessary to speak Dankali. As soon as we got out of the *pirogue* I made for the bushes, thinking that there I should surely find some firewood.

A native ran up to me and very insolently asked me where I came from, what I wanted, and so on.

'Who are you yourself, who speak like a sultan?' I retorted.

'I am an Italian soldier. Give me your papers and follow me to the post.'

'How do I know you are an askari? You have no uniform. Go back to your post yourself, and think yourself lucky that I don't give you a lesson in manners.'

So saying, I made as if to go towards the clump of bushes. At this the native threw himself upon me, and tried to snatch the revolver I had in my belt. Naturally, a struggle ensued. He called to his aid the sailors of the *boutre* which had put in a few minutes before us, and five of them came running up. I had only Abdi to help me, for Kadigeta had run off towards the sea. My attacker held his ground, clinging like grim death to my revolver. He knew that if only he could keep me from using it, the five Dankalis would soon master us. But my crew had been watching from the ship, which was not far from the coast, and as soon as Mhamed Moussa realized that there was a fight, he began to fire off shots to frighten my aggressors. The arms on board were Gras rifles with cartridges filled with black powder, and the detonations made a terrific row. Soon the *boutre* was smoking like a warship in some old print of an engagement at sea. Terrified, the five Dankalis threw themselves flat on the ground, and the self-styled askari let go and nipped off, mother naked, into the bushes, leaving his white *chama* in Abdi's hands.

We did not wait for a more glorious victory, but ran towards the *pirogue* which Kadageta held ready to push off, and as fast as we could paddle we rejoined the *boutre*. I was just throwing a leg over the gunwale when a volley of shots was fired from the shore. I saw half a score of red tarbooshes appear from behind the dunes. They were the native soldiers of the Italian post, who had come to their comrade's rescue, thinking he had been attacked. They treated us to some pretty sniping, and bullets fell thickly round us. It was fortunate that we were already under sail, for it would not have been easy to manœuvre under the circumstances.

As soon as we began to move, I could not resist replying, for nothing is more irritating than to be used as a target. With the back-sight at eighteen hundred yards, we kept firing off our six rifles. The *boutre* was soon smoking like a crater; the noise of the shots excited us, we had not had such a good time for long. I knew very well that at this distance my shots were harmless, and so were those of the Italians. We rounded off the fête by an imitation of heavy cannon.

This was done by throwing a dynamite cartridge, duly attached and with the wick alight, into the water. This apparatus floated, and when it exploded it made as much noise as a forty-pounder. From a distance it must really have been terrifying.

Soon the dialogue was cut short by increasing distance, and we had a hearty laugh over our battle. On counting the empty cartridge-cases, I found we had fired a hundred and twenty-five shots. A genuine battle, and no mistake. What I didn't know, and what I was to learn only on my return, was that the Italians did not treat it as a laughing matter at all, and that the whole colony of Eritrea was in a ferment over it.

I consulted my chart to see where this henceforth historic battle had taken place, and found that the spot was called Takalaï. Quite near there was an Italian military post, occupied by a detachment of Tigrean guards. Needless to say I hadn't known this.

Much smoke had resulted from this visit, but no fire, for we had not got a single stick of wood, and I didn't think it would be prudent to put in again until we had passed the Italian frontier. I stood out to sea at once to make the people on the coast think I was making for Arabia, so that they would not follow me overland, which they would not have failed to do if I had continued on my way directly northwards. I was far from suspecting how this very decision was to render this adventure still more complicated. While I was struggling with the askari, or perhaps as I fled, I had lost a slipper, like Cinderella, or, strictly speaking, one of my Catalan sandals. This sandal was to appear as evidence against me later on, and it, too, led to complications.

It had been very lucky for me that I had obeyed my impulse and left my ship outside the anchorage, for if I had been inshore I should have been caught like a rat in a trap, and should have fallen into the hands of the Italians. The misunderstanding provoked by my landing might have been cleared up easily enough, but

I should have had to explain the nature of my cargo, and there's no saying how the affair would have ended. Often in my life I have been stopped on the edge of disaster by some such impulse.

For two days and two nights after this adventure at Takalaï I was obliged to beat about in bad weather. Our position at midday two days later indicated that we had only got forty miles farther north. There was a strong southerly current against us.

CHAPTER XVII

THE MIRACULOUS CISTERNS

ON CONSULTING the book of the words I found there was mention of ruins and cisterns on the island of Errich. This island was supposed to be the antique Pharos of the Ptolemies. Perhaps there would be water there, since they spoke of cisterns. We drank terribly in this sultry weather. We had to allow ten litres of water per man per day, for drinking only, for we washed with sea water.

This evening, threatening storm clouds were once more massed on the mountains, but I was not to be caught a second time. It was only three o'clock in the afternoon; I had plenty of time to find an anchorage behind the island of Seïl Bahar before nightfall. There was a vast emerald green bay there, sheltered from every wind that blows, a mute invitation to sailors to spend a peaceful night. The water in it was clear, calm and deep, and the passage leading to it was wide. A *boutre* was moored at the end, surrounded by *pirogues* like a hen surrounded by chickens. I decided to join her. But no sooner had we entered this pretty lake than on all sides I saw the yellow splatches denoting submerged rocks. If the light had been bad and we hadn't noticed them, we should inevitably have been ripped up. By keeping a look-out from the masthead, we were able to reach the healthy, clear water where the other *boutre* was anchored, but it was only after much meandering.

They were Sudanese who were fishing for a kind of sea slug in order to secure the horny membrane which the animal uses as a peduncle to help him to move about, and as a lock when he is resting or when danger threatens. This organ looks like the plectrum of a mandolin, so you can understand what enormous

102

quantities of them are needed to make up an appreciable weight. This substance is very expensive, and is used in India as an aphrodisiac. When it is burned over live coals the smoke, which is strongly ammoniacal, is considered a sovereign remedy for colics, fevers, etc.

The two crews were soon bartering fish for tobacco and exchanging news. Suddenly the khamsin began to blow with terrific violence. What a delight it was to listen to it whistling harmlessly through our rigging, while the *boutre* sat comfortably astride on her two anchors, and think what unholy weather it was outside.

The *nacouda* of the other *boutre* was a very old Sudanese, who had been sailing these waters for forty years. He said that it was quite true that there was drinkable water in an island to the north. Naturally, he could not indicate it on my chart, which was a complete puzzle to him. He carried his charts in his head, and looked with some contempt on the piece of parchment by which I set such store. The explanations he gave me were perhaps quite clear to him, but I didn't follow them very well, especially as he answered yes to all the questions he did not understand. However, I concluded that the island he referred to must be the island of Errich, which was marked on my chart as having cisterns.

Next morning, there was a good land breeze blowing, and we soon reached the bay to the north of this island. There was a shallow lagoon which we had to cross in the *pirogue*. I landed at the foot of a hillock on which, sure enough, there were remains of walls. These must be the ruins my chart mentioned. They were on the highest point of this flat and barren island. There must have been a town there in olden days; one could still see traces of foundations and lines marking out streets and squares. The sun was beating vertically down, and the ground was so hot that we could not put our bare feet on it, but were obliged to wear thick-soled shoes. Mhamed Moussa, who had no shoes, walked cautiously in the shadows of stones or on tufts of grass. Suddenly he vanished from sight as if the earth had swallowed him up. But almost immediately his head reappeared above the ground. He had merely fallen into one of the famous cisterns. I then discovered several of them, all exactly alike. I explored them, not that I hoped to find water—I saw how ridiculous that would be—but out of that curiosity that old things never fail to excite.

These cisterns were in the form of amphoræ, ten feet in diameter. The walls were of baked clay, all in one piece. They were in a perfect state of preservation, without a single crack. The clay for these cyclopean potteries had probably been fired on the spot. They were three-quarters full of sand, and of course there was not the faintest trace of water in them.

It became so unbearably hot that in spite of my desire to potter about among the ruins, I was forced to go back to the ship to quench my thirst. The climate of this island must have changed considerably, for a city could never otherwise have been established in this desolation of burning plains, which stretched as far as the eye could reach, unbroken by a human habitation, a herd of goats, or even a tree. Archæologically speaking, this excursion had been very interesting, but as far as getting water was concerned, I was no farther on. I had just time before nightfall to get to the Kohr Nowarat, in the middle of which was the island of Badhour.

The Kohr Nowarat was a sort of large lake, connected with the sea by a very deep straight which, unfortunately, was barely eighty yards wide and strewn with rocky islets. In the middle of this stretch of water was the island of Badhour, like a fortress surrounded by moats. On the most southerly point of the island, a small village of half a score of huts could be seen. We anchored near it and I went ashore to see if there was any chance of getting water.

We did not meet a single man on the way, only women. They were dressed in ample black robes, of much the same style as those worn by the women of Upper Egypt. They were very Arabic in type, but nearly as brown-skinned as the Dankalis. The children, not at all shy, played round us; the boys were naked, while the little girls wore a loin-cloth. All the men were away fishing for trocas (sea snails) or mother-of-pearl. There were no old men, for the men who follow those occupations die long before they reach old age, generally blind. I saw two or three blind men crouching at the doors of their huts. Their blindness was in the early stages, when the eyes become opaque like those of a boiled fish. This disease of the eyes is due to their work as divers in waters infested by a sort of jelly-fish to which I have already referred when describing the trocas fishers. But hereditary syphilis may also have something to do with it. To even up the balance, the women live to be incredibly old. They looked as if death had forgotten to call for them. The Arab proverb that cadis and old women have to be beaten to death with sticks must have some truth in it.

I learned that there was still water on Badhour from the year before. This year's water had not yet arrived. They spoke about water exactly as if it were a crop that ripened at a given season, and indeed their water did come rather in that way, as you will see. The inhabitants of this island bore no resemblance to those of the adjacent coast. On the mainland, the natives were Sudanese with an admixture of Egyptian blood. In the old days, in the time of the Khedives, they were slaves; to-day they are to be found among the lowest classes in the towns. In Cairo and Alexandria they fulfil the functions of porters, night-watchmen, orderlies and so on. They are magnificent specimens of male perfection with their coal-black skins and beautifully muscled bodies, and dressed in Oriental garb they are most decorative as they stand at the doors of the big hotels. Nowadays they are also in great demand in the dancing establishments from Khartoum to Cairo. But the inhabitants of Badhour are very different, and have the most profound contempt for their neighbours on the continent, as Arabs have for everything that is African.

For a long time this island was the port of concentration for the caravans coming from the Sudan, and it was from here that they set sail for Arabia. Badhour was the central market for working slaves as Tajura was for luxury slaves. This traffic was openly carried on until the making of the Suez canal, and continued for some time after that. Indeed, it is said to flourish to this day, although it is now forbidden.

There were about twenty huts all told in the village, all belonging to the same family. The 'ancestor' was a woman so incredibly ancient that she might have represented a statue of old age. She was very tall, and generally walked nearly bent double, but when she drew herself to her full height, she was terrifying. She did not look at all like a woman, but like a man, a man who resembles a horse. Her immense eyes were further lengthened towards the temples. Strange fires must have burned in those eyes many, many years before. Now they were blurred, the pupils covered with a bluish film, as if they had ceased to look on anything living, or show interest in any human being. Before me I felt I had the spectre of a dead world, with a withered heart incapable of any emotion, a creature older than time, which had lost all its instincts and forgotten all its affections. The others addressed her with great respect, in some unknown tongue in which were mingled a few words of Arabic. They explained to her that we wanted water, for this life-giving element belonged to her. The fleshless spectre was the guardian of the treasure.

Without a word she got up, leaning on her two sticks, and we followed her towards a sort of amphitheatre hollowed out in the centre of the island. It looked like a disused quarry, with vertical sides about twenty-five feet high. At the foot of this circular wall, little heaps of stones like tombs were arranged. There were nearly two hundred of these heaps, a few yards apart.

A flock of white goats was drinking from little clay troughs filled by women who drew the water in leather bags from a deep hole. This water was brackish and had a strong magnesia content; it was undrinkable. This, we were told, was only for the cattle; there was much better water. Salah had a smattering of the language of Badhour, for he had lived for a long time in the Sudan. He acted as interpreter and arranged the price. After long palavers, during which the old woman did not move a muscle, it was agreed that I should pay a thaler and a half for the right to take water from one of the cisterns closed by the heaps of stones. There were different qualities, it appeared, and this price was for one of the best.

The old woman went up to one of the heaps, bent down and with careful gestures removed the stones one by one, while we formed a respectful circle round her. We felt a sort of awe, as if it were a magic ceremony, and she was going to mutter an incantation so that the clear water might gush forth. One has to be in this arid country, burnt by the leaden sun and dried by fiery winds, to understand the emotion we felt at the sight of those rocks which were to give us water. At last all the stones were removed, and a screen of branches appeared. Under it was the mouth of a hole twenty inches in diameter. This was the cistern. A hollow about seven feet deep stretched in a vault under the rock. In the foot of this hole was a sheet of water, so clear that I had to drop a pebble into it to convince myself that it was really there.

A man lowered himself into the hole and drew some water. It was very good, pure as the water of a mountain spring. We had the right to take all we wanted, until the cistern was empty. It appeared that when these cavities were emptied, they gradually re-filled, the water oozing out of the rocky sides. However, at this time of year many were dried up. So it really was water of the previous year we had taken, for the next rains would not fall until September, when they would refill the mysterious reservoirs which fed these miraculous cisterns.

CHAPTER XVIII

THE LEGEND OF CHEIK BADHOUR

THE NIGHT of the Friday on which the body of the Prophet (on whom be prayer and peace), was brought to rest in the Kabba in Mecca, the Holy City where he had been born, a miraculous star waved its golden hair across the sky. The constellation of the Lion was completely covered by it. Led by this divine sign, two hundred pilgrims set out for Mecca across the murderous deserts of Nubia. Two moons had waxed and waned since they had left their villages, when they stopped on the shores of an unknown sea, where blue fishes flew through the air like the birds of heaven. Before this stretch of water with its limitless horizon from under which the sun rose each morning, they gave themselves up to discouragement, and for the first time lost faith in their celestial guide. And that night, the miraculous star failed to appear.

The oldest of them, Cheik Badhour, realized the sin they had committed in letting insidious doubts filter into their hearts and destroy their faith, and he decided they must do penance. Perhaps Allah in his mercy would take pity on them and send them help. He led his companions on to a peninsula in the form of a plateau which jutted like an immense nave into the sea. There, all swore to await death in unshakable faith in Him who had no ancestors and who will have no descendants, in Allah, for there is no god but Allah, and Mohammed is his prophet. In vain the burning heat of the sun and the devils of thirst tortured them; not one, not even the youngest, uttered a single complaint.

When Friday evening came, the sun set in a welter of crimson and, their minds already a little crazed with the approach of death, they thought they saw the orb of day expiring in his blood, like the lamb whose throat is cut on the day of sacrifice. However, they said the prayer of El Acha, just as usual, all lined up behind Cheik Badhour, who conducted the ritual Raka, reciting verses from the Koran. Suddenly, the sky was rent asunder by bands of jagged fire, the earth trembled and the sea lashed itself into tremendous waves. But the faithful remained prostrate, humbly waiting for Allah to work his will.

In the morning, a radiant sun rose over a glassy sea, but the peninsula on which the faithful had been kneeling had broken off from the mainland and was now entirely surrounded by water. They understood that God had pardoned them by saving their bodies from the loathsome beasts that crept, howling, round their retreat every night. So they all forced themselves to a supreme effort, and started to hollow out their tombs. In them they would lie and await death, since such was the will of Allah. Hardly had they scratched the stony soil with their bleeding nails than it became softer, and little pools of clear water formed. This miracle saved their lives. They were able to subsist until a vessel came one day and took them to Djeddah.

And from that day the cisterns have remained, one for each tomb. Down the centuries they have given the water which is life to those who passed through this thirsty land, and never once have they all dried up. Their lesson to men is that faith is precious to believers as the spring in the desert, and that by faith one can move mountains.

CHAPTER XIX
THE HAND OF DESTINY

ONE CAN look to the future with a lighter heart when one knows that the water-barrels are full. The miraculous cisterns of the island of Badhour had taken a weight off my mind, and since our call there we had tacked night and day, with the tenacity of an insect which keeps doggedly climbing up a slope, heedless of the fact that it always falls back to the bottom again. In spite of this, we were all in high spirits. Perhaps the water of Badhour inspired in us some of the faith to which it owed its origin, and we did advance, though with maddening slowness.

I ventured into the Bay of Berenice, which is noted on my chart 'unhealthy bay', which in naval terms means strewn with uncharted rocks. Nevertheless, I crossed it without encountering a single obstacle, and reached the end of the bay, where I anchored on the sandy bottom. There were plenty of rocks under the water in the natural harbour where in days of old had stood the town of Berenice, to which came the caravans from Upper Egypt, with merchandise for export to Arabia and Persia.

The solitude was most impressive. The arid plains stretched up to a distant chain of mountains all bristling with sharp peaks and gigantic needles. On the steep slopes of one of these mountains was an enormous rock shaped like the handle of a dagger. For this reason the sailors who prepared the chart of this region had called it the 'Dagger of Berenice'. Over all was the sand, levelling everything into a monotonous plain. Only a few summits of volcanic hills which seemed to have slipped down into the plain emerged here and there like islets, and the setting sun stretched out their shadows fantastically over the level sand.

The climate here must have changed too in the last few thousand years. No water was now to be found, and that, of course, means death and abandon in these fiery latitudes. This deserted corner of the world might have served as an indication of what our whole planet will perhaps look like one day, when all the water in it has dried up. This shroud of yellow sand stretching illimitably where whole tribes once lived their busy lives in prosperous cities, this silence untroubled even by the hum of an insect, these barren and skeleton-like mountains against the copper sky without rain or cloud, all these things so motionless and changeless seemed to be asleep under a magician's wand. Everything was of the same colour, that ghostly yellow of the Egyptian soil which deepens to golden at the sunset hour, when the sky becomes stained with rose and purple. The blue of the sea, the agitation of the waves, and the dazzling whiteness of the foam which hissed over the sand, made a startling contrast of life in face of all this death. I had seen the volcanic chaos in the south of the Red Sea, and it had made me think of the creation of the world, when the mountains emerging from the generating warmth of the sea had not yet taken form, but this landscape suggested rather a world too old, a world expiring, on which no indication was left that men had once lived there.

The aspect of nature had changed abruptly as soon as we passed the twenty-third line of latitude. The nights were not so hot now, and the air was drier, so that our skins were freed from the constant moisture and eruptions whose itching had made our nights an agony. All this now disappeared as if by magic.

My men had never been so far north, and they were full of astonishment at the lengthening of the days, the lingering twilights, and the fact that the Pole Star climbed ever higher in the sky. As soon as the sun had set and the desert sand had breathed all its heat into the transparent air, a cool breeze came down to the sea and a heavy dew fell over everything. I took advantage of this little land breeze to set sail. I was certainly a little rash to navigate by night in those ill-reputed waters, but the joy of getting on my way, steering straight north with a bellying sail after so many weary days of tacking, this joy that only a sailing-ship can give to a mariner was too irresistible for me to listen to the voice of prudence. Anyhow, life would be pretty dreary if we always acted reasonably; it does one good to be a little mad at times.

Nothing happened to punish our temerity. Mile after mile the *boutre* moved forward, silent and swift, over the calm waters of the bay towards the north-west, this north-west so jealously guarded by that everlasting contrary wind, and my heart sang with triumph. At noon we were right out at sea. The weather was still very fine, but the wind had shifted round to the north. I held on my route on the starboard tack, all sails set, full and by, running six knots like a steamer. The crew, having no work to do, lay in the shade of the sails, playing games which ashore would be disdained by children of eight.

At such moments the slightest incident, even if it is only the sighting of an old plank floating on the water, creates a passionate interest. But for the marvellous weather and the idle condition of our minds, we should never have bothered to manœuvre so as to pick up the object which we saw floating a few cables' lengths away, and which proved to be an empty packing-case. It was in perfect condition; a single spar had been prised off its lid to take out the contents, and it was full of small fishes, which had been overjoyed to find this providential refuge from their enemies. Poor things, they could not have foreseen that they had simply exchanged one danger for another, and that they would be eaten just the same, only fried. In this life it is always the unexpected that happens. I myself had no idea that by picking up this empty box I had changed my destiny, or rather I did not know that Fate had sent it across my path to save me from a terrible danger into which my rashness was to lead me. The cabin-boy was just about to chop up the case to light his oven fire, and I had given him leave to do so, when the idea struck me that we might use the case to hold our sack of biscuits. So I had it put in the hold alongside the eight cases of hashish, which were very similar in size and appearance. In this way, our biscuits would not be broken to fragments as always happened when they were in a sack, for the men kept walking over it.

Towards evening, the breeze hauled to the north-west, and began to blow with its habitual violence. Farewell our pleasant idleness; it was once more the struggle with sea and wind, under reduced canvas and with the hatches fastened down. No fear of our amusing ourselves picking up empty cases now. The farther north we got, the more violent became the wind. There was not a cloud in the sky, only a faint mist which never lifted round the horizon. Probably it is this atmospheric condition which gives North Africa its magnificent sunsets, which are always pointed out to tourists as the classic background for the pyramids at Giza. Out here in the open sea, this dimness prevented me from seeing the outline of the mountains and finding out exactly where I was.

For six days I had not been able to identify a single characteristic peak, and the indications on my chart did not at all coincide with what I could see. For instance I read 'sharp peak', 'haycock', 'hummock', and when I looked, expecting to see them, I saw mountains of an entirely different shape. All the same, my observations were exact and my calculations correct. We were undoubtedly in latitude 24° 15'. I began to look out for the lighthouse at Sanghaneb, which stands in the middle of the Red Sea on a reef. But in the evening, as the sun set behind them, a chain of mountains stood out against the red sky with sharp peaks, haycocks, hummocks and all the rest of it, such as I had vainly looked for two days before.

Could I be forty miles farther south than my astronomical point indicated? My self-esteem as a sailor suffered a rude shock, but what bothered me most was the brutal snatching away of my illusions; I felt as if some malevolent hand had pushed us forty miles back in one second. All the same, I could have sworn that my calculations were right. But in that case the mountains of Elba must have changed their position, unless I had made a mistake in the date. I verified all my preceding calculations, and found that for a week I had made my corrections with twenty-four hours of difference. I had marked my departure on Friday, 10th July, whereas it had really been the 9th. As the difference in the declining of the sun was about 45°, I had imagined myself to be forty-five miles farther north than I really was. Honour was safe; I had just to swallow my disappointment.

CHAPTER XX

FIRST CONTACT WITH THE CUSTOMS

WE HAD just caught sight of Sanghaneb on its reef, looking like a statue wearing a black and white checked dress. At midnight three days later we sighted the light of The Brothers. We had been tacking for about a fortnight since our visit to the island of Badhour, and though we had husbanded our water very carefully, there now remained only enough for seven days. Prudence demanded that we should renew our supplies without delay. We had to settle this question before going into the Gulf of Suez, where we could not have the slightest contact with the population on either side. I decided to go over to the coast of Arabia, where I could show myself without fear, as there would certainly be a watering-place at the foot of the Antar mountains. I ought to have known that at sea one can count on nothing.

Hardly had we started on the port tack when the wind hauled to the north more and more as we gained to the east. We could soon hardly manage to keep our helm north-east; that meant we were really going east when you take into consideration the lee, the current, and all the little side-issues of sailing close to the wind. It was most discouraging; you might almost say we were going back to Djibouti. We had to change our tack so that the wind would be favourable to us. But it increased in violence, and at sunset a hurricane was blowing. The sea became very disagreeable, with short, choppy waves, as the wind struck obliquely the heavy permanent swell from the north-west.

It is useless to describe what followed. Everything not made fast was swept from the deck. A heavy sea carried off the oven, which had been left in the fo'c'sle, and unfortunately our bread was still cooking in it.

116

We should be reduced to a diet of dates and boiled grain for a long time. Cheery prospect. But that was not the greatest disaster. The hoops of a two-hundred-litre water-barrel had just burst, eaten away by rust, and all the contents of the barrel had been lost. We had only twenty-five litres of water left. We had now no choice but to make with all speed for Kosseir a little Egyptian port opposite The Brothers.

The Brothers were two flat islets, two madreporic tables in the middle of the sea. On one of them was a lighthouse. I thought for a moment of going and asking water from the lighthouse-keeper, but it would have been quite impossible to put in at the islet in such weather, for the sea was smashing and raging against it in an immense welter of foam. If it had been calm I might also have asked water from a steamer, but that, too, was out of the question. There was nothing for it but to put in at Kosseir. It was an Egyptian port, so there was bound to be a customs house and excisemen who would search my boat, since I was penetrating into Egyptian waters. This idea filled me with misgivings, and I nearly gave up my dangerous project; perhaps it would be better to go off before the wind, and seek a watering-place, no matter where, on the coast of Arabia. But the idea of losing all those miles for which we had fought so hard against the wind was too painful. No, any risk rather than that. Needless to say, I was trying to marshal any arguments I could find to justify the crazy rashness of what I had decided to do.

If I came successfully through the visit of the customs at Kosseir, it would be a feather in my cap, and would be of the greatest help to me in affronting the dangers of possible encounters in this accursed Gulf of Suez, one hundred and eighty miles long. Besides, if I got to Suez with my papers not visaed since my departure from Djibouti, as if I were a liner from the Far East, my little twelve-ton *boutre* would be looked upon with the greatest suspicion. To-day it would seem much more natural, since Alain Gerbault has set the fashion for long trips in sailing-boats, but at that time I risked drawing on myself a lot of most undesirable attention. I thought for a moment of putting in at some solitary point and hiding my cases before entering the harbour of Kosseir, but there is no shelter on the African coast at this part, and even if the weather had allowed me to carry out this project, some one would probably have seen me and wondered what on earth I was doing, and once suspicions were aroused, it would have been all up with me. Once more I had to walk straight into the danger and bluff for all I was worth. So I put myself into the skin of a man with nothing to fear, and boldly entered the port.

It was a very small harbour, with just room for a few coasters. The village, or town if you like, consisted of an agglomeration of tumble-down dwellings, but on the quay was a large, yellow-painted building with a wide-open door. Near it was a sentry-box containing a guard wearing a tarboosh, and two old cast-iron carronades stood facing the sea, on a neat little gravelled esplanade, fenced off with chains. How well I knew this classic arrangement. Here was housed the official element of the port. My heart sank; I longed madly to turn and flee while there was yet time. Heaven alone knew what dangerous variety of civil servant was concealed behind these yellow walls.

Two large, half-dismasted *boutres* rocked indolently in front of the quay. The arrival of my sailing-ship, with her rigging different from that of the barks in this region and flying that practically unknown flag, the French tricolour, set the whole town in a commotion. In two minutes the quay was thronged with tarboosh-crowned gentlemen, neat and shining as English policemen. They rushed hither and thither, very agitated, then got into a boat and made for us. Among them was the Health Officer. He was a young Egyptian, who lolled in the stern of the boat with an important air. He addressed me in English, the only language a civil servant of distinction would deign to speak.

I asked humbly if he would mind speaking French or even Arabic, with an apologetic smile to excuse my temerity. He looked at me with some surprise, and abandoned the starched correctness of his attitude as if it were not compatible with the vulgar languages referred to. Yes, he spoke French. Two men came on board and conscientiously sprinkled the deck with some foul-smelling disinfectant. Until a few years ago this ridiculous rite was imposed on all the liners passing through the canal. It had the advantage of being very expensive. But much I cared for the evil smell of their preparation, or its exorbitant cost, or all the petty annoyances invented by the Health Service to hinder ships. I was ready to take everything smiling, and even be grateful so long as they left my cases alone. As the doctor left he announced, as an agreeable surprise, that the police and the customs people would be coming on board. Devil take it, I hadn't thought that this little port would be quite so full of officials.

Just to be prepared for the worst, I left the lateen yard at the top of the mast, with the sail tied round it with wisps of straw. If the customs became too inquisitive, I would take French leave of them. If I carried off one of the excisemen with me, so much the worse for him; I would drop him at the first port of call. I was sure of being able to escape in this manner; these functionaries would be too surprised to offer any resistance, so accustomed are they to the patient submission shown by ships to their maddening and ridiculous tyrannies. Only, if I were obliged to do this, all my plans would be frustrated, for I could no longer dream of going to Egypt.

At last a large launch arrived, with a beautiful green flag on which in large white letters was the beloved word CUSTOMS. It was full of native customs employees, accompanied by an officer in full uniform, very spick and span. As soon as they came alongside he addressed me in French, which he spoke very correctly. The doctor must have told him, and I must say he did not seem particularly anxious to play at being an Englishman. I helped him on board.

'Have you any cargo?' he asked.

'No, I am in ballast; I have only provisions for my crew.'

I felt that it was on the tip of his tongue to ask a very natural question, 'What are you doing here?' So without giving him time to utter it, I explained that I was pearl fishing. This occupation has a dash of romance about it; people are apt to think at once of the Arabian Nights, and then, too, I had a crew of men of a race unknown in Egypt, which added to the picturesqueness. He looked at me with interest. Here was a pleasant change from the dull routine of his duties as customs officer. His natives, however, had not come under this romantic spell, and most prosaically they began to go systematically over the ship with the joyous activity of fox-terriers looking for rats. They opened the crew's sea-chests, sounded the empty water-barrels, unfolded the spare sails, and so on.

'Would you like me to have everything that is in the hold brought up on deck?' I asked in my most dulcet tones. 'That would make it easier for your men to make a thorough examination.'

'No, no, it is not at all necessary,' replied the officer, impatient to get back to my stories of pearl fishing. 'Just open these packing-cases. What do you have in them?'

'Ship's biscuit. But you can see for yourself; there is one that was opened this morning.'·

And I showed him the case Providence had sent me.

'But if you like,' I added, 'I'll open all the rest; it's quite simple. I have also,' I continued without waiting for an answer, 'a fairly valuable lot of pearls. Have I any formalities to go through for them?'

'Ah, you have pearls?'

'Yes, I'll show you them. But perhaps we had better

wait until your men have finished their inspection; I should prefer to be alone with you.'

These men are very 'gleg i' the uptak''.

'Certainly, you are quite right. Anyhow, they have finished. There is no point in opening the other cases, seeing that this one is open. Let's look at your pearls.'

He sent his men ashore, and when we were alone I showed him a small lot of pearls I had luckily thought of bringing with me. He had never seen pearls gathered in a heap like that in their red rag which set them off so well. Naturally, he asked the inevitable question amateurs always ask:

'What are they worth?'

I named a figure. He took one up and rolled it lovingly in the palm of his hand.

'And what is this one worth?'

I looked at him with a smile, then, after a short silence:

'Let us say it is worth the pleasure of making your acquaintance. I shall be honoured if you will accept it as a souvenir of my visit to Kosseir.'

He protested half-heartedly, but his face shone with delight.

'You got these pearls in Egyptian waters, I suppose?'

'H'm . . . yes,' I answered at random.

'That's all right, then; you've no duty to pay on them. At least I don't think so, for the question has never come up before. Just as well to say nothing about them at Suez. You can easily keep them in your pocket.'

He then invited me to go ashore with him and visit the commander of police. We were now as thick as thieves. I took two Somali sailors with me as escort, just to fix the eyes of my hosts on something picturesque and new to them, and keep them from thinking too much. The Chief of Customs, for that was who my amiable friend turned out to be, was a fat young man, very Egyptian, indeed Oriental, who let the Arab peep through as soon as we had exchanged half a dozen

sentences in that tongue. He was surprised to hear my
men call me Abd-el-Haï, and stupefied when I said
carelessly that I was a Mohammedan. This put him
quite at his ease, and it was agreed that I should dine
with him that evening.

When we reached his house, he became wholly
Egyptian. He took off his military uniform, and put
on a long silk *gandoura*, thrust his bare feet into heel-
less slippers, and ensconced himself luxuriously among
the cushions of his divan. His servant brought a narghile and the traditional Turkish coffee, with a multitude of little dishes containing fritters and such-like
dainties, cooked in the native fashion. The doctor
arrived and made himself quite at home, smoking the
narghile and idly eating fried fish and oily fritters with
his fingers. We spoke Arabic. Where was the correct
Englishman of an hour or two ago?

When the mouthpiece of the narghile was passed to
me, I assumed my most innocent air and asked:

'What is it? Is it hashish?'

'Unhappy man,' replied the Chief of Customs, half
laughing, half shocked, 'you obviously don't know that
hashish is absolutely forbidden in Egypt.'

'Really?' I laughed. 'I didn't know. All the same
I have read that it was smoked in Egypt, and I should
have liked to see what it looked like.'

'Of course it is smoked, a great deal, even . . . but
you must never speak of it. The very word is taboo
in Egypt.'

The doctor smiled and said nothing. After this,
seeing dinner-time was still a little way off, we went to
see the Police Commissioner. He was a Maltese, and
like all the Maltese in the Government services, he was
more English than any Englishman. He affected a cold
disdain for everything Egyptian, and spoke to the
natives with the chilly politeness with which one would
address a well-trained servant to whom one only gave
orders, and he never looked at them, as was only fitting
when dealing with impersonal beings who only spoke

in the third person. The vestibule of his house was cluttered up with golf clubs and tennis rackets, and on the wall were English prints representing stories of mail coaches and the Pickwick Club.

When we entered the reception room, which had a large bay window, we could see nothing but clouds of smoke coming from behind *The Times*. There were comfortable armchairs, whisky, soda, pipes, and a prevailing smell of Virginian tobacco. Presently *The Times* was lowered, and the commander deigned to realize that we were in the room. There was nothing English about his appearance, though his blazer bore the coat of arms of an Oxford college on the pocket. He was swarthy and oily as a Bolivian, and though he was carefully shaved, his face was blue right up to his cheek-bones. He had bushy eyebrows, jet-black eyes, and a vast nose with wide, hairy nostrils, from which I could not tear my fascinated gaze. He spoke Italian in the coppery voice of a Southerner. My mind instantly flew to the insolent gondoliers of his native island.

When we had entered the room, across the perfume of Virginian tobacco I could detect an odour which reminded me of the scene at the farm at Steno, when Petros Caramanos burned something under my nose. Almost at once, too, a servant dressed like the 'boys' of the real Englishmen at Aden, came in to remove a superb narghile. H'm, I had little doubt about the sort of tobacco this Maltese smoked when he was alone. My companion immediately put him at his ease by begging him to go on smoking his narghile. The commander laid down his meerschaum—from a famous London maker, I noticed—which he had probably lit when he heard us coming, and replaced between his lips the jade mouthpiece of his water pipe. Once again we had to eat oily fried dainties with our fingers, and I started to speak of pearl fishing, of divers, of sharks, and so on. They asked me to bring in my Somalis, whom I had left at the door. The commander examined them in an odd fashion, dilating his nostrils as if he could sniff mysterious effluvia. He was so astonished that he resumed his Oriental form, and belched loudly after the radishes. This involuntary sound, so very un-English, recalled him to realities, and he tried to cover it by a fit of coughing. For a few minutes he was again the stiff Englishman. Then he started the inevitable gramophone, and when I was leaving I presented him with a pearl.

During the dinner at the house of the Chief of Customs, we spoke of trade and business.

'You should have brought a cargo of coffee up from Abyssinia. It is worth here three times what it fetches in Djibouti, and I should have helped you to get out of paying the duty of five francs the kilo. Just think, what a profitable deal. . . .' And so on, and so on.

And for two hours we spoke of trading, but the word 'hashish' was never mentioned. It was a word which was taboo, right enough. Obviously he looked on me as an idiot who did not know the first thing about this precious commodity. Besides, hashish could only come from the north, and could only be had from Greeks, in whose hands was the monopoly. It would have been ridiculous to speak about it to a Frenchman.

Before I left he gave me a letter for a friend of his in the customs at Suez, to whom he recommended me warmly. And next day I joyously set sail, my papers duly stamped to show I had gone through the customs. During this stay I had been able to renew my stores and fill my water-barrels with distilled water, for there was no other at Kosseir. What I had specially appreciated was the green vegetables, which were brought by camel from the interior. They came from regions watered by the Nile, by a road which stretched for a hundred kilometres, for Kosseir was the point on the coast nearest to this generous river.

CHAPTER XXI

TWO TYPES OF ENGLISHMEN

THE WIND was more manageable now, and I was able to make a long tack with the helm set due north, but during the night the weather changed again, the wind became violent and the sea got very rough. I swerved and tacked towards the land. For three days we battled against a raging wind. At times the sea was untenable and nearly swallowed us up bodily. We only just managed to keep heading north, and in two days we only advanced a few poor little miles. I began to wonder if I should ever be able to enter the Gulf of Suez by the strait of Jubal. It seemed nearly as bad as the Bab-el-Mandeb. But on my chart I saw the great archipelagos and the labyrinths of reefs in the Bay of Gimsa, to the west of the strait. I thought it would be safer to pass through them than to affront the choppy and dangerous waves raised by the north-west wind between the island of Chadwin and the coast of Arabia. It really seemed useless to continue this exhausting struggle, so I decided to give up for the night and seek shelter behind the island of Safadja, in the large bay which stretches at the foot of a picturesque mountain and is sheltered from all the winds. The mountains were still of the same nature, so tortured and bare that they looked like the skeletons of mountains, with giddily soaring needles and deep, narrow ravines down which rivers of gravel streamed towards the sea.

Low buildings and wooden huts clustered round a tall factory chimney. There was a mine of some sort there, for I could make out the wagons of an aerial railway suspended above the chaos. The island was deserted, in spite of the scaffoldings of oil wells which rose on all sides. These were doubtless borings for petrol, for we were now in the region under which flowed the deep layer which extends as far as the Farzan Islands. Bad weather forced me to stay in this shelter for two days, and we took this opportunity to repair the rigging, and do the thousand and one tedious little jobs which are always put off on some pretext or other. These scenes had one beauty before, that of solitude, but that has been for ever destroyed by those hideous factories, and an indescribable melancholy now hangs over them. Nevertheless, the colourings remain splendid, and every evening I was forced to marvel afresh at the exquisite and unreal tones, so fanciful that no name exists for them, and which are only to be seen here on these northern shores of the Red Sea.

As the wind continued to blow as violently as ever, I was forced to conclude that this was its normal speed, and to make the best of a bad job. I could only navigate by day in the labyrinth of reefs into which I was about to venture, but the comparative calm of those inland seas and the frequency of the land breezes would make up for the time lost by the nightly halt. There is no use describing the days which followed, spent in the delicate manœuvring of the ship through the narrow channels strewn with coral rocks.

One morning the cabin-boy, having gone as usual to pump water out of the hold, reported that there was much more than usual, which rather alarmed me. But this water proved to be brackish, so it couldn't all have come from the sea. I then discovered that the hoops of two more barrels had burst, eaten away by rust like the other one. This was a disaster, for in this region there was not the smallest watering-place; all water had to be distilled from sea-water. And there was no hope of getting water before Suez. I bound the staves of the remaining barrels with tightly twisted ropes. Here I was once more faced with this terrible water problem. There was only one thing I could do, and that seemed to me quite natural; namely, go and get

water from one of the numerous encampments round
the wells.

In order to get to the nearest one we had to sail
dead against the wind up a channel barely three cables'
length wide and more than two miles long, between
reefs which could be clearly seen through the transparent water. Our rigging obliged us to wear, so the
short tacks we had to make did not get us very far, for
at each change we lost about as much headway as we
had just gained. We took more than three hours to
clear the three miles, and we had tacked more than a
hundred and fifty times. This was a very tiresome
manœuvre because of the lateen yard, which had to be
changed over each time, and also because of the sheet
on the front of the mast, which whipped furiously in
the wind as soon as the sail sagged. It took the whole
crew to master it and pull the sail taut. If it had contrived to escape during this manœuvre, not only would
the men have risked being stunned while trying to get
hold of it, but during this time the ship would have
drifted and we should have been on the rocks. At last
we got safely to the open sea, but the hands of all the
crew were raw and bleeding.

Soon we reached Abou Mingar, and I saw metal
tanks on the beach, reservoirs for the petroleum, I
supposed. There was a whole litter of machinery lying
there in the open; enormous black pipes ran over the
sand and disappeared underground, and a horrible
smell of naphthalene filled the air. We anchored right
in at a little landing-stage. Nobody on shore seemed
to pay much attention to us; the long-shirted coolies
went on pushing the little wagons slowly along, singing
the while to keep themselves awake. At last a European, a workman in khaki shirt and blue trousers,
signed to us to go elsewhere. A little farther away two
other men in sun-helmets and shorts, obviously
Englishmen, watched to see that their order was obeyed.

What could I do? I changed to another anchorage,
and immediately went ashore, intending to speak to the

two indifferent Englishmen. But the workman who had signed to us to move intercepted me. He was a sort of foreman, of the classic type of worker in the Egyptian ports, speaking all the Mediterranean tongues. It was difficult to tell whether he was Maltese, Greek, or Italian. His accent was a mixture of the accents of all these tongues, no matter which he spoke. One might call it the Egyptian accent.

'What do you want?' he asked me in a surly tone.

'First of all to see the man who is in charge here.'

'The manager isn't here; he is inland at the extraction well. It's about five miles from here, an hour by the little tram.'

'But who are these gentlemen over there?'

'They are English engineers.'

When I said I needed provisions, he explained with satisfaction that I could get nothing at all here, but only at the mine, where there was a canteen where one could buy all sorts of things. Only it was necessary to get a permit to go there.

I introduced myself to the two Englishmen. They looked at me with withering scorn, and the bored suspicion with which you might regard an unfortunate commercial traveller who came to your door trying to sell you something. Once in my adventurous life I had hawked coffee, and all the horrible memories of that time rose in my mind. I told them that I was French, that I had come from Djibouti, and I explained the accident that had left me without water. They listened to my story with perfectly expressionless faces. Then one of them deigned to remove his pipe from his mouth and answer in painfully correct French:

'No visitors are allowed on the concession, and I can't take the responsibility of allowing you to go to the mine. You must send an application to Cairo.'

I pleaded for water at least, since there was none on the coast, and in no country in the world does one refuse water, even to a dog.

'Quite impossible,' he replied briefly.

And to indicate he had said quite enough, he replaced his pipe in his mouth as if he were locking a door, and turned his back on me. I treated him to a few choice insults in order to cool my helpless wrath, but he had ceased to understand French. Tranquilly he resumed his study of a map which his colleague was holding open on the back of a negro commandeered as desk.

As I returned to the quay I saw a small steamer come in. She was a very old tug which went the rounds of the different boring wells and concessions in the Bay of Gimsa. The captain was also one of those men of indefinite and interchangeable nationality, but he was a sailor. He gave me water, potatoes, and even a loaf.

. . . . . .

The smell of oil, the factory noises, and the sight of all this machinery tended by grimy-faced men disgusted me. For more than a month I had been living with the desert and the sea in absolute freedom, and it was very disagreeable to have the spell broken by the presence of my fellow-creatures. The landscape remained the same, but the divine character with which my imagination had invested it had gone. While I was alone in the midst of these solitudes, I had felt myself right in the middle of this vast universe, in which some mysterious instinct urged me to lose myself. Woe to the man who has once experienced the bliss of this divine communion with nature: every time he is compelled to return to the herd he will suffer from an awful solitude. I now turned the helm towards Arabia. The coast of Asia was still mercifully free from industries, there was no fear of seeing other factories there, or of encountering unfriendly English engineers.

But in less than two hours it would be dark. I should never have time to reach it and find an anchorage; it would be better to try to get through the strait of Jubal during the night. Perhaps for once the wind would have lulled a little. But such hopes are snares: the reality is always very different. It was already almost night when we got round the southern point of Shadwan Island.

This big, mountainous island guards the entrance to the Gulf of Suez as Perim guards the Strait of Bab-el-Mandeb. It consists of a chain of reddish hills separated by deep ravines. The rock is absolutely bare, without the faintest trace of vegetation, and these mountains descend to the sea in a vertical wall, forming sheer cliffs which spring from the water without shore or coastal reef. This wall lies in the axis of the strait, like a ship riding at anchor. A lighthouse with red lamps has been built on the most southerly point, facing the open sea, to indicate the strait to ships entering the gulf. The coast on either side is hidden behind the horizon; all one sees are the vast reefs which stretch out into the water for over six miles. During the day the great mass of the Sinai Mountains can be seen to the east, and very far to the west the ragged peaks of the Egyptian mountains. The island of Chadwan is clearly visible in the day-time, and a ship has only to enter the strait boldly, leaving the island to port; but by night everything is obscure, and nothing indicates this deep channel which is ten miles wide, and one has only to drift a little to lose sight of the island entirely. Ships then risk being ripped open on the rocks which lie under the water. You can see how important the lighthouse is.

When I arrived to windward of the island, the last glimmer of twilight enabled me to make out its lofty tower built at the foot of the mountain, some sixty feet above sea-level. Near by was the little square house where the keeper lived, and when I looked through my telescope I saw a man watching us through his. This hermit, tucked away on his solitary rock, takes an interest in everything that appears on the surface of the sea, just as sailors do during a long voyage. A little below the house was a small wooden platform built out over the sea. Probably this was the landing-stage where the ship which brought the keeper's stores anchored.

The native sailors recount a story that there are seals living round this islet, and some of them declare that they have seen the females suckling their young. Perhaps what they have seen are sea cows, strange-looking creatures with vaguely human busts, which haunt these seas, and round which the mariners of old wove the first legends of mermaids.

Mhamed Moussa was telling the others stories which might have come out of the Odyssey, of which, naturally, he had never heard. The ancient legends had been handed down by word of mouth, according to the immortal tradition of the popular story-tellers. The others were drinking in his words with wide-eyed interest, transported into a magic world, their imaginations afire with the wildest dreams. Before this rocky island dimly visible through the gathering darkness, amid the roar of the surf and the eerie cries of the great gulls wheeling in the beams from the turning lantern, these simple stories take on an impressive grandeur which no written word could ever convey. Probably I was affected by the glamorous atmosphere created by this admirable audience, which listened with such avidity to the singing voice of Mhamed Moussa coming out of the darkness.

We had hardly emerged from the shelter of the island when the wind began to blow with renewed fury. The sea poured out of the strait in an impetuous torrent, the great billows tumbling over each other in their haste. I had just time to tack to avoid breaking the mast, yard, and bowsprit. I had been expecting bad weather, but not this tumultuous, raging sea, in which it was impossible for a little ship to live. I went back into the shelter of the island. In the darkness there was only one hope—to find the little landing-stage and moor the *boutre* there. But now the night was very black. Before me, on the island side, was a thick curtain of obscurity into which the red lamp of the lighthouse shot out its fiery rays, all sparkling with tiny stars, which were the white wings of the sea-gulls thrown for a second into dazzling relief. In these circumstances it was impossible to judge distances, but as I knew the coast was very steep I approached without fear in search of the wharf which would save us. Kadigeta, the lynx-eyed young Dankali, lay in the prow trying to pierce the darkness.

At last we saw it before us. We ran down the sails and let the *boutre* carry her way. Abdi dived with the end of a rope in one hand and swam like a porpoise towards the land, while we played out the cable. He vanished instantly into the night, while the rope continued to run out. From a long way off we heard his voice calling that he had not reached land yet, and the coil of rope was finished. We had to pull it all in again with him at the end of it. During this time we had drifted, and a current was now bearing us rapidly away from the island. We were already so far away that it no longer sheltered us from the wind which started driving us out to sea. We could hardly see the island, having now come into the zone where the red glare of the lantern beams enveloped us as they touched the water. The current must have been swift indeed to have pushed us so far in such a short time. We had to try at all costs to get back to the island, otherwise the sea would carry us off like a piece of driftwood on a river towards the south.

It was new moon, the season of high tides, and I must have arrived just at the moment of the ebb. We crowded on sail and started tacking to regain the miles we had lost. At regular intervals the sails were lit up by the red ray which passed over us. Then little by little as we won our way back, the beam only gleamed on the top of the white triangle of canvas; then we remained wholly in the shadow while the rays passed over our heads, carrying their comforting message to sailors away on the horizon. I wondered if we would be lucky enough to strike the exact spot where the wooden jetty was built. That was the whole question. We had to lower the sails as we got near the mountains,

because of the puffs of wind that fell from them in
sudden gusts and also because of the eddies. We
should have to approach at a good speed, then lower
the sails at the last possible moment and let the *boutre*
carry her way, in order to strike the wharf. But to
carry out this manœuvre successfully, it was necessary
to know exactly at what point we wanted to touch land,
and in this obscurity we could not see twenty yards
ahead.

I leaned over the helm, gnawing my nails with
anxiety, my eyes fixed on this threatening darkness.
Suddenly I saw a little, twinkling star appear a little
above sea-level, some distance from the red globe of
the lighthouse lamp. It waved slowly up and down
and I realized that it was a lantern carried by somebody
on foot. It moved slowly along, sometimes disappearing behind the rocks. Then it remained stationary. It
was undoubtedly a signal meant for us. Probably the
lighthouse-keeper had been watching our manœuvres.
This unexpected assistance cheered us up, and for
another hour we tacked towards the light. But as I did
not know how powerful it was, I could not estimate
our distance from it, and though it glimmered feebly
enough, it was sufficient to dazzle us and make the
surrounding darkness still blacker. I thought I was
still a long way off when I suddenly saw its reflection
on the choppy water, and realized that the wharf was
only twenty yards away. I had just time to lower the
sails before we were right in under the wooden erection
covered with seaweed. The tide was out.

A man was crouching on the little platform ready to
seize the rope we slung him. He moored us solidly
and called out 'All right'. Then before I had time to
collect my thoughts, he had taken his lantern and started
back up the mountain-side, like a peaceful citizen going
home to bed. As he went he threw me a cordial 'Good
night'. The wind began to try to push us out to sea
again, but this time there was nothing to fear—we were
securely fastened. I watched the light going up the

mountain-side and vanishing. The man had entered his house. Another type of Englishman, this good fellow . . . a hermit and a sailor.

Even if the position we were in had allowed us to sleep, the deafening noise made by the screaming sea-gulls wheeling unceasingly in the rays of the lantern would have kept us from closing an eye. I was afraid, too, that the currents would be reversed when the tide changed. In that case nothing could save us from going on the rocks. I could not see them, but I could hear the wind whistling through their crannies, and the suction of the air when the swell penetrated into them, then the heavy crashes of the waves dashing against them, followed by streaming and spraying. My men were very uneasy. In vain I explained to them that all these strange sounds were·produced by the force of the water in the hollows; they were sure that there were seals and other sea-monsters concealed there. Abdi said he had seen one holding our mooring-rope between his teeth, and he was certain that it was these monsters who kept trying to push the ship out to sea. All this, accompanied by the most terrifying details. I could understand their condition of mind very well, for I myself was so influenced by the strangeness of this place that all the stories I had heard haunted my mind, and if I had been obliged to dive down into this black water, I could not have done it without a shiver of fear. I rather enjoyed being in the grip of this vague super-stitious fear, for in spite of science and learning, the human soul has a natural thirst for the marvellous and the unknown.

Towards morning the rope which attached us to the jetty, which had been kept taut by the wind constantly driving us away from land, slackened and the ship stopped swinging. As I had feared, the current had begun to flow in the contrary direction. I should have liked to go and thank the Englishman who had saved us, but I felt that it would be imprudent to wait here any longer. This time the strait seemed calmer. In

these regions the aspect of the sea changes with disconcerting rapidity. We went up the channel in a long
tack, making good progress; in the morning we had
passed the northern point of the island and on the
starboard tack I ventured in among the reefs of the
inner sea which stretches to the north-west. There I
could work profitably to windward in these waters
which are always calm, despite the strong breeze
blowing.

CHAPTER XXII
THE STRAIT OF JUBAL

I WANTED TO gain the shelter of the southern part of the big island of Jubal before night fell. At the point which was marked as anchorage on my chart I saw with disgust that there was a cluster of buildings, but, though I scanned the spot most carefully through my telescope, I could not see any signs of inhabitants; everything looked deserted. I anchored in front of a pretty beach all littered with machinery of all kinds, elevators, cranes, and so on.

We went ashore. The first thing we noted was that there was no trace of footprints in the sand, which was as smooth or as ridged by the wind as in the most deserted islands of the Red Sea. I saw a big building the door of which stood wide open. I went into an engine-room containing a horizontal Diesel engine. A workman's bench and all the usual tools were lying about as if the workmen had just gone home to dinner, but everything was thickly covered with dust, and the machinery was all festooned with spiders' webs. Outside, compound tackle was hung on lifting-jacks complete with chains, and a half-full barrel of oil stood with closed tap.

I could not believe my eyes. No doubt a watchman would soon be appearing. I fired off a shot to attract his attention and sent a man up to the higher ground to inspect the surroundings. But he could see nobody, and my shot remained unanswered. The island was deserted all right; everything looked as if it had been abandoned suddenly. I was strongly tempted to lay hands on all this material left only in the charge of God, and the pillaging instincts of my sailors, accustomed to stripping wrecks, were strongly excited at the sight of all this tempting booty. I had some difficulty in making them see reason. My virtuous remonstrances were not at all dictated by a lofty moral sense; I should have laid hands on all this treasure trove without the slightest scruple, if only to wreak vengeance on the two English engineers for their reception, had I not realized how impossible it would be for me to put in at Suez with such an odd cargo, so little compatible with my alleged business of pearl fishing. This eccentricity would inevitably have drawn upon me an attention I was far from desiring. I therefore contented myself with taking a few tools, which are always useful, and various bits of wood which might come in handy for repairs. I was obliged to promise my men that we would stop here on our way home, and if the legal owner had not come to claim his property, to allow them to load it on the *boutre*. There was an assortment of copper plates which so tempted them that I had great difficulty in preventing them from carrying them on board at once. The most valuable discovery we made was that of several barrels of fresh water, and on them we pounced with considerable satisfaction.

We went off before dawn. The wind was not yet violent, and after a three hours' tack we reached the edge of the reef of Schab-Ali, which runs along the coast of Asia for about twenty miles, eight miles from the shore. This reef was formed of a series of madreporic tables joined together by rocky spikes between which there was no clear passage. Behind this barrier, on which the waves broke, was a little inner sea of calm and limpid blue water, in which ships of small tonnage could come round the most violent head winds. In this sheltered zone other beds of madrepores show their wide yellow patches just under the surface. At this season, when the Red Sea was at its lowest level, there was very little water covering the reefs, and at low tide some of the rocks and tables emerged completely. There were generally sea eagles perched on them, which gave an appearance of lively animation to these strange silhouettes. We went into this inner sea by a narrow opening in the southern extremity of the reef. The wreck of a steamer was spitted on the rocks, so perfectly preserved that for a moment we had the illusion of having arrived just after the disaster had taken place. Two enormous herons had taken up their abode on the deck of the wreck, and were walking about with great dignity; from a distance we thought they were men. As we came nearer they flew heavily away, followed by a whole flock of screaming birds.

I had to yield to the prayers of the crew and go and inspect these sad remains more closely, for Mhamed Moussa and Abdi came from Cape Gardafui, notorious for the number of wrecks which take place every year, and flotsam and jetsam had an irresistible attraction for them.

In reality this ship had been abandoned for many years. Every part of it was eaten away by salt and burned by the sun. All that remained was the shell, held together by the reefs which surrounded it on all sides, giving an appearance of life to this rusty phantom by preventing the waves from breaking it up. No doubt in a night of fog, that fog which consists of sand blown from the desert by the west winds, they had not seen the lighthouse on Chadwan, and driven out of their course by the violence of the wind, had run in here between the reef and the mainland, and only realized their error when they ran aground. I was always saddened by the sight of those dead ships, those corpses which remained upright as long as they could and seemed to struggle desperately not to go under and disappear entirely from the eyes of men, but to stay there as a warning to others. In the empty hold, through which the waves washed with curious sucking noises, in the dismantled alleyways, everywhere ghosts seemed to flit about. Firan found some bones in the fo'c'sle. Much moved, we all ran up to see them. They were the bones of a dog, or of a bitch rather, for in a corner we picked up two tiny skulls and fragments of bones broken up by the birds of prey. I imagined the death of this poor beast, which had remained alone on the wreck, unwilling to abandon her little ones which she had hidden in a corner known only to herself, where she had put them when the water had begun to fill the ship. It was strange to find these bleached bones after so many years, these touching skeletons which had remained to tell their sad story.

Since we had stopped in any case, I thought I might as well examine these great rocky plateaux which encumbered the sea in every direction, and which I had never been close to. I took the *pirogue* and set out. They were veritable gardens under the sea, pushed up to the surface for the moment. The strangest thing about them, however, was that their surface was covered with great tridacna, those enormous shells which pious sailors used to bring home to act as fonts in their village churches or the chapels of their castles. Some of them were huge, measuring nearly three feet at the longest part. They were all half open, letting the clear water wash over their inner mantles, on which the sun set curious shadows. Each one gave out a veritable glow of its own colour, as if the whole mollusc had been an electric lamp. There were shells of every shade from violet to dark red, but the colours most frequently seen were green, yellow, and orange. As I glided silently in my *pirogue* over these submarine flower-beds, covered by about eighteen inches of water, I had the impression of moving over a very gaudy carpet. Every shell seemed to be the opening which led to the splendours of some fairy palace, and I believe that they must have inspired all those pretty legends told by sailors of old, of nymphs and mermaids which haunted grottoes of mother-of-pearl, jade, and crystal. While I was dreaming of all these splendours and wonders which the imagination can create out of nothing, my men were thinking of something more practical. They took on board as many of the shells as possible, opened them and scooped out the flesh, which they hung in strips to dry in the sun. Alas, the enchanted palaces now looked like socks hung out to dry on washing day. Their beautiful phosphorescent lights had vanished.

During the night a land breeze came down, most exceptionally, from the mountains of Sinai; we who had just come from the burning tropics shivered under its chill caress. Although this wind was in our favour, we could not take advantage of it at once, for because of the rocks surrounding us we were obliged to wait until dawn. But this pretty east wind lasted all fore-noon and took us up as far as Tor, a port in the neighbourhood of Sinai, which was a starting-point for pilgrimages to the Coptic monasteries. Really, when one looks at these lofty mountains, so arid and rocky, one can't help wondering what possessed Moses to bring his people here and make his laws in such a place. But the climate must have changed here too.

At noon the north-west wind established itself definitely, but no matter how violently it might blow, we could not loiter in anchorages any longer; we had lost a lot of time already and the 18th August was approaching. At all costs we must get on northwards. I could hardly hope to arrive in time, but at least I wanted to be as little late as possible. For four days and four nights we went from one side of the gulf to the other, tacking painfully, with the *boutre* constantly on her beam ends, in spite of the fact that we changed the ballast over to the windward side every time in order to lessen the list so that I could keep all the sails spread to keep the *boutre* from drifting.

I was rash enough to pass over the Cheratib bank. There was quite enough water for our small vessel, but I did not know in what a witches' dance the sea indulged when the north-west winds blew strongly, with the southern currents. For two hours I remained captive in this infernal spot, obliged to navigate with the lateen yard half-way up the mast to avoid smashing all the rigging. When we got out the *boutre* was leaking in a very alarming manner. We had to pump every hour, and each hour it took longer to empty her. Everybody listened in gloomy silence to the beating of the valve, and a general sigh of relief hailed the gurgling of the rose at the bottom of the hold. Seeing that the leak seemed to be getting worse, I thought it might be as well to find out where it was, and on examination I discovered that a piece of caulking-cord had been torn away, and the action of the water kept pulling more and more of it off, thus enlarging the leak. Once the hold was emptied, we could hear the water spurting in near the midship-beam. Just at this point there was a considerable weight of ballast consisting of a great coil of chain on which rested a two-hundred-litre barrel of water, the only one we had left. The ship was pitching so abominably that there could be no question of shifting this enormous weight. I steered for the shore. When a ship has sprung a leak, however small, instinctively one makes for land. I hoped, however, to find a sheltered place where we could try to shift the ballast. Of course I might have emptied the barrel, but where would we have got a fresh supply of water?

Under Cape Safrana the sea became calm and the wind seemed to slacken; when we were a cable's length from shore I was able to lower the sails. For a few minutes Abdi had been busy preparing a sennet of oiled cotton ; I realized what he wanted to do. First of all, a man dived and passed a rope under the ship. He attached it to each side about where we supposed the leak to be. Then Abdi muttered a prayer, took a deep breath, and dived with all his materials for caulking. The rope which had been passed under the keel supported him while he worked. After diving several times, he managed to stop up the whole length of the opening with his sennet of cotton. This was enough to keep out the water. We went out to sea again, a heavy load off our minds.

I was awakened during the following night by the crew, in a great state of excitement. A white light gleamed on the horizon before us, and from time to time a bright beam crossed the clouds. We had reached

Suez. It was the 16th August; we had been thirty-six days at sea. I had promised Alexandros to be here on the 18th. As I have already said, I gave this date quite at random, in order to appear business-like, but really without having the slightest idea if I could keep the appointment. I don't think he had taken me very seriously either, and yet here I would be exact to the minute. It was rather amusing.

Now that the end of the voyage was in sight I felt much more at ease. Up till now the constant worries of navigation, the ever-renewed wonders of these coasts I had not known before, had made me forget the practical aim of the voyage. But now I was obliged to turn my mind to it. The sporting side of the enterprise, the adventurous attraction it had had for me— all that faded into the background. Now for business. I had put my holy all into this speculation; these eight cases represented my entire fortune. If I failed it meant ruin. Good-bye to the sea and the open air, good-bye to the life of freedom I so loved. I should be obliged to accept the slavery of some dreary job and become a domestic animal. This prospect revived all my courage and energy, which had faltered a moment before the painful necessity of mixing with men who lived for filthy lucre, and fighting them with weapons I hated to use.

I thought of these Greek cafés of which I had had a glimpse at Suez, and of the bar at the Piraeus. It seemed to me now that all the men in them had had sinister and evil faces. Had I been dreaming, and would I have a painful awakening? The real dangers were now about to begin, and I feared them infinitely more than those of the perilous voyage I had just made. I should have to struggle now against cowardice, cupidity, trickery . . . a crooked fight amid the filth of a sewer.

CHAPTER XXIII

THE HIDING-PLACE

AT DAWN the white lights of Suez faded before the golden glory of the sun, and the town suddenly appeared out of the desert in dazzling clearness. The mountains of Ataqa to the north-west of the bay turned to a vivid rose, and the gulf, smooth as a mirror in the calm of the transparent air, gleamed with delicate mother-of-pearl reflections under the fairy-like delicacy of the sunrise hues. Gradually sky and sea became blue, the land merely ochre, and the north wind began to blow.

At this moment I noticed a small white sail leaving the coast of Asia. A fishing-boat, I thought, which had been waiting for the wind. I was still more than thirty miles from Suez, and could see nothing clearly yet. The crew took it in turns to climb to the mast-head, each one wanting to be the first to have a good view of this town of which we had been speaking so long, the goal of our voyage, reached after so many struggles. I had decided long before that I would not go into the harbour with my cargo. Though I had passed through the customs at Kosseir, that was no guarantee against a visit from the customs at Suez. In all countries which have only a veneer of civilization, the officials imagine that they establish their prestige in making themselves as much of a nuisance as possible. So I thought I would imitate the turtles, find a deserted beach, and deposit my riches in the sand. The sail I had seen upset my plans; but for it I should have been near the coast already. The best thing to do was to let it pass; after that I should see. I hugged the wind in order to advance as slowly as possible until these tiresome fishermen should have disappeared.

But, alas, my *boutre* appeared to interest them, for

they came nearer and nearer until they were only two cables' length off. It was a simple bark with a lateen sail such as I had seen round the liners when we had called in at Suez. I could see the men squatting on the after-deck, their eyes fixed on us. There were six of them, all dressed in blue *guellabias*, with tight little white turbans on their heads. Then the bark continued towards the north-west, while I let my *boutre* bear away to get as far as possible in the opposite direction. When she was out of sight I steered for the coast of Asia. The wind was favourable, so I reckoned we should have time to deposit my cases somewhere before darkness fell.

Already the big petroleum tanks at Port Tewfik could be seen above the horizon, and soon the tops of the masts of the ships in the roads were outlined against the sky. Finally, the white town itself came into view. We had gone as far as was prudent. I steered due east. The coats of Asia was barely ten miles away; we should reach it in an hour and a half. Suddenly a multitude of white sails like a cloud of butterflies blown by the wind appeared from the north. They were fishing-boats. Every day they left Suez about midday, as soon as the wind had steadied, and came down to fish on the shores of the gulf fifteen or twenty miles south of the town. In less than three-quarters of an hour they were opposite us, between us and the coast of Asia, and already several of them had lowered their sails and begun fishing. There was no use thinking any more of seeking a hiding-place on this coast. These fishers would not move before the next morning. If I was imprudent enough to start any manœuvre which might attract their attention, they would realize that my *boutre* did not belong to the ordinary flotilla of Suez, and next day we should be the staple subject of conversation in all the native cafés frequented by sailors. So I had to go back to where I was. I steered westward in the direction which had been taken by the first boat we had seen that morning. I realized now that this vessel was not like those I had just seen. She differed in form and in tonnage, and her manœuvres had been rather odd. These boats really were fishing-boats.

In these countries routine is a law; everything is done in accordance with changeless traditions. Originality is wholly unknown. This applies even to the fishing; each man does not fish according to his own ideas, but according to a local method followed by everybody. I had just had the proof of this in the great number of little boats which had all remained near the coast of Asia. So this solitary vessel had had other business than catching fish. While I fled westward, I reflected: Alexandros was expecting me on the 18th and it was now the 17th. Knowing that I was coming by sea with my precious cargo, he must be thinking that I should soon be putting in an appearance. Could I guess what plots might not have been hatched, if he had babbled to the *habitués* of these strange cafés he frequented? These idle people had all the time in the world to plot, for they did nothing else. They knew the country, they were in touch with accomplices all over the place, and if they knew my secret, I must seem a ludicrously easy prey.

In the end, I was quite sure that this ship had been sent to look out for me. But just why? She had undoubtedly been waiting for me, she had come close enough to identify me, and after taking a good look, she had disappeared. Had she gone to warn the coast-guards? No, that would be ridiculous and wouldn't put anything in Alexandros' pocket, for the reward given by the customs for information was on the scale of a thaler per *oke* of hashish captured, whereas if he bought my merchandise, he would have a profit of three or four pounds sterling per *oke*, that is twenty or thirty times as much. I went off into a long series of suppositions, each as absurd as the rest—a dangerous exercise because it induces auto-suggestion, and often leads to irreparable blunders. Here were the facts:

A bark had been watching for me and had just
ascertained that I was in the gulf. That could not be
altered. But this bark supposed that I had my
merchandise on board; that I could change, and I
should lose no time in doing it. I went on my way,
making more or less for the north, so that from a distance I should seem to be heading for Suez, if, as was
very probable, I was being watched. But as soon as
darkness fell, I crowded on sail and dashed for the
coast of Egypt. I did not know the first thing about
the nature of this coast. I merely presumed it was
deserted, at least at night.

After the fading of the twilight, a little young moon
lingered in the sky, then vanished behind the great
range of Ataqa and left us in darkness but for the stars.
I kept sounding in order to know when we approached
the shore, for we couldn't make out the low-lying coast
at the foot of the mountains. The water grew gradually
shallower, and at ten feet we lowered the sails. All the
manœuvres were carried out in the most absolute
silence. I had oiled all the pulleys so as to avoid the
creaking and rattling which generally accompanies the
lowering of sails. Ahmed's exuberant nature caused
him to make enthusiastic exclamations on every occasion, and it needed a resounding box on the ear to
silence him. The anchor was cautiously lowered, it
dipped under water, found the sand, and there we
were motionless, in the midst of a dead calm. We
were towing the *houri* after us. I had had it lowered
that afternoon, as it is practically impossible to lower
a boat silently. In it I embarked with Abdi and Ali
Omar, the only two on whose coolness and courage I
could absolutely rely. Abdi always ignored danger,
and believed himself invulnerable when he was with
me. Ali Omar was genuinely brave, and used his
courage with intelligence.

In spite of the shallowness of the water at the point
where we had left the *boutre*, we were still far from
the coast. Long after the silhouette of the *boutre*

had vanished behind us, the land had not yet come into sight. Suddenly, Ali Omar stopped paddling and pointed to a vague dark mass a hundred yards to our left. I had brought my night glasses with me, and I recognized the outline of a ship. Her mast had been removed, probably to allow her to hide more easily. I could see her lateen yard quite plainly jutting out over the stern. It was the boat we had seen that morning, I did not know why she was lurking there dismasted, but of one thing I was very sure, she was not engaged in fishing. At the distance at which we were, our *houri*, which was very low in the water, could not be seen. Silently we glided to the right and were soon swallowed up in the night. After half a mile of this ghost-like progress the keel of the *houri* grounded on the sand. We moored it to a paddle fixed upright in the sand, and advanced slowly through the shallow water, stepping delicately so as to make no noise.

Stinging skates, surprised in their sleep, began swimming through the cloudy water. At the risk of being wounded by their poisonous touch we went on, silent as before. The danger was that we might step on one of these flat fishes, half buried in the sand, so Abdi insisted on going first to have the honour of brushing these dangerous sleepers out of our way. Indeed, in this way, only one of us risked being stung, and since Abdi wanted to be the one, Ali Omar and I gracefully conceded him the honour. At last we reached firm ground. I had not the faintest idea where we were, for the night was very dark in the shadow of those mountains which blotted out a good part of the sky. Underfoot was a gravelly soil, strewn with sharp fragments of shells. Here and there round us were little, whitish dunes, and after that, darkness, silence, and the unknown. Through my glasses I could make out other vague outlines of dunes, and it seemed to me that we were on a sandy plain, which was utterly deserted.

We eagerly investigated to see if the soil was suitable for the proposed burying of our goods. At every step we took forward, we felt the sand with our hands to discover its nature, and I had the disagreeable impression that though my hands touched gravel, my feet were gradually sinking in as if there was mud underneath it. I made an effort to free myself, and sank farther in. The oozing mud was soon up to my knees, and I was still sinking. Luckily there was a dune very near, and I managed to reach it before my legs were completely imprisoned. There, the ground was solid. Abdi and Ali Omar had had the same experience. We had to retreat, for we were on shifting sands whose depths I did not know. We happened to find the traces of our footprints and followed them safely back to the sea. We had had the luck to land just where there was a strip of solid ground in the middle of a quagmire. If we had landed at another point, I don't know how we should have come out of the adventure.

We had some trouble in finding the *pirogue*, owing to the darkness, and it was one o'clock in the morning when we got back on board. I still had time to hoist the sails and be out of sight before dawn, for I was most uneasy at the presence of the other ship, though I tried to find a normal explanation for it. By seven o'clock in the morning we had crossed the gulf and anchored on the Asiatic coast, three cables' lengths from an absolutely deserted beach to the south of Ras Sudr. The fishing-boats had disappeared; they must have gone back to Suez before dawn, and I knew they would not return before midday.

The sand on the beach was firm and dry, and went up in a gentle slope towards a little rocky wall twenty yards from the sea. This was the boundary of a desert plain. At the foot of this little cliff, which was only about fourteen feet high, I dug a hole in which to put my eight cases. While the men were hollowing it out, I examined every inch of this plain through the telescope, right up to the chain of mountains away in the east. I left a man on guard on a small mound and came back to where the men were digging. During this time, the cabin-boy had amused himself by picking *bil-bils* off the rocks which emerged from the water, for the tide was out. These bivalves were exceptionally big, which led me to suppose that no one fished them here. Naturally, I opened some of them from idle curiosity, and to my great surprise found several small pearls embedded in the flesh. Probably it was not known in this country that these bivalves contained pearls. I made a mental note of this fact for future use; for the moment we were too busy arranging for the bringing of our goods to land to bother about anything else.

We could not get all these cumbersome cases into the *houri*, indeed, it could only take one at a time, which meant that the disembarking of the hashish would take too long. But since they were zinc-lined, why should I bother putting the cases in a *pirogue*? Why not just throw them into the sea? They would float, and helped along by the sea breeze swimmers could easily push them towards the shore. In a few minutes my cargo was in the sea, and the crew, in the highest spirits, frolicked through the water, pushing the cases before them. When we were about to lower them into the hole prepared for them, I was surprised to smell the familiar odour of hashish, and I noticed, on examination, that the salt water which dripped from them was strongly impregnated with this odour.

In a flash I realized what had happened. What a disaster; the water had seeped into the cases! Perhaps they had been badly soldered, or more probably the heat at Djibouti had dilated the cold air which had been enclosed at Steno, thus opening the joinings. All my merchandise was perhaps spoilt, for I remembered that Petros had particularly warned me not to let the hashish get wet. There was no time to be lost; the most imminent danger was the spoiling of the hashish. We ripped open the cases, which now seemed too securely closed for our taste: we were in such a hurry to rend them apart. Only one was still all right; the other seven had let in water and all the little sacks were soaked. But the sun was already high in the heavens, and briskly dried the four hundred packets spread neatly out on the sand. It was quite an imposing display. I just thought of the thunder-struck joy of a company of coastguards, if they had happened to pass at this moment.

I had made up my mind once and for all, and would take the consequences, whatever they were. I would risk my life in this affair, and was determined not to be captured tamely. The sacks would take at least an hour to dry. If any one happened to pass during this time and threatened to bother us, I would stop him, by ruse if I could, but by force if necessary, for I was very sincerely determined to see this business through, cost what it might. This decision taken, I immediately recovered all my serenity. I kept with me Abdi, Ali Omar and two Dankalis, with all the arms which were on board, and Mhamed Moussa returned to the *boutre* with the rest of the crew. He had orders to get ready to put to sea, and to run south before the wind, then to beat up northwards. I kept the *pirogue* with me to go and join him out at sea whenever our work was finished, if Fate allowed us to finish it. I sent away the *boutre* because I did not want to attract attention to the point on the beach where we were. If any excisemen, or even innocent passers-by, were to come along the coast, they would naturally follow the little path which ran parallel to the shore on the top of the little cliff, some fifty yards back from where we were. If they saw a ship at anchor, they would naturally approach the edge of the cliff in order to hail it, or simply to get a nearer view, whereas if there was nothing on the sea or on the part of the beach visible from the path—for our merchandise, being right under the foot of the cliff, could not be seen from it—they would have no reason for going out of their way.

I dragged the *pirogue* up the beach and hid it under the cliff. Our sail had now disappeared, everything was calm in the limpid morning air, and as far as the eye could reach over the sandy plain, there was no sign of life. Out at sea, cargo boats passed by, indifferent to everything but the route they must follow. We carefully turned over all the sacks so that they could dry through and through. Ali Omar kept watch, lying on the top of the cliff. Suddenly he rose and glided towards us, wearing an anxious expression. My heart gave a horrid jump, as if I had been stabbed.

'You have seen something?' I asked.

'Not on land, but over there a steamer which is not a cargo is coming down from Suez, keeping very close to the coast.'

From where I was, only the smoke from her funnel was visible. I climbed up the cliff, and sure enough I saw the yellow funnel of a little vessel with a single mast. I could not see the hull, but the funnel, clearly shown up by the sun, was obviously yellow, denoting a coastguard. They were certainly inspecting the coast, and would be sure to have powerful telescopes. I had the empty cases piled into the trench, and since I was afraid we should not have time to pack the sacks into them, I had the latter covered with a thin layer of sand. From a distance they would thus be invisible to any one who did not know they were there. We ourselves crouched down in the space left in the trench, so that nothing remained to attract the eye to this spot.

The steamer approached, very rapidly now, and her white hull confirmed that she was a coastguard. I could even see the big searchlight on the top of the foresail, and her war flag on the gaff. She was following the coast less than a mile out. What a lucky inspiration I had had in sending away my ship! Half an hour later, her presence would have compromised everything, hopelessly, too, for there would be no question of engaging battle with a warship. When she was just opposite us, I was afraid she was going to stop. I thought I could hear all our hearts hammering in our chests. But the white foam churned up by her stem rolled on, she passed . . . she was gone . . . she had seen nothing.

'*Al amdul illah*,' sighed my men.

I had passed an agonizing five minutes, but once the danger was past our luck seemed to me miraculous, yet at the same time quite natural. I felt as if I had never for a moment really believed that a catastrophe was possible. A sort of presentiment had assured me that all would go well. I remembered the case we had found floating on the sea. Why had Destiny sent it to me if my enterprise was not going to succeed? Fortunate optimism, thanks to which I could keep up my courage in trying moments. But this respite to our anxiety did not last long. I had my eyes fixed on our sail, away out at sea to the south. The coastguard had seen it too, and seemed to be making for it. Was she going to take it into her head to hail her? In that case, the absence of the captain and four of the crew would seem a little curious, if the ledger was looked at. What explanation would Mhamed Moussa give? Even if he said we had all died of cholera that would complicate the situation frightfully, and goodness knows what would be the end of it all. However, the gravest danger, and the most immediate, was past. We hastened to profit by this fact, and bury the accursed sacks, which were now dry. Rapidly we arranged them in their cases and at last the sand covered everything with its secret mantle. But as often happens when things are unpacked, we could not get them all in. Perhaps the merchandise had swollen a little. I had twelve little sacks over. I decided to keep them with me; they could act as samples, so that I could arrange the sale of all the hashish as soon as I arrived. They went into quite a small parcel, which could easily be disposed of in case of danger.

Meantime, the coastguard was nearing my *boutre*.

Mhamed Moussa ran up the French flag, and I saw
him lower it three times in the regulation salute. My
blood ran cold. For sheer nerve, this would be hard
to beat. How infinitely I should have preferred him
to take his chance of passing without attracting special
attention, as if the *Fat-el-Rahman* was just an ordinary
Arab *boutre*. These French colours, this regulation
salute, might intrigue the patroller, or it might be that
those on board had nothing to do and might seek
amusement by visiting this courteous sailing-ship.
But the patrol boat must have been in a hurry, for she
contented herself with replying to the salute and
keeping on her way south. I dropped my field-glasses,
and we danced a wild war-dance of joy on the beach,
finishing up with a general bathe, with acrobatic diving
and wrestling. This relaxing was necessary after the
nervous tension we had endured for nearly three-
quarters of an hour. The *pirogue* seemed lighter than
a wisp of straw in our joyful arms as we carried it
down to the water, and driven by three paddles she
fairly flew towards the *Fat-el-Rahman*. Mhamed
Moussa said he had thought of saluting the coastguard
when he had seen her change her course and come
towards them. He remembered having seen me do
the same thing with an English battle cruiser when we
were gun-running!

With light hearts, strong in the innocence of our
empty hold, we sailed gaily towards Suez. The sun
was setting as we rounded the red lighthouse at Port
Tewfik, a big construction in the very middle of the
bay, bearing the keeper's house and the great lantern.
The roads were full of shipping, the red and green
lights of beacons began to twinkle, and in the background the circle of shining points which indicated the
town spread out along the horizon. It was very calm,
as is the rule in the bay of Suez at night, and we lay
there motionless under the red glare of the lighthouse.

This afternoon on our right, I had seen great
stretches of sand on the coast of Asia, where it would

be very simple to hide our compromising samples, for my men did not want to spoil the joy of entering this great unknown port by worrying about them. I readily agreed to hide them ashore for the time being, since the calm would keep us there anyhow until morning. Once we had gone through the customs we could easily go in the *pirogue* the following night and fetch them. I took Abdi and two Dankalis and went to carry out this last formality, while the *boutre* remained absolutely still, without even being anchored. Two hours later we were back. Some distance from the sea I had come on a little hillock it would be easy to find again, as there was an old iron barrel half buried on it. In this rusty old tub I had hidden the packets.

On the morning of the 18th, we anchored at last at Port Tewfik, in front of the Hygiene Department's yellow-painted buildings at the entrance to the canal.

CHAPTER XXIV

SUEZ

IT TURNED out just as well that I had relieved the *boutre* of all her cargo. Native customs agents came and poked into every hole and corner of the *Fat-el-Rahman*, even into the compass. Not that they had the slightest suspicion of anything, but it amused them to rummage, or maybe they hoped I would offer them baksheesh to go away, and not turn everything upside down. I might have saved myself by doing this if I had had anything on board, but the very fact of having paid would have engendered suspicion. The classic trick of the amiable customs officer has been too often played. After settling with him, one can expect a surprise visit.

At last about noon I was able to set foot on Egyptian soil, in order to go into town. Port Tewfik is a town which sprang up when the canal was being pierced. Everything is new and modern in it, and it contains nothing but houses for government employees and garden cities for workmen. These last are quite smart, consisting of gilded cages of barracks in which the men who work on the canal live with their families, with tiny gardens where the women-folk can squabble while the men are working at riveting metal plates or having a drink at the pub. I looked for a restaurant where I could have a real meal with white bread, hors d'œuvres and a table-napkin, but it was in vain that I strolled up and down avenues bordered with flowers, lawns and bronze statues. I should have to go to old Suez, about two and a half miles inland.

A local train runs between Port Tewfik and Suez. At the station the platform was crowded with native workmen and clerks coming back from their work at the docks. I looked at the Arabs dressed in long shirts.

They were handsome and well built, but very dirty, as was natural in a country where they could not live without clothes. I was deeply absorbed in my meditations, when some one slapped me on the back. I started as if I had been shot, and looking round, recognized Alexandros.

'I arrived this morning,' he said in answer to my look of surprised interrogation; 'I came to Port Tewfik to wait for you, since you had made an appointment with me for the eighteenth. Did you have a pleasant voyage?'

'Not bad. And you?'

I was disconcerted at the lack of surprise he showed at finding me up to time. Any one might have thought I had only to take the train. To tell the truth, my punctuality was a matter of chance, but otherwise it would have been a remarkable achievement. This man with his placid smile, his big nose, his sleepy eyes and the slight trembling of his tobacco-stained fingers which constantly played with his amber rosary, brought back vividly to my mind the atmosphere of the cafés I had seen in his company at Port Said. How indeed, I thought pityingly, could this poor devil, already half dotty, have the slightest idea of what a struggle against wind and waves meant? The train was about to start, and we got in together. We did not speak; I looked out the window at the lagoons crossed by the railway on the long jetty which connects Port Tewfik with the mainland on which Suez is built.

Everywhere where there is salt water I seem to find a friend, a silent accomplice. I was studying now how I could make use of this lagoon, for I should have to get my hashish in somehow, and all my thoughts were concentrated on finding a vulnerable spot, a breach by which I could enter the fortress. When I have an idea in my head, I examine everything solely from the point of view of utility to further it. It comes between me and the outside world like a kind of filter, and only what can serve it is allowed to come through. It is almost a disease.

On the embankment over which the train was passing there was a road alongside the railway, separated from it by a simple railing. We took only seven or eight minutes to reach Suez.

Suez is an old Arab town, with a European quarter, but it has remained essentially an old city belonging to the times when sailing-ships brought spices and perfumes and the good coffee from Mocha to it. The European streets are round the station. The Rue Colmar, the principal street, is like a provincial High Street. Nothing is lacking to complete the illusion: there is the draper's with all the latest novelties; there is the 'Parisian Milliner's'; the tailors' dummies smile idiotically, and there is a little boy in a Norfolk suit among them; the big clock indicates the watchmaker's shop; passing the grocer's one gets a whiff of salted cod; a withered old maid keeps the haberdashery store, and her cat sleeps in the window. All the shops have little bells that tinkle when you open the door, and pedestrians stroll along the middle of the street.

We went straight to a square in which was situated a café which reminded me very much of those in Port Said, except that the customers here were peaceful tradesmen and clerks waiting till it was time to return to their shops and offices.

Yet they had the same lazy look as if they spent their lives here before a glass of water, a cup of Turkish coffee, or a game of tric-trac. Most of them were on the terrace, so Alexandros led me into a dark corner inside, practically deserted. We sat down and he assumed a conspiratorial air I found quite uncalled for, since nobody knew me and in my khaki clothes I passed quite unnoticed. Perhaps it was he who was too well known, but I couldn't help thinking that he simply took a childish pleasure in playing at conspirators.

The proprietor of the café was a Greek, needless to

say. He came and shook hands with Alexandros; they conferred in low tones, then sent off the waiter, also a Greek, on some mysterious errand, making him take off his apron and go out by a side door. When we were once more alone Alexandros plied me with questions.

'No, I have nothing on board, as you may well suppose—only a madman would be crazy enough for that. But don't worry, "everything" is where I can lay hands on it, and have it brought into town whenever I wish.'

This statement, my mysterious affirmation that 'everything was where I could lay hands on it', made a great impression on my companion. I spoke to him of the little sailing-ship I had seen in the gulf, then of my encounter with the coastguards, and by the banality and vagueness of his replies I concluded that he did not know much at all about Suez. On the other hand, he chattered constantly about Port Said, which did not interest me in the slightest. I got quite worried and wondered what sort of imbecile this man was, and what possible use he could be to me. At this moment the waiter returned, muttered a few words in Alexandros' ear, resumed his apron, and went bounding off with a trayful of coffees.

I looked inquiringly at Alexandros.

'To-night at eight,' he replied, 'we are going to see a man who may buy your entire cargo.'

'So you are taking no further interest in the affair?' I asked.

'Ah, yes! I should just think I am! But here I can do nothing without the man I speak of. He holds all the traffic that goes on in the Gulf of Suez in the hollow of his hand.'

'So smuggling goes on here?'

'Yes, but all the merchandise comes down through the Canal. Sailors, stewards, fishermen, firemen, engineers, all kinds of people throw packets of hashish into the sea wrapped in rubber so that they will float and not be spoilt by the salt water. They throw them at given points and a ship goes and picks them up.'

It dawned on me as he spoke that the ship which had so intrigued me had probably been engaged in this sort of fishing. And she had been anchored beside the shifting sands so that she could hand over the spoils to an associate. All this was logically probable but not certain.

CHAPTER XXV
THE CONSULATE

As I COULD do no more business with Alexandros for the moment, I left him and went to pay a visit to the French consul. When I reached the door leading into the courtyard, a servant came and opened to me. He was an old negro, who had doubtless been in the service of the consul for a long time, to judge from his familiar manners. He wore a chechia with a tricolour cockade and a wide red woollen girdle, and he saluted with the negligent familiarity of the porter of a ministry. All this indicated to me that I was in France; I felt quite at home, and a gentle emotion filled my heart. I went in and the chancellor came to meet me, smiling and amiable, delighted at my visit. He was not a Frenchman, but an Egyptian, a Copt from Tor, a little seaport at the foot of the Sinai mountains, and his name was Spiro. He had been in the consulate from his earliest youth, and the various consuls, who generally come to Suez to wind up a peaceful career, had brought him up, educated and formed him, so that now he was the perfect chancellor. At the present time, the consul might just as well not have existed; everything would go on just as usual, for Monsieur Spiro knew everything and did everything at every hour of the day.

He was about thirty, but did not look more than eighteen, and was a bachelor. He was so well groomed that he looked as if he had just stepped out of a band-box, and the first things one noticed about him were his perfectly cut jacket, his white waistcoat and the sublime crease in his beautiful putty trousers. He had a Jewish cast of features and the bronzed skin of the Arab, in spite of his hatred and avoidance of the sun. His jet-black hair showed an obstinate inclination to curl, but was severely fixed down with some perfumed cream. A bowl of roses stood on his desk, and the room was as scented as a lady's boudoir. Later on, I had a lot to do with Mr. Spiro, and I got to know him very well, and appreciate his good points.

The first of these was that he was infinitely obliging. He would unhesitatingly make use of all his friends in order to do you a service, and he had a host of 'intimate friends'. He spoke of them in dithyrambic terms, and seemed to find humanity endowed with all the virtues. He never made the smallest disparaging remark about any one, and if you went so far as to criticize somebody in his presence, or to repeat something not very flattering, Spiro excused him with indulgent smiles and protesting airs, without, however, going so far as to contradict you, for he could not bear not to agree with everybody. This exquisite chancellor spoke all languages, starting with Arabic, French and Greek, which were his mother tongues. He spoke them faultlessly and without accent. Then he also spoke all the languages of the Mediterranean basin, including Turkish. He lived in the Arab fashion, under the care of an old woman whom he called his servant, but who might well have been his mother. He remained a bachelor, nobody understood why; for he was a good-looking and charming fellow and had an excellent position. His intimate friends, of course, hinted all sorts of things, basing their observations on the boudoir-like atmosphere of his office, his love of dress and his feminine daintiness in everything he did. I didn't believe a word of it, only Spiro was as defence-less and timorous as a woman. He was afraid of everything, and trembled as soon as he could no longer smile.

After a little amiable chat, I asked to see the consul, but Spiro said with an air of great mystery that probably the consul was still having his siesta, as it was only four o'clock.

'The *Paul-Lecat* came in at eleven o'clock last night,'

he explained; 'that meant a sleepless night, you understand, for it takes over an hour to go out to the roads
with the *Hélène*, the Messageries tug.'

'Is the consul obliged to go on board all the steamers?'
I asked.

'Oh, yes, it's very hard,' replied Spiro, raising his
eyes to Heaven; 'just think, to be obliged to go out to
the middle of the roads twice a week in all weathers.'

'Yes, indeed,' I replied, trying to keep my face
straight, 'I quite understand that if the consul was on
the *Paul-Lecat* yesterday he must prolong his siesta.
I shall come back to-morrow morning.'

'Not at all, not at all; wait a minute, the consul will
be in at any moment now. Besides, he only nearly
went on board the *Paul-Lecat*, for at the last minute
the weather was a little threatening and his housekeeper refused to let him go.'

'He is very subject to colds in the head,' he added,
'and one has to be so careful in this climate. . . .'

Spiro stopped speaking, and even breathing, put a
finger on his lips, and a slow smile overspread his face.

'Hush. . . . I think I hear him coming. . . .'

Monsieur du Gardier, the French consul, was a
man about fifty, wearing enormous horn-rimmed
spectacles. He was a distinguished and cultured
gentleman, with very pleasant manners, who had
entered the consular service in order to shelter himself
from the storms of life. He had no ambition, and
wherever he was sent, the authorities forgot him, and
now he had been forgotten at Suez for I don't know
how many years. He welcomed me with that cordial
simplicity which is so valuable an asset to men in his
position, as it always flatters equals and encourages
inferiors.

Naturally, I spoke of pearl fishing, to explain my long
cruise in these little-frequented waters. I recounted
the adventures of the voyage, exaggerating my find of
pearls in the *bil-bils* of the Gulf. Spiro had been
allowed to remain and take part in the conversation,

and he listened to my story with appropriate gestures and changes of expression. He smiled blissfully, shook his head gloomily while raising horrified eyes to the ceiling, clasped his hands with so compassionate an air that the tears came into his eyes, or else shuddered and threw hunted glances all round him. All this mimicry was so expressive that it seemed affected, but poor Spiro was quite incapable of irony. He was simply polite, and seeing his chief following my tale with attentive interest, thought it the correct thing for him to allow his own emotions full play.

Du Gardier belonged to a very old and noble Breton family: Brittany has produced many a corsair and sea-rover, and he said with a proud smile that he had some of the blood of those old sea-dogs in his veins. He had a passion for the sea, and spoke of it lyrically, like Chateaubriand.

'Ah,' he sighed, 'how I should like to live your life; it is the life of my dreams. How I envy you the excitement, the risks, the adventure of it all. But what can I do?' and with a vaguely discouraged gesture he indicated the office, the papers, all the comfortable accoutrements of a rich old bachelor.

Spiro assumed an admiring air as he listened to his chief's profession of faith, glaring before him as if he saw through the smoke of his cigarette wild-eyed pirates swarming on board a ship with pistols between their teeth. But what can a man do when he has a severe housekeeper who puts a hot-water bottle in his bed, makes him drink hot milk and forbids him to go out if the weather is damp? How, I ask you, is a man to become a sea-dog in the circumstances? Du Gardier himself realized that his lyrical ravings sounded a little absurd in this old-fashioned and luxurious dwelling, where he let himself be petted and tyrannized over by his old nurse, as in the days when she put him to sleep in his muslin-curtained cot. I found him touching rather than ridiculous. If he had become a self-centred and fussy old bachelor, an elderly child who was never naughty, it was due to the too soft life he had led, in which there had been no obstacle, no struggles, no poverty.

I thought of the poor boys who are fetched from the door of their lycée by a servant, cross the road in the care of a policeman, and who are brought up in cotton-wool until they reach manhood. Then their parents manage to get them off their military service, and they are finally carefully planted, as in a hothouse, in some comfortable and easy job, where they are sheltered from all the storms of life. It is not surprising that they reach old age with the souls of little children. All the manly virtues have died, and they are without resistance or defence, like hothouse flowers or cage birds. I always feel deeply sorry for such men, and the parents who sacrifice their children through excess of affection seem to me to do them a great wrong. Their affection is really nothing but cowardice and selfishness, they want to spare themselves the worry of seeing their children encounter the risks and trials which alone form the character and the will and make men.

Du Gardier introduced his brother. He was a painter, an official artist. Every year he came to visit his brother and paint a series of harmless little pictures of a size convenient for packing. He was the living image of his brother, except that he did not wear spectacles. They had a great affection for each other, and lived there very happily, treated as irresponsible children by their old nurse. The painter had just come in from his morning period of work from ten to twelve, after which he lunched and went out again. He was severely scolded because his shoes were wet, and his brother packed him off at once to change.

Like the consul, he had several orders, and like him was very 'Civil Servant'. He sent pictures to the *Illustration* and had won medals at the Artistes Français. He did allow himself to wear a flowing tie, as a sign of his profession, but his bohemianism stopped there. This eccentricity was quite sufficient, so everybody at the consulate thought, to show how up-to-date and enterprising are the Government services. He called himself a modern painter, because he put a little purple into the shadows on his seascapes, but his wild audacity as an Impressionist went no further.

The consul was astounded to know that pearls were to be found quite close at hand in the Gulf, and Spiro opened eyes like saucers to show that his surprise was as great. I had to promise to take them out pearl fishing one Sunday, so that they could see the operations for themselves. Du Gardier declared that he would invite all the 'best people' in Suez to come on this expedition, and he seemed very proud to have found a compatriot engaged in such romantic pursuits.

CHAPTER XXVI

STAVRO

ALEXANDROS WAS still sitting drowsing at the Greek café, but I could not persuade him to take me to see the person to whom he had that morning referred until darkness had fallen. We walked towards the Arab quarters; a vague odour, mixed with the smell of incense, stagnant water and fried oil, pervaded the narrow streets, which were almost deserted; it was the odour of the attractive blue smoke. But here it seemed a natural part of the atmosphere, it was the smell of the native town. Alexandros smelt nothing—he was probably too used to it, like the rest of the inhabitants; it needed a foreign nose to perceive it.

We came out at a fairly wide street, with four-storied houses on each side. They had long balconies on each floor, joined together by vertical beams, which made the houses look like cages. There lived the Arab, Greek, and Maltese clerks, in a word, all this cosmopolitan crowd which constitutes the population of the seaport towns of Egypt. We kept close to the walls on Alexandros' advice, for an open drain ran down the middle of the street and rubbish of various kinds was constantly thrown into it from the windows on each side, so that one ran most unpleasant risks of intercepting the bundles.

The street sloped downwards and I could see the calm waters of the lagoon lapping against the last cobbles. The end house stood out black against the sky. The tide was high, for the walls of this house were only a few yards from the water, which surged silently up and down, influenced by the sea tides. It was as if the sea were stretching out stealthy tentacles to play with the reflection of the last gas-lamp in the street. Here lived the man we were looking for.

Privately, I approved his choice. This house was so
near the water that on this calm evening the sea looked
as if it were lying before the door like a dog curled up
at his master's feet. The dead calm of these waters,
which had nevertheless come from contact with the
mighty deep-sea waves, reminded one of the well-
trained silence of poachers' dogs, or of horses loaded
with contraband. The black profile of this house
looked mysterious against the star-studded sky, before
this mirror of silent, deep and secret water. A very
narrow dark street separated the house from its neigh-
bour, and behind it were waste lands which were
doubtless flooded at the equinox.

Although it was still very early, the end of this little
transversal street was absolutely deserted, and there
was no sign of life in the house into which we were
about to enter. Alexandros knocked at a little door in
the side street. Several minutes went by. If I had
been alone, I should have knocked again, but Alexandros explained that it was by the fact that we knocked
only once that we would be recognized as friends, and
we waited. Sure enough, in about five minutes we
heard steps coming along a passage, then without the
slightest sound of key being turned or bolt shot back,
the door opened a few inches. Alexandros was
recognized and we were allowed to enter.

I saw a fat woman of about forty, wearing a black
handkerchief on her head like the peasant women I had
seen in Greece. She welcomed me with a smile, and
by the light of the smoky lamp she held in her hand I
saw a kind, fat face, peaceful and waxen as the face of
a nun. She was dressed entirely in black. We followed
her into a big room with bare rafters, lit only by a tiny
lamp burning before a gilded icon. There was a vague
smell of tar in the air, as if we had been on a ship. She
lit a big, hanging petrol-lamp which dispersed the
shadows.

In the middle of the room stood a round table, and
straw-bottomed chairs were set against the walls.

There were two windows with beautifully laundered white curtains, and between them stood an old-fashioned commode with bulging drawers. On it was set the little altar of the icon with its ever-burning lamp. Above it hung an ancient gun with a very long barrel. I wondered if it was an *ex voto* or a relic. Above that hung a portrait in crayons of a gloomy-eyed old man, wearing the bonnet of the mountaineers of Crete. This was the ancestor, the father of the master of the house, an old mountain chief, leader of the Christians in rebellion. For thirty years he had defied the Turks, then was betrayed and captured, and shot at the age of seventy. The gun which gleamed against the wall in the peaceful light of an altar lamp had killed more than six hundred Turks, and the family venerated it as a relic. Alexandros told me this story in a low voice, while my eyes wandered round the room. At the other end was a dark mass covered with a cloth; it was a row-boat. Perhaps this was what the silent water was waiting for on the threshold of this mysterious house.

A glass-panelled door opened and a sort of giant came in. He had to stoop to enter and come in sideways. On his head was an immense black hat with a very wide brim, which cast a shadow over the upper part of his face like a black mask.

'Welcome!' he cried to me, 'I am glad to see you. I congratulate you on your successful voyage. Last night I dreamed of a big cupboard full of bread, and this morning I saw a dead black cat. Both of these are signs of luck; we shall overcome our enemies.'

He sat down. He was wearing a flannel shirt without a waistcoat, and a wide black woollen sash. He took off his hat when he saw that we were bare-headed. His skull was small and his forehead receding, almost entirely covered with a stubble of coarse hair. His deep-set eyes gleamed from under bushy eyebrows. He had grey-blue eyes, which looked at you very straight and frankly. At this moment he was in high good humour; you could feel that he had laid aside all distrust. His heavy moustache fell over a jutting and obstinate chin, and his aquiline nose cast a dancing shadow on the wall. He was immensely big and strong, built like a wrestler, and I was really afraid that the poor little chair would be crushed like an egg-shell beneath his weight.

This was Stavro, the son of Dimitri, the old man who had died for liberty, after killing six hundred Turks with his gun. He saw that I was looking at his father's portrait, and said warmly:

'Ah, there were men in those days. They lived to fight and die nobly. To-day we kill ourselves in the struggle to live too well. I was only eight when my father was put to death. There were twelve of us; I was the youngest. I saw him fall under the Turkish bullets when he came to the help of the base slave who had betrayed him into an ambush. These are things which form the character of a child. . . . My eldest brother brought me here, and I was educated in a French school. That was in the time when every one in Egypt was proud to speak your language. Now one must speak English, kiss the feet of the English Government officials, and spy for the English soldiers. I tell you, in this country if you want to get on, you must be either a pimp or a police spy.'

'But what about the natives, the Arabs?' I asked. 'Are they too what you say?'

'You bet they are. It's all they're fit for. White-livered, cowardly, lazy, vicious dogs. But I exaggerate; if they even had vices they might have some personality, but they haven't even that. They will lend themselves to any vice for a few pence, they only work under the threat of the lash, they are beasts of burden, and the English are right to treat them as such.'

'But how do you manage your affairs if you have to do with such people?'

'Ah, that's the trouble. There are two ways of smuggling. The first, which is the usual way, is to make an arrangement with the police and the customs. All their employees live off bribes. They make money and build palaces, but their associates, the smugglers, come inevitably to ruin, for as soon as they are known to be rich, they are betrayed. I knew a man who worked with a supervisor of customs who was sent to another post one fine day. The officer who took his place showed up the whole concern. Everything the man possessed, lands, property, etc., was sold, and the State made over three millions. It was all a plot; the head of the customs were in league with the two inspectors. The customs protect and fatten a smuggler in order to eat him up when he is worth while. The second way, which is my way, is to work alone, and never to have a share in any deal which includes an employee of customs, for if they are false to the duties for which they are paid they are traitors, and a traitor would kill his own father, or else they have agreed with their chiefs to pretend to betray, and that is just about as despicable.

'I have here men from Arabia, staunch mountaineers, or sailors from the Hedjaz. Some of them are fishermen, others work all over the country in mines or quarries. Never on any account do I employ an Egyptian. The fishing-boat which so alarmed you yesterday morning belongs to me, and I knew this morning that you were at Suez.'

'So you were expecting me?' I asked, smiling.

'Yes, of course, and you can thank your lucky stars you came direct to me. If you had made the slightest attempt to deal with any one else, I shouldn't have given much for the result. But although you didn't know it, I was watching over you, first because you are French and I like the French, and secondly because of the extraordinary thing you have done in contriving to get your merchandise as far as this without knowing anything of the hashish business. You are a marked man, born under a lucky star, and the cunningest will come off second best when they try to down you.'

'So you believe in predestination?'

'I can't imagine not believing in it. Those who smile at such convictions have never reflected on the determining factors of their actions or tried to understand the marvellous way they spring out of each other. That is because they live too artificial a life, run into the social mould, like one brick out of thousands for building a wall. As soon as a man resumes his individuality, as soon as he faces life as a free man, when he uses his will-power to stimulate his fighting instincts, he develops like a plant in fertile soil, and it is then that he feels the hand of Destiny upon him guiding him through his struggles. If he really studies himself, he will hear the echoes of an ancient instinct which guides him to act as is best for his own safety.

'I believe in dreams, too; the mind conceives them outside all the rules of reason and logic, which are fundamental bases for life on earth, but which are no earthly use for trying to penetrate into the beyond.'

I sat listening to this giant with the narrow forehead putting forth ideas I had often had myself since I had been tackling life single-handed. A girl, his niece, brought in refreshments. There was no mistaking that she was the daughter of the fat woman with the ivory-pale face. Like her mother and her uncle, she was enormous. Two others, her younger sisters, came and shook hands with me. All three were dressed in black like their mother. This was the family of Stavro's eldest brother. When he died, leaving a wife and four children, these three girls and a boy, Stavro was only eighteen. He nevertheless assumed the responsibility of his entire family, as well as the charge of an older invalid sister. Although his education had been fairly complete (he had attended the lycée at Cairo until he was sixteen), he had had to give up all ambition, and start work immediately as a common sailor in order to earn their daily bread. He had never married, in order to be able to keep the promise he had made to his brother on his death-bed. Since then he had lived like an old bachelor, devoted to his nieces, his ailing sister and his sister-in-law, who in return managed his house. These women dressed in mourning, with the black handkerchiefs of widows on their heads, glided about silently through the shadowy, white-washed rooms and gave this smuggler's house an atmosphere of serenity and peace, like the smell of cold incense.

Alexandros sat silent in his corner, evoking in my mind the shady cafés where he seemed so entirely in his element. I thought how different this smuggler and his house were from anything I had expected. I thought of Stavro, of Petros in his farm at Steno, and then of good old Papamanoli, and I felt that they were of a very different kidney from Alexandros and his like.

Now we began to talk business: we discussed prices, and Stavro changed completely, becoming the keen, grasping, shrewd fellow he had to show himself in order to succeed in his dangerous profession. I knew very well that I was at his mercy, and was only too pleased to accept the price he offered. I made a deal for the small quantity I had left in the old iron barrel.

'You must deliver the goods to me in town, for I can't undertake to send some one out to sea to fetch them. In two days the whole native town would know what you had come for, and the police would keep an eye on you. Your great advantage is that nobody dreams that you have any connexion with hashish, and you must contrive to avoid losing this trump card. You have seen the French consul, who will introduce people, acquaintance with whom will help to keep you free from suspicion, for the French element of society here is considered incapable of any fraud. They are looked upon as imbeciles who are too idiotic to extract profit from anything, and you must do everything possible to make yourself appear the stupidest of the lot. As for Spiro, he is a gem of a fellow; I see him sometimes at the barber's, and we speak Greek together. We are very good friends, and he may be useful to us, for one can discuss anything with him.'

'What! He would accept a present?'

'Oh, heavens, no! Never on this earth! Don't go and suggest any such thing to him, or he will die of terror at the idea of compromising himself. I only meant that by nature he loves to be of service. He has a timid admiration for me; he knows very well I am a smuggler, though he never says a word about it. This idea gives him little thrills of terror which he finds rather agreeable since the danger is imaginary; in that he is like all fearful and effeminate creatures. So he is quite fond of me, and without seeming to, he often gives me precious hints. Besides, I only see him at the barber's; in the street we don't know each other. I occasionally send him a basket of choice fruits, just as a friendly attention, that's all.'

At this moment, the door opened and a young Arab came in. He was dressed in a blue *guellabia* which had faded from repeated washings and which was much patched, but very clean. He was barefooted, and wore a tight white turban. He had a very attractive little face, deeply bronzed by the sea air, with the features hard and sharp as if they were carved out of teak. He was not an Egyptian, but a mountaineer from the Hedjaz. When he came up to shake hands with me, I noticed that he had only one eye.

'This is Djebeli,' said Stavro; 'if everybody had what they deserved he would be a king, for not one man in ten thousand has a heart like his. I once saved his life; he knows it, and would think it the most natural thing in the world to lay it down for me, if need be. I'll tell you his story one day. I asked him to come to-night so that to-morrow you would be able to recognize him. You will hand over the goods to him.

'Alexandros will go away. If you were to be seen with him in the cafés he frequents, all would be lost. To-morrow morning you will see Djebeli basking in the sun near the station. He will see you without your having made the slightest signal to him. You will follow him at a distance, and he will lead you to the spot at which you must land with the merchandise. It is at the sea-wall which is being built; he will sit down for a moment at the place. Observe him from a distance; don't go near the wall yourself. Only, make good note of the spot, for after dark it isn't easy to find. In a street near by is a little eating-house for coolies, kept by a Greek. There you can safely speak to Djebeli and make your arrangements. The landlord is in my pay, so you have nothing to fear.'

As I looked at this serious and reserved little Arab I thought of my Abdi; there was a sort of kinship between those two whole-heartedly devoted beings, who attached themselves by instinct. I said good-night to all the family and took my leave, for Alexandros had already been gone for some time. As he was about to open the door, Stavro stopped to give me the final instructions.

'Be very careful of the sentinel who may be on the sea-wall. He must not see you coming, for on the water you will be clearly visible, while he will be in the shadow of the rocks. Besides, these brutes are very quick to fire a shot, since their heads have been stuffed with tales of submarines.'

'I know,' I replied; 'don't bother about that; I'm well accustomed to dodging such people.'

'All right, then, I shan't worry. God be with you.'

The fat woman in black murmured a few words in Greek, perhaps to tell me she would pray for me before the icon. As I left I saw the three pale-faced girls gazing at me anxiously. The noiseless door opened upon the night, then closed behind me. I was alone in the silence, as if all I had just left were only a dream. The mirror-like lagoon was still there, but the level of the water had gone down a little. I thought that the sea, having shown she was there, faithful and reliable, was now going away.

I went back to Port Tewfik by the last train, thinking over that last warning: 'Be very careful of the sentinel.' Bah! Since luck was on my side, why hesitate? Perhaps Stavro was right, everything is written. And in that case——

CHAPTER XXVII

THE SEA-WALL

I HAD ARRANGED with Djebeli to be at the sea-wall
at ten o'clock in the evening, when the moon set. I
had allowed plenty of time so as not to have to hurry.
The place where the hashish was hidden in the barrel
was more than six miles away, and if the weather was
calm, all would go well. I could be there and back in
four hours. During the day I had minutely inspected
this wall—a long rampart of huge rocks thrown in
great numbers across the roads, in view of future
constructions at present held up by the war. I had to
engrave every detail on my memory, for in the darkness
I should not be able to distinguish anything clearly.

At five o'clock I embarked in the *pirogue* with Abdi,
Ali Omar, and a Dankali to go and fetch the twelve
sample sacks. We gradually worked away from the
Fat-el-Rahman, pretending to be fishing, so as not to
attract attention. The north wind blew more strongly,
and when we were far enough off to be invisible from
Port Tewfik, we dropped all pretence, and made
straight for our objective. The *houri*, driven by three
paddles, flew before the wind. Little by little the sea
got rough, but as we were going with the swell that did
not bother us. Night came down too quickly for my
taste, for I should have liked to arrive in the neighbourhood of the barrel before it was completely dark. I
was afraid I might have some trouble finding it on this
monotonous stretch of sand.

The outside lighthouse of Port Tewfik was my first
guiding-mark for approaching the coast near our warehouse. The rising tide took us much farther in than
the last time, but at last the keel of the *pirogue* scraped
against the sand. We left her there and set off on foot
up to mid-thighs in water. The moon was almost

new, and shone faintly, casting light shadows before us. The sandy desert stretched as far as the eye could reach. I recognized the nature of the soil in which I had left my sacks, but I could see nothing which resembled a barrel. Ali Omar who, like most natives, had an instinctive sense of direction, assured me we were much too far south, so we returned towards Suez along the edge of the water. Suddenly Abdi stopped, dropped on all fours and calling to us, pointed out fresh footprints in the moist sand. When one is engaged in this sort of nocturnal excursion, the least thing assumes an alarming importance, and immediately my imagination was off at the gallop. These were not footprints left by us on the former occasion, for we had never walked in this direction. I concluded that fishers came here. After all, what more natural? We were no longer in deserted regions far from the habitations of men. A footprint on the sand was nothing to worry about.

The sight of a black object looming up before us made us drop sharply flat on our faces. We watched for a minute. It looked like a man crouching, absolutely still. It was probably the barrel, and I was tempted to spring up and make sure, but I was kept back by fear of the consequences if it were a man. If it were a local fisherman and he saw us, he would recognize us as strangers, and our nocturnal excursion would become a subject for gossip in the native cafés and we should fall under suspicion. So I left my men lying there, and walked openly along the shore so as to pass within about twenty yards of the black object. I should thus see what it was: if a man hailed me, I should answer his greeting and walk calmly on. I soon saw how unnecessary and ridiculous all our alarm was. It was simply the barrel, which looked odd in the moonlight, because of the curious shadows cast by the faint glow.

We ran up. Nothing moved; everything was as we had left it, but the mysterious footprints stopped there.

I broke into a cold sweat; I was convinced for twenty seconds that we had been seen from the lighthouse, and that some one had searched for and found our hiding-place. When my groping hands encountered the little sacks, I felt that a miracle had taken place, so sure had I been that they were gone. I had put them almost openly into the barrel, barely covered with a thin layer of sand. This was what had been the saving of them, for it was obvious that some one had come and searched all the sand round about; the traces were very clear. How true it is that the most obvious hiding-places are the best.

I drew out the sacks; there were only ten. In vain I ran my fingers through the sand in the barrel. I was sure I had put in twelve, and Ali Omar declared that he had counted them also, and that there had been a dozen. So the hiding-place was not so good after all; it had been found, but the thief had only taken two sacks, doubtless meaning to come back for the rest. I was very upset. This discovery depressed me to an unreasonable extent. Ali Omar was wrong, perhaps, but it was not the moment for conjectures. We put the flat cakes into three india-rubber bags which Djebeli had given me to protect the hashish against the risks of a nocturnal transport in a small boat, then with a certain satisfaction we got into the *pirogue* and faded into the night.

There was a head wind now, and as we were going against the swell it was not so pleasant. We had to collect in the stern so as not to ship water. In spite of this precaution, I had to bale all the time. I blessed the india-rubber bags. However, as we got into the middle of the roads, the waves became higher and the wind more violent. For a ship of ordinary size it would have been just a ripple, but for our slender *pirogue*, overloaded as she was, it was worse than really bad weather. The Dankali in front of me had to stop paddling to help me to bale. In spite of our efforts, the *houri* was half full of water, and of course the heavier she got the more water she shipped. We should never arrive, I thought despairingly.

Twice a wave broke over the prow and filled the *pirogue*. We all jumped into the sea in order to empty it by swinging it to and fro. The india-rubber sacks had been washed overboard; luckily they floated, but they were already some distance off when Abdi managed to seize them. We re-embarked, all except Abdi.

'Go without me,' he said; 'I'll swim back: the *pirogue* is overloaded as it is.'

So saying, he gave us an energetic push off, and dived to prevent any argument. He vanished into the darkness. For a time we could hear him singing what I called Abdi's song, the only one he knew and which he carolled in the most critical situations with the care-free joy of a house-painter sitting on his scaffolding. Then his voice was lost in the growl of the sea roused to fury by the wind. The *pirogue*, being lighter now, kept on her way more steadily. We shipped less water, and the red lantern of the lighthouse grew farther away from our stern, while the first steamers loomed up under the double stars of their harbour lights.

I was perishing with cold, I shivered violently and my teeth were chattering, but I did my best to paddle. At last the sea grew a little calmer as we approached the end of the roads. After wandering about a bit, we made out the sea-wall, which the town lights in the background made even more difficult to see. I rounded the end of it a good distance away. One man paddled while Ali Omar and I lay flat peering over the side trying to make out the form of a sentinel on the black reptile. When we were a hundred yards from it and directly opposite the point where Djebeli should be waiting, we advanced at right angles. Thus we were only a pin-point on the water, but even that seemed to me too much.

Suddenly we saw a little red glow giving intermittent flickers in the shadow of the wall. It looked like a

lighted cigarette, and I guessed it was Djebeli. We
advanced more quickly, for the light seemed to beckon
to us. When we were twenty yards from the wall, a
white form rose up, and I recognized the *guellabia* of
Djebeli. Without a word we handed over the rubber
bags. He pointed to the end of the jetty and whispered
rapidly:

'Be careful, there is an askari there. Go right out
and don't answer if you are hailed. It doesn't matter
about me, I know him.'

But no voice came out of the darkness, and at one
o'clock in the morning I was back on my *boutre*. Abdi
was not there. His absence completely spoiled any
pleasure I felt at the success of this first attempt to
deliver my cargo. When I thought that in a swift
pirogue we had taken three hours to cover the distance,
I wondered what the poor fellow would do, with only
his own strength to rely on. Not one of the crew was
able to sleep; we all anxiously watched this black water
and stared into the darkness, lit up intermittently by
red and green flashes of light from the fire-buoys. Big
steamers passed, going into and coming out of the
canal, swift launches set us rocking at their passage,
but though the wind fell as dawn approached, the sea
did not give up Abdi.

CHAPTER XXVIII

STAVRO AND I CROSS SWORDS

EVEN MY coffee had a bitter taste, and the splendour of the rising sun, which spread a carpet of gold and rose over mountains and desert, seemed a cruel mockery, jeering at the pain and sadness in my heart. The sun was now entirely above the horizon, and the sea stretched calm and shining, without the slightest ripple to break its surface, much less anything that might be the head of a swimmer. All the same, I could not believe that Abdi had met such a stupid death. Abdi drowned! It was too absurd. He had once stayed in the water for fifty-six hours, and had not seemed to find that very extraordinary. We kept cheering each other up by pointing out how likely it was that he would reappear, and the various daily occupations on board and the busy life in the roads took our minds off our anxiety.

I told myself firmly that until the following evening there was no need to begin worrying, and I let it go at that. But that did not prevent my mind from being pervaded by a horrible depression and haunting fear of disaster. When I went to take my siesta I could not sleep, and lay gloomily staring away over the desert quivering with heat, which stretched to the south on the Asiatic shore. It was there, on these monotonous beaches which began opposite us and stretched far beyond the horizon on the other side of the canal, that Abdi had left us the night before. Suddenly I saw a black dot standing out against the yellow sand. I dashed for my glasses. It was difficult to see in the shimmering heat which distorted everything, but I finally made out the silhouette of a man. It was Abdi; I was sure of it. It was impossible to identify him, but something told me it was he. An hour later I

could see that I was right. He walked along the shore,
stooped, stopped, ran after crabs like a man collecting
bait, then when he was on the other side of the canal,
opposite us, he glided slowly into the water. From
time to time, his head emerged above the surface, then
he dived again. A quarter of an hour later he was
alongside.

'It's quite simple,' he explained; 'I couldn't swim
against the wind when you left me, or rather I didn't
want to. I preferred to go ashore and come to Suez on
foot. But as I walked along I met three men going
south. I lay down in the water until they had passed,
then I amused myself by following them at some
distance, guided by their footprints. They had not
seen me. They stopped at the iron barrel, turned up
the sand all round it, pulled it out, turned it upside
down, then went on towards the south.'

Abdi agreed with me that our sacks had been discovered by the man whose footprints we had seen, but
that he had not been able at that moment to carry off
the merchandise, so, thinking it was a safe hiding-
place, he had left them where they were and come back
later with friends. We had preceded them by two
short hours. Abdi had lain down behind a sand dune
and watched till dawn, but nobody had come back;
the three would-be thieves had remained in the
south.

I was far from easy in my mind. What if these
charming persons hunted about until they found where
I had hidden my cargo? I trembled for my cases, for
once their existence was suspected, it would be child's
play to find them. All anybody would have to do
would be to plunge an iron rod into the sand. In this
way they could go over vast stretches in very little time,
for the field of investigation was not so great. Only
the sandy parts were possible as hiding-places, and
there were not many of them. I was thoroughly upset,
and wanted to be off at once, but we were in a harbour;
we should have to go through a host of formalities

before we could leave, and this sudden departure would seem very odd. I thought it best to consult Stavro on what was to be done. He was the only person who could help me. I had to go to his house anyhow that evening to settle up for the hashish already delivered, so I could tell him of my fears.

After dinner I went to Suez. I took Abdi and Ali Omar with me, so that they would know where Stavro's house was. They followed some distance behind me. The summer twilight lingered in the streets of the native quarter. The heat of the day breathed out from the walls and ground like an immense sigh of relief. The dim light faded softly into night; it was the daily truce from the burning heat of the sun. The street which ended in the sea was deserted as far as passers-by were concerned, but it was buzzing with popular life. The lofty many-storied houses showed twinkling lights at their countless windows, behind the climbing plants and the lattices of the wooden balconies. A vague rumour rose into the air, composed of the clattering of dishes, jazz tunes from gramophones, crying children, scolding women, laughter, the coughing of an invalid, the buzzing of a sewing-machine, in a word, the vast symphony, not always harmonious, of a working-class population in shirt-sleeves and slippers, pleased to be home after the day's work.

A woman's silhouette appeared on a balcony, and with a graceful gesture threw down a package of rubbish into the street, where it scattered in a musical tinkle of broken glass. At every doorway were men sitting smoking blissfully, astride chairs, inhaling the warm air in which floated a smell of stagnant water. As I got near the end of the street the animation decreased, until it died away completely, leaving the end house deserted, standing tall and silent before the sleeping water of the lagoon. I turned into the side-street and was abruptly swallowed up by its shadows. The same woman with the black handkerchief on her head came to let me in. This time her welcoming smile was

almost gay, and she led me at once into the room where
the icon kept watch. She addressed me in Greek, then,
laughing when she saw I did not understand, she told
me in Arabic that Stavro was absent, but would be in
presently. My two men were left squatting in the
passage.

At last the master of the house arrived. He looked
even bigger than before. What a magnificent-looking
brigand! He swept off his felt hat with a dramatic
gesture, and greeted me in jovial tones. He called his
sister-in-law in a terrible ogre's voice, but she came
tranquilly along like one well accustomed to such
thunders. Stavro held out to her a tiny package
wrapped in tissue paper, which had been completely
hidden in his large hand. It contained two little
candles as big as my finger which he had bought for
the altar of the icon.

I told him Abdi's story of the men he had seen
during the night near our hiding-place. He shook his
head as if he were reflecting deeply, but I had the
impression that he was embarrassed rather than
perplexed.

'I don't think there's much to worry about,' I said.
'I expect you know who they were, and I am surprised
they haven't already reported the result of their investi-
gations, like those in the *boutre*.'

'Whatever do you mean? Do you think I would be
such an ass as to risk having our deal fall through, for
the pleasure of double-crossing you? In our business
one must be honest and able to give one's entire and
unreserved confidence. Ordinary trading is made up
of mutual trickery. The good tradesman is the one
who is the most skilful at taking in or in interpreting
the terms of a contract to his own advantage, without
overstepping the legal limit, playing the game of
commercial struggle for which laws were invented.

'In our case it is quite different. We are outside the
law. The only rule in our game is loyalty to one's
given word. Take my word for it, when men feel the

necessity for writing down their bargains it is because
later on they want to be able to ease their consciences
by putting their iniquities down to the score of what
is in the contract. Don't make the mistake of confusing
smugglers with those who get their living out of
smuggling. I sent away Alexandros because he belongs
more or less to the latter category. He's not a bad
fellow, but just a weak-kneed creature who would die
of hunger if we did not give him a few crumbs to pick
up. Only he lives in this dubious society you have
seen adorning the terraces of the cafés. Sometimes we
need these wastrels, but we have to be very prudent
about how we use them.'

'I quite agree with you, and I did not mean, and I
have never even thought, that you could play me false.
But why don't you tell me what you think about those
men prowling round in the dark? You seem to find it
quite natural.'

'Yes, you ran a terrible risk, for if they had found
your cargo, what could you have done? Thank your
stars you only lost two *okes*. I'm afraid the place where
you have hidden the rest of the goods is not so safe as
you thought.'

I couldn't help thinking that this man had been trying
to find where my treasure was, and that perhaps at this
moment he knew my secret. I said, smiling:

'Why don't you tell me frankly that the two *okes*
were brought to you this morning?'

'Had you appointed me guardian of your merchandise
or given it to me to put away in a safe place?'

'No, but I came to deal with you for the selling of it.'

'After asking advice from the electricians in the canal.
One of them told me how you had spoken to him about
your plans. So all that concerns me is to pay for what
you bring me.'

I was furious, and had some trouble in hiding my
discomfiture. It was true, I had acted foolishly; I could
not but admit the justice of the logic of this man who
was defending his own interests by taking advantage

of my weakness. I felt that he would be relentless and that I should have to go very warily.

'I see,' I replied, trying to keep my smile unchanged, 'that in your—I mean, our business, there are rules by which one must abide. Thank you for the lesson, and now pay what you owe me, for I must be going; I did not sleep so well as you last night. . . .'

My smile must have been a pretty wry one, for Stavro observed me mockingly, then said in a friendly tone:

'Don't be angry; what's the use? You were wrong to accuse me of double dealing. If I had been a twister I could have got all your cargo yesterday without having to pay a cent. I should simply have played on your fear of the sentinel. As you may suppose, he had been paid to let you come near. Djebeli knows him, and an occasional thaler keeps friendship warm. We could easily have staged a sham seizure of your sacks as you were handing them over to Djebeli. You would have fled, only too thankful to get off so cheaply with nothing but the loss of your hashish. But that would have been a robbery, since you had confidence in me. Only don't forget that all the lazy dogs who live from smuggling would not hesitate to use such methods, or even to do away with you if they could do it without risk.'

More and more I felt that I was in this fellow's hands. I felt the complicated netting of this cunning snare into which I had put my head closing round me. I felt like the little fish in the fable which struggled in vain to free itself, and to whom the fisherman consolingly said: 'No matter what you do, you'll be fried this evening.'

'I'm not angry,' I said after a few moments of silence; 'I have no reason to be; we are talking and you are teaching me many things, and since you are so wise in this game, tell me frankly what should I do?'

I felt ruefully that this question was an admission of weakness and would give him the advantage over me.

But since I could not have the upper hand even in appearance, it was better to go to extremes in the other direction, and let him think that I capitulated unconditionally. This would flatter his vanity, and when a man is flattered he can be more easily led to commit blunders. In such conflicts, when all seems lost, the thing is to gain time and lull the enemy into satisfaction over his victory. During this interlude one sometimes manages to hit on a means to turn the tables.

Stavro assumed a thoughtful air, and hummed and hawed like a doctor with a puzzling case, to conceal his satisfaction in having me at his mercy. Then, stroking his moustache, he said:

'I think, since you ask my advice, that if you have hidden your cargo in the sand somewhere on the coast you had better fetch it as soon as you can, to-night if possible, and take it far away. I know the objections you will raise to that—the time for the formalities to get out of the harbour, etc. Never mind, give me a man who knows where the cases are, and he can take a *boutre* out to fetch them.'

'All right; so you are buying the lot?'

'Of course; why should I take any interest in the affair otherwise?'

'That's true. . . . How much will you pay me in advance?'

'What, you want something on account? Ah, I can see you have no confidence in me.'

'Which of us two,' I retorted, 'lacks confidence? You show me the way, since you are afraid to advance me anything.'

'After this, what can you expect me to do? Please don't make any mistake; there's no question of mistrust; I'm sure you are perfectly loyal. I'm just wondering where I am to get the money. You probably think I am rolling? Well, the thirty pounds I have just paid you for the ten *okes* delivered last night were lent me by my sister-in-law.'

'That doesn't concern me. When a man comes

forward as buyer and claims to be the only man with whom to deal, surely he has the money to pay with. Don't let us waste time haggling—that's good only for Armenians or Arabs. Come to the point: give me five hundred pounds and I'll show you where the three hundred and eighty-eight *okes* are.'

We argued for half an hour without being a whit further on. Sick of the whole business, I was trying to disengage myself with vague promises, which would permit me to leave on good terms with my adversary without committing myself.

'All right,' I said, with an air of acknowledging myself beaten once more. 'But it's such a fine night, it's a pity it's too late, for by the time we've found a boat——'

'A boat?' interrupted Stavro. 'But there's your boat, all ready, complete with sails, oars, a box of biscuits, and a little barrel of water.'

And he waved his hand towards the mysterious bark which lay opposite the icon. I began to laugh as I looked at it, and asked:

'And is it on wheels?'

Without answering he opened the shutters of a wide window, in the embrasure of which, behind the boat, were piled old brooms, brushes, and boxes of all sorts. The window opened onto the lagoon and the water came right up to the wall outside it, but like all the other ground-floor windows, it had thick iron bars across it. I looked at Stavro uncomprehendingly.

'Ah, you are worrying about the iron bars?' said the Greek, smiling; 'look how we dispose of them.'

Then I realized that the bars were not embedded in the wall, but turned on a pivot, leaving a wide opening yawning over the water. Two hooks fixed in the roof-beams carried tackle so that by four men (and Stavro equalled any two ordinary men) the boat could be launched in less than a minute. It was all marvellously organized.

'Do you often use it?' I asked.

'Very seldom; only in exceptional circumstances like to-night.'

'Never mind all that to-day,' I interrupted; 'I am like the Jews—I never do business on Saturdays. Be ready to-morrow night and I'll send you two men to show you the place.'

'But Saturday finishes at sunset,' joked Stavro.

'For the Arabs, perhaps, but I am neither Jew nor Arab, and my Saturday goes on till midnight. Anyhow, I am dead tired; I'm sleeping on my feet.'

He accompanied me to the door, still trying to persuade me.

'Come along, now, think it over. Your lucky star inspired you to bring two of your men with you. We are four. In one minute the boat will be in the water. It is high tide, the moon has just set, it is barely eleven o'clock. In three hours we should be at the hiding-place, for the wind is in the north.'

I admit that I was tempted to yield. The romantic side of the adventure, the impromptu voyage, the secret window, the mysterious black-draped boat—all that might have come out of a story by Alexander Dumas, and interested me intensely. But the faithful Sancho Panza within me warned me of the folly of delivering my secret to this man who burned to learn it. You never know where cupidity will lead. I liked Stavro, and he had declared himself an honourable bandit, a man of his word, but money was after all his chief interest. And he was a man, subject to temptation. If he found himself in possession of such a stock of hashish, representing such a large profit, he might fall. Better not to tempt the devil, I wisely concluded. Besides, I'd just had a marvellous idea.

CHAPTER XXIX

THE MIRACULOUS CATCH

At last the door closed behind me, and I was once more alone in the street with my two men. At the moment of parting, Stavro had wanted to win over my two sailors, who looked upon him with the greatest distrust because they had thought at one moment that I was about to come to blows with the giant, so he presented Abdi with a water pipe made out of a coconut, such as the sailors in these parts smoke. Abdi did not smoke, but he was touched and delighted by this present, and he wanted to squat down on the pavement immediately in order to try it. As soon as we were on board he stirred up the ashes of the cook's fire to find glowing coals, and woke up all the crew. Some of them, rudely recalled from slumber, consigned him to all the devils, but they got no peace until every one had tried the new pipe. Finally Abdi, having made himself exceedingly sick, was satisfied.

Early next morning I went to the consulate, knowing that Spiro would be there after mass. I went to invite him to accompany me that afternoon on a pearl-fishing expedition, the first in the gulf. I wanted the consul to find the first pearl, to give a sort of official consecration to the enterprise. Spiro was wild with enthusiasm. The consul was at the ten-o'clock mass, but he was sure he would be delighted to come.

'Can I ask some friends?' he asked.

'Friends might be rather in the way,' I replied; 'I want to do things very discreetly; there's no use advertising to all and sundry that there are pearls in the Gulf of Suez. I intend to ask for the monopoly of mother-of-pearl fishing, and such a revelation might make the Government ask too big a price.'

'You are right, that is most important,' said Spiro, lowering his voice, and looking round furtively, as if some one were listening at the keyhole.

'But I have an intimate friend who is a police captain, and he would simply love to come. I have spoken to him about you and he is dying to know you. He is also a friend of the Assistant-manager of Customs, the young man whom the inspector at Kosseïr recommended to you, and who would be very pleased to come too.'

'All right,' I answered, 'you can bring those two friends, but no more.'

'Needless to say,' I added, 'I ask you to say nothing about the expedition to anybody.'

'Have no fear on that score . . .' and as I went out Spiro accompanied me, walking on tiptoe, and speaking in a whisper, to show that he knew how to keep a secret.

It was agreed that he would telephone me at Port Tewfik to let me know the consul's answer and at what hour we could leave. He also promised to arrange with another of his intimate friends, who was in the harbour service, so that my *boutre* could leave the roads without any formalities.

On my way to the station in the Rue Colmar I passed before Stavro's shop, for in ordinary life he was a greengrocer. I went in on the pretext of buying vegetables, but really to see him. I saw him in the shadows of the back shop, looking at me with alarmed eyes. He seemed to find that my visit was rather compromising, but he must have realized that I had a good reason for coming, for he vanished into a sort of kitchen, beckoning me after him. I disappeared in my turn behind the piles of tomatoes, leaving Ali Omar to make the purchases.

'Here is why I have come,' I began without introduction; 'your friend Spiro and probably the French consul are coming for a sail in my *boutre*. I am to take them over towards the mountains of Ataqa. I

couldn't refuse, besides, I think it adds to my prestige
to be seen with Government officials as much as
possible. But I am rather at a loss, for how can I ask
such an illustrious company to get into my *pirogue*?
I need a boat which holds five or six in which to take
them out to my ship. I should take this boat with
me, in case my guests wanted to go ashore at the foot
of the mountains.'

'It is indeed a good idea to take them for a sail. I'll
send Djebeli to find you the sort of boat you need.
To save time, perhaps you will send one of your men
to fetch him; he is probably in the Arab café beside
the level crossing. But I beg of you, don't come back
here. In spite of all these innocent-looking vegetables, I am well known as something quite different
from a greengrocer, and the Government officials
would think it most peculiar to see us so friendly
two days after your arrival, and suspicion would fall
on you.'

'Don't worry, I'll be like Spiro henceforth; I shan't
see you in the street.'

Ali Omar soon found Djebeli and told him Stavro
wanted him, then we went back to the *boutre*.

My idea was to offer my guests any pearls we might
find in the oysters we fished, as a graceful way of
thanking them for saving me from undergoing the
tiresome formalities of leaving the roads. But I was
rather afraid we mightn't find any, as generally happens when one counts on something in advance. But
since I wanted to give them a present, why not give
chance a hand by putting the pearls I had among the
oysters? The chief value of these pearls in their eyes
would be that they had been found in their presence,
so it was preferable to put them into oysters beforehand, to make the illusion complete. This trickery was
justified, I thought. I sent two men to the inner
harbour of Suez, for the sides of the quays were
covered with *bil-bils* at low tide. There were assuredly
no pearls in them, but the shells were enormous.

They were soon back with a big basket of these bivalves. I let them open in the sun, then I slipped in
the pearls. In this way I was sure, even if the expedition were unsuccessful, that my guests would not be
disappointed.

At eleven o'clock I saw an orderly from the consulate
making signs to me from the quay. Spiro had sent
him to tell me that the consul could not come. He
was very sorry, and asked if I could put off the excursion
until another day. I replied that we could easily make
another excursion, but that I expected Spiro and his
friends at two o'clock. I was rather relieved that the
consul would not be with us. I had felt rather a cad
mixing this charming fellow up in such an affair. He
had struck me as so absolutely honourable, and he had
received me so frankly and trustfully that my little
comedy seemed rather cheap. But what was I to do?
It was the only way out of a difficult situation. That's
the worst of the sort of adventure into which I had
entered. I was often obliged to do things which my
conscience found just a trifle shabby. The risks were
nothing, but these compromises with my principles
were very disagreeable.

To be sure, there was still Spiro, but somehow I
didn't seem to have the same compunction about him.
Perhaps because he had the soul of a child, and I felt
I was going to amuse him. Anyhow, whatever the
reason, I did not have the same scruples about him as
about Du Gardier.

The boat I had ordered arrived, rowed by two Arabs.
I had bought beer, cakes, champagne, and ice, for I
did things on a grand scale, since I had thirty pounds
in my pocket. At last my guests appeared. Spiro was
walking ahead in the shade of a parasol. He wore a
black jacket, tennis trousers, and a straw hat. He had
a flower in his button-hole and a smile visible two
hundred yards away. After him came the two young
effendis of the police and the customs. They had with
them two servants laden with packages of food. I

insisted on these men remaining ashore, for they would have been very much in my way. Naturally, I pretended it was because of the secrecy it was necessary to observe. Spiro immediately looked like an Egyptian Guy Fawkes.

Presently we were all installed on board the *Fat-el-Rahman*, which trailed behind her the boat in which the two Arab rowers were already asleep. I had put up an awning, and we spread on the after-deck a fine Persian carpet Spiro had had the good idea of bringing. We skimmed lightly over the calm waters of the roads with all sails set. I had the pleasure of meeting the customs boat going out to visit a big steamer just come up from the south. The crew recognized the languid gentleman reclining on my deck, and saluted us respectfully. I chuckled inwardly.

We had soon left the bustle of the roads behind us. Spiro was in poetic mood, and compared the swollen sails to butterflies' wings, the sea to heaps of precious gems of sapphire and emerald; admired the grace of the gulls' flight, and so on. The others had brought a portable gramophone, for it would be impossible to admire the beauties of nature except to the accompaniment of potted music. They played Arab songs and tried to astonish my men, whom they took to be absolute savages. They were delighted with the Arcadian simplicity of their dress, consisting of a simple twist of material round the loins, and they exclaimed admiringly over the smooth texture of their skins. Then we lay drinking beer and smoking gold-tipped cigarettes while Firan and two Dankalis acted the clown, dancing the most grotesque dances of their country for our amusement. I had not told any of them the real object of this excursion, but they had seen me put the pearls in the *bil-bils* and they guessed that some good farce was being prepared, so they did what they could to add to the gay atmosphere of the outing.

The reader has of course guessed what I meant to

do. I wanted to go to the beach where my cases were buried and see if they were still safe. If so, I should try either to change them to another hiding-place or to take them on board. I skirted the coast, pretending to be searching for a suitable place to begin pearl fishing; we were already out of sight of Suez. At last the beach came in sight. My heart beat fit to burst as I took my telescope and swept it over the sands. All my men shared my emotion and all instinctively tried to hide it by singing more loudly than ever. I took the *boutre* in as far as I dared, and anchored in shallow water. I then noticed two men hiding under a rock. They got up as we approached. They were only a few yards from where our cargo was buried. Ali Omar nudged me and pointed out to sea, and I saw a sail making for the point where we were. I easily recognized the *boutre* that had so worried me the day of my arrival. I wondered if the two men were waiting for it. Decidedly, I must get my cases away. But first of all I must get rid of these two men. Aleady the very official-looking tarbooshes worn by my two guests had had their effect, and the men were cautiously edging away towards the back of the dunes.

'Look at those two Arabs,' I said to Spiro; 'I don't want them to go and spread the news that we are fishing for pearls.'

'Don't worry, my friend will say a few words to them, and I guarantee they won't linger.'

But the unknown pair seemed to have good eyesight, and to have already recognized those on board, for they now broke into a run, and fled northwards.

'If you are not afraid of the sun,' I then said to my guests, 'we'll begin fishing on the reefs behind this promontory. I have already found interesting shells there and perhaps we shall be lucky again. You can go and watch the divers at work and see the whole process.'

Spiro and his two friends installed themselves in the

stern of the boat I had borrowed, not forgetting their precious sunshade. We glided towards the reef, followed by the two Dankalis in the *pirogue*. They had their *mourailla* with them, through which they inspected the bed of the sea, and also a *harba* with which to harpoon dangerous beasts, and placed on their nose the *kartoum*, a pair of horn tweezers which they generally wore as a sort of pendant round their necks. Of course I had hidden in the *houri* the *bil-bils* containing the pearls, for use in case we didn't find any. Once we were round the point we could see nothing but the top of the *Fat-el-Rahman's* mast rising above the spit of land. The divers intoned the *bismillah* commending their souls to God, then took immense breaths and dived.

There were *bil-bils* in plenty where we were, and very soon they had a large pile in the *pirogue*. They brought the *houri* alongside the boat, and one of the divers began opening the shells. This is always an exciting business, like a game of chance. To my great surprise, right at the beginning we found some very pretty baroque pearls; my guests were in the seventh heaven. Then one of the Dankalis opened one of the oysters prepared beforehand, and before I could stop him had squeezed the pulp and produced a superb round pearl. Spiro thought a miracle had happened.

'Really, what a marvellous thing, I could never have believed that I would see such wonders with my own eyes. What is this pearl worth?' And he rolled it lovingly in his fingers.

'Ask your jeweller,' I returned smiling.

'No, no, never; if you want to give a present, my friends must come first.'

'Wait a bit,' I returned, 'we haven't finished; perhaps we'll find others.'

And we started fishing again. This time my spectators were thrilled; the gambling spirit had been aroused, and they were quite unconscious of the lapse of time. When the next lot were opened, we didn't find much, and I saw the disappointment on their faces. I couldn't leave off on this disappointment, so the divers were sent down a third time. I had resolved to sacrifice my other two pearls. The time passed like a flash for Spiro and his friends, but not for me; I kept anxious watch on the promontory which separated us from the *Fat-el-Rahman*. As soon as the cases were on board and securely stowed in the hold, Ali Omar was to appear on the crest and signal to me.

The Dankalis had been diving for an hour and a half, when at last I saw Ali Omar waving from the top of the promontory, and I heaved a mighty sigh of relief. I called up the divers with the *bil-bils* they had amassed, into which they slipped the two containing the pearls. The two Egyptians were burning with impatience, like two gamblers waiting for the last hand to be dealt. What an explosion of joy when the other two pearls appeared!

'What a pretty ring this will make! What a magnificent tie-pin! What an original souvenir—pearls one has fished oneself!'

I can safely say that never had I presented pearls with more cordial goodwill. When we got back to the *boutre* it was nearly sunset. A wink from Ali Omar and the satisfied air of all my men told me that everything had been carried out as per programme, and that my eight cases were now in the hold under our feet. I was the only one who noticed that the skin of my Somalis' shoulders had been scraped, and that Abdi was wearing a bloodstained rag around one foot. As they did not have the *houri*, they had carried the cases on board on their shoulders, having taken the *boutre* as far inshore as her draught would permit.

We opened tins of food and gaily drank our champagne, and our return was marked by a general contentment; everybody was delighted with the excursion. It was after midnight when I anchored in the old place in front of the Health Office quay. I was now in a position to resume my discussions with Stavro. He could search every beach on the coast, and much good might it do him.

CHAPTER XXX

THE KING OF THE SMUGGLERS

I WASN'T EASY in my mind all the same, for my situation was rather like that of a man compelled to smoke while comfortably seated on a powder barrel. I decided to take Stavro's advice, and not deliver the goods in small quantities. The least accident might bring about a catastrophe. I should go that very evening and try to make some new bargain for my cargo. I was in a strong position now; I could afford to wait.

When I reached his house, only his sister-in-law was there; he was absent, and I didn't believe a word of the explanations given me for his sudden departure. I didn't insist, but one thing did strike me as queer, and that was that Djebeli also had disappeared. Ali Omar searched for him in all the Arab cafés, but in vain. I should have to resign myself to waiting; there was nothing else to do.

Three days went idly past. I began to be a little anxious. Really, it was too peculiar that Stavro should choose this moment, when he was on the point of concluding a most profitable deal, for making this mysterious voyage. My sailors had been lavishly tipped by my guests on Sunday, and the money burned holes in their pockets, so they launched themselves enthusiastically into a life of pleasure. They adored the cinema, which they now saw for the first time, and all the little side-shows in the streets. I managed with difficulty to prevent Kadigeta from yielding to the blandishments of an Armenian dentist who wanted to pull out two splendid canines in order to replace them by two teeth of glittering gold. Abdi found nothing better to do than to have a molar extracted by a charlatan dressed in magnificent embroideries. His tooth

had been perfectly sound but he was charmed by the
shimmering costume of the operator. He was very
proud of this exploit, and never tired of recounting it.

Next day all except Abdi looked ill and depressed,
and nobody seemed to want to go ashore. What had
happened? Abdi alone was in perfect good humour,
and was singing his song while pretending to smoke
his beloved coco-nut pipe. Probably their money was
all done. I finally got at the truth. Abdi, with a
paternal smile, brought up to me Firan the cabin-boy,
who had been lying for twenty-four hours in the
fo'c'sle like a poisoned rat. His comrades had thought
it was time to make a man of him, and all had gone
into a distant quarter where for a few sous sailors could
buy the illusions of love. They had all come back in
a fine state, all except Abdi, who had been having his
tooth pulled during this time. Luckily, there wasn't
much harm done; a little disinfectant was all that was
needed. At heart I was glad this had happened to give
the crew an idea of the dangers and temptations which
beset a sailor ashore.

At last Djebeli reappeared. I saw him fishing
placidly from the end of a quay. He had come to tell
me that Stavro expected me to dinner at his house that
evening. In the big room where the bark and the icon
stood opposite each other, the round table was set for
two. The black-handkerchiefed sister-in-law made me
sit down, and Stavro arrived a minute after. He was
freshly shaved and wore a white shirt, but he un-
buttoned his waistcoat and his faithful woollen girdle
reappeared, covering his ample stomach.

'Well, what news?' he asked with a jovial air.

'Nothing much,' I answered, 'except that I was
getting a bit tired of waiting and was seriously thinking
of going away.'

'Why be in such a hurry? It appears that you had
a wonderful time on Sunday. I have just seen Spiro
at the barber's and he told me all about it, and showed
me the pearl he had fished himself. He has been telling

the whole town. Not bad for a start; my congratulations.'

The fat woman brought in a steaming tureen, the good old family tureen of white china with a pewter ladle, and we sat down opposite each other. The women, according to the old Oriental usage, ate apart, after they had served the men. In Stavro's house all the old traditions were respected. His nieces were cloistered like nuns; they only went out once a week, and that was to go with their mother to church. No men ever entered the house; my presence was quite exceptional.

There were two decanters of Samian wine on the table, one of them representing a woman with a dress adorned with flowers, and the other a similar figure with dress strewn with fruits—Spring and Autumn, no doubt. Stavro poured out the golden wine, and laughed at me the while with his little grey eyes. If I hadn't had my hashish safe in my hold I should have thought he had managed to play a good joke on me.

'What has become of Abdi?' he asked, for he had a special liking for Abdi.

'He is on board with the others, who are all ill.' And I recounted their unfortunate escapade.

'All the better, all the better,' he said sententiously. 'That will oblige them to keep quiet, for it's a bad thing to let them loiter in the Arab cafés. I know they are very faithful to you, but there are people who have got things out of them without their suspecting it. Too much has already been said about your Sunday's excursion. I have heard various things—oh, nothing precise, but for any one who is in the game, more than enough. It's time that was stopped. Well, have you decided to sell me the lot?'

'Yes, certainly, but I must have half the money in advance.'

'Still harping on that idea? Of course you are easier in your mind now.'

'I never was anxious.'

'Well, after all, I agree with you; you are right to ask it. I like men who can look out for themselves.'

We had now reached the cheese, and were savouring an immense slice of Roquefort. The wine in the allegorical decanters had reached a low level, though Stavro drank nothing but water. I felt that I had better go slow, for my head was beginning to swim a little.

'I've just got back from Cairo,' went on Stavro. 'I went about our business, and I am going to introduce you to a man who will pay the lot. He belongs to Petros Caramanos' country, and the farm you went to belongs to him. He allowed his tenant to sell you the four hundred *okes* just to see what you would do with it.'

'Yes, I know,' I replied; 'they telegraphed to him.'

'Ah, you knew that?' said Stavro, surprised.

'Yes, I knew,' I replied, with a Mona Lisa smile which was intended to convey to him that I knew lots of other things as well.

'It was only natural, since he was the owner of the hashish,' said Stavro. 'In any case, he would soon have crushed you if you had tried to dispose of it except to us. But he finds what you have done absolutely extraordinary, and he wants to meet you and become your friend. I think it is to your own interest to name him a reasonable price in order to get rid of your whole cargo at once.'

Though the generous wine had instilled a blissful contentment into my veins, I still knew what I was doing. I was interested to have at long last the explanation of the telegram sent from Steno. It was to announce me to the 'King'; these people were perfectly organized and I was in their hands. They had allowed me to act up till now, while keeping watch on my movements, and now that I was so deeply involved that there could be no backing out, they had only to dictate their conditions. If they had found my cases, the whole question would have been settled. They had been sure that if they let me come they could easily lay hands on my cargo, knowing I had no choice but to bury it in the sand. But they had not found it, so I could still fence. Did Stavro suspect it was back on board my *boutre*? I did not think so, for his vague allusions and ambiguous remarks were all bluff. If he really had known, he had only to say so openly, and I should have had to give in. No, he thought that I had merely changed the cases to another place. I had to play the game warily. Stavro and his associates were not rascals; they had tried to take all advantages over me, but that was good warfare, and I had retorted by defending myself with some success. Now we could treat on equal terms.

It was agreed that we should go to Cairo together next day, so that I could make the acquaintance of this king of smugglers. We took the train at seven o'clock next morning, Stavro travelling in a different compartment, for it was not prudent for us to be seen together. He only rejoined me outside the station at Cairo; we took a carriage, and the coachman set off immediately without asking for an address.

We soon turned into a street which seemed one long row of funeral undertakers' shops. These strange shops are only to be seen in those Egyptian towns where there are many Greeks. The carriage stopped before one of them, a vast room which stretched back into the shadow. Behind big plate-glass windows was an imposing array of coffins of all sorts. Some were daintily padded, and open like jewellers' boxes, showing an attractive lining of pastel-coloured silk. Two or three of the finest were laid on trestlés, to show off to full advantage their gilded carvings, wrought-metal handles, and ornamental nails.

In the midst of this macabre scene some people were sitting round a little table, drinking coffee and chatting gaily. Right at the back was an immense desk at which sat a man of about forty, who had a decided and soldierly air. He was talking to two ladies in deep mourning. This was the owner of the shop, busy with

customers. Stavro shook hands with the coffee-
drinkers as we went in. They were compatriots,
tradesmen from round about who had popped in for a
minute's chat. Some of them spoke French, and Stavro
introduced me as a tourist come to see the Pyramids.

At length the owner passed on the ladies to a
salesman, who would help them to choose a coffin for
the dear departed, and came towards us with out-
stretched hand, smiling, affable and familiar. He said
to me at once, as if I were an old acquaintance:

'Let's go to the house. My wife will be delighted
to see you and to speak French, for she was brought
up in France.'

In front of the door stood an imposing hearse to
which were harnessed two magnificent horses of the
most impeccable black. I was prepared for anything,
and I almost expected my new friend to invite me to
get into this gala vehicle. I had used up my faculty
of astonishment since I had entered this strange shop.
But no, the hearse was not for us; it had only come to
fetch its trappings. A landau, probably a mourning
one but comfortable for all that, carried the three of
us off towards the new quarters of the town, and
stopped before a huge house with pink marble balconies.

The staircase was also of marble, adorned with
bronze statues holding electric torches. A porter
saluted us respectfully at the door. We reached the
second floor, and entered a room positively bewildering
from its profusion of mirrors. Everywhere were bear-
skins, Persian carpets, palm-trees in tubs, and such-like.
Then I was ushered into a drawing-room decorated in
the most atrocious taste by a very expensive upholsterer,
with a profusion of bronze and terra-cotta statues, the
latter painted like anatomical mouldings. My host
invited me to sit down in a gilded armchair upholstered
in yellow silk, opposite an immense cabinet full of
silver dishes, gold cups, and so on, which looked like
a goldsmith's showcase.

Gorgis, the master of the house, was very proud of

all this luxury, and greatly enjoyed the admiration in which he believed I was plunged. He was very parvenu, poor man, but in spite of his immense wealth he had remained a man of action. He rather resembled Petros Caramanos. He was so proud to show me all his riches, his vanity was so harmlessly obvious, his way of seeming to say, 'Just fancy, I'm the man who made the money to buy all this' was rather childlike, and provoked my sincere liking rather than otherwise. We spoke of my visit to Steno, of Papamanoli, of Madame Smirneo; indeed, I gave him all the family news, for Petros was his second cousin.

Stavro was ill at ease in the midst of all this luxury. He kept rolling the immense brim of his black felt hat between his great fingers, and very soon, muttering something about important business, he left me alone with Gorgis.

He introduced his family, three blooming children The youngest was still in the arms of his English nurse, while the eldest, though he was only eight, greeted me like a little old man of the world. His wife was a pretty woman, a little plump, in accordance with Oriental tastes, and most elegantly dressed. She spoke French perfectly, without the slightest accent, and we discussed music and literature. Gorgis did not take much interest in this sort of thing, so he disappeared.

At last it was dinner-time. Dinner was served in a vast dining-room, with crystal-shelved cabinets containing complicated silver-ware all round the walls. The table was oppressively well supplied with silver and innumerable glasses of every size, and the meal gave me the feeling that it came from a good caterer for banquets. There was the inevitable lobster, and elaborate ices. I was horrified at the way the children pecked at the sweets, then threw them to the dogs.

After dinner Stavro came to fetch us, and we went to a sort of music-hall, where Gorgis had booked a box next that of the Khedive. Gorgis laughed heartily at everything, and enjoyed himself like a child; I couldn't help remembering that he had been an ordinary sailor. Stavro, in spite of his gigantic frame, seemed much more refined in type, probably because after all he was a man of education. The secret jealousy which he felt for the lavish wealth of Gorgis could be read in his mildly ironical smile at the noisy mirth of the ex-sailor at the vulgar farces played by the clowns. He threw me a meaning glance from time to time, as if to indicate how much above such childish nonsense he himself was.

When we started to speak of business Gorgis was anything but a child. Assuming a lordly and generous air, to make Stavro's canniness seem more petty, he accepted the price I suggested straight away, and agreed to pay half the money in advance. When Stavro wanted to bargain and scrimp over details, he told him to be quiet, and there, in the box at the music-hall, he drew an enormous wad of bills from his pocket with a careless air, and handed me five hundred Egyptian pounds. I had some trouble in finding a place for all this paper in my pockets. Next day we were to arrange for the delivery of the goods.

A room had been booked for me in rather an ordinary-looking Greek hotel owned by a friend of Gorgis. Before we parted for the night Stavro, who occupied the next room, gave me a long harangue about his friend, and his absurd taste for unsuitable and excessive luxury. They had been sailors together, and little by little Gorgis had organized their business, and in ten years he had amassed a fortune.

'I only got the bones to pick,' said Stavro a little bitterly. 'He's a marvel in business, there's no denying that, but selfish—he thinks only of himself. Do you think everybody is happy in his house? He keeps his poor wife short of everything, and treats her like a slave. Yet when it is to show off he doesn't care how much he spends; he just flings his money away. You must have noticed that to-day. One thing I must say: he is honest as the day. He keeps the accounts and

nobody has ever been a penny the poorer for that.   In
so far as that is concerned you have nothing to fear,
especially as he feels you are a man of a certain social
rank, and he is flattered to do business with you.'

It was true that all the time I had been with the
two partners, I had noticed that it was always Gorgis
who decided, always Gorgis who paid. He had that
assurance which comes from the possession of much
money, and which gives a certain prestige which takes
the place of distinction. He was known and bowed
down to wherever we went. The gigantic Stavro
trailed after him like a little boy. I had the advantage
of being a novelty, and especially of possessing four
hundred *okes* of hashish which they hadn't managed to
steal from me. Alone in my room, I counted my
banknotes over and over again. I could hardly believe
they were real, so little real hope had I had of bringing
my enterprise to a successful conclusion. The future
seemed brighter now.

CHAPTER XXXI

THE BEDOUINS

EARLY NEXT morning I was awakened by a knock at my door. It was Gorgis. A car was waiting, and whisked us off out of the city, south towards the out-skirts of Cairo, covered with kitchen-gardens and fields of clover. Here and there were hamlets with clay houses surrounded by manure-heaps. We reached a station on the line to Helwan. There we took a local train. I wondered why we did not go on in the car —perhaps so as not to attract attention.

Three-quarters of an hour later we got out at a little station right out in the country. On the deserted platform were heaps of vegetables and wooden cages containing hens and rabbits. We set off on foot across gardens and green fields, following winding paths. At last we crossed a wooden foot-bridge over the canal which watered all the country-side. On the other side, without any transition, was the desert. We walked up a dried river-bed towards a chain of neighbouring hills. I wondered where we were going. Stavro had removed his coat, and mopped his forehead, puffing and blowing. I was suffering martyrdom from my shoes, as happens each time a return to civilization compels me to wear the cursed things. Gorgis, who seemed quite at ease, walked ahead, swinging a cane and poking fun in-cessantly at the weighty Stavro.

What very odd tourists we must have looked in this stony desert under the burning sun. But there was nobody to see us. What reason could any human being have for coming into these solitudes? And yet the rich valley of the Nile was close at hand, stretching green and smiling at our feet, with here and there a rich red patch, where the plough had turned over the alluvial earth brought down from the plateaux of Abyssinia by

the river. The irrigating canal we had crossed a little
before drew a mathematically straight line between life
and death, as if some invisible barrier existed between
the teeming life of the plains and the barren stretches
of the desert towards which we were making our way.
We advanced in silence, all our attention taken up by
selecting flat spots on which to put our feet. I could
hear Stavro behind me grumbling and swearing at the
rolling rocks on which he twisted his feet.

At last by this gentle slope we arrived at the foot of
the cliff which crowned the vast plateaux of the hinter-
land. I turned round to admire the vast Nile valley,
which stretched to the horizon which was blurred by
that tenuous mist which rises from all the lands watered
by its muddy stream. There it lay, majestic and all-
powerful, spreading over the plain in a long curve, as
wide as an estuary. Hundreds of white sails, those
great triangular sails of the flat boats of the Delta, taut
on their lateen yards, were coming up the peaceful
course of its yellow waters. Other sails flitted across
the fields along the innumerable and invisible canals,
looking like butterflies in clover fields. The chalky
cliff behind me was all hollowed out by the galleries
of disused quarries. The blocks of stones for building
the Pyramids were hewn out of this living rock. The
same scenery had spread before the eyes of Pharaoh's
slaves as they glided the great cubes of stone down this
slope to the brink of the river where they were awaited
by great, flat-bottomed boats exactly like those of
to-day. The same north wind had brought them there,
and the same tranquil current would take them back
as far as Giza.

Suddenly we came on a sort of crevice in the cliff,
into which was inserted a narrow ravine. It was so
burning hot here that I thought of an oven door, but
hardly had we passed the entrance when we came out
on a vast sandy circus, covered with harsh, dry grass.
A herd of camels was peacefully grazing; we were
surprised to see them, yet the camel is such an

extraordinary-looking animal that its presence rather contributed than otherwise to the desolate appearance of this waterless desert. A clump of thorn bushes and of greyish shrubs showed that the scanty rains must linger in the hollow of this basin. Towards this oasis, if I might call it an oasis, Gorgis now walked.

A Bedouin, dressed like those of Upper Egypt, came out of the bushes and strolled tranquilly towards us. He was carrying carelessly on his shoulder a Remington rifle, with the barrel pointing to the ground. He seemed to know my two companions very well, and greeted them with great deference. Then he turned and walked away, motioning to us to follow him. We were approaching a camp. I could see plump, bronze children running about naked, hiding behind the rocks to watch us pass from a safe distance. At last we saw a house, or rather a hut made of planks covered with corrugated iron. All round were the nomads' dwellings, light, dome-shaped tents made of mats thrown over curved branches. As we came near men came out of these tents with the dazed air of those just awakened from sleep. Probably these Bedouins lived by night and slept all day.

The wooden hut was forty feet long by eighteen wide, and was partitioned off into two rooms, with a small window at each end. There was no furniture, and the floor was of beaten clay. In a corner were a few blackened stones and open tins, which were probably used as pots and pans. A Bedouin brought an old chair and two empty wooden cases, and invited us to sit down. Gorgis manifested considerable impatience, tapped angrily on the ground with his foot, and asked in furious tones:

'Why is Omar not here? He knew very well we were coming this morning.'

'Be calm, my master, he is coming,' replied the Bedouin tranquilly, continuing to sweep up the rubbish which littered the ground, with a palm-leaf broom.

I noticed how different was the Arabic spoken by these natives from that spoken in Cairo. This was the dialect of Upper Egypt, and I had some trouble in understanding it.

At last Omar appeared, surrounded by a troop of Bedouins. I wondered how so many people could suddenly have sprung up in this seemingly deserted place. He was very tall, like many Egyptians, with very broad, square shoulders. In spite of his slimness he gave an impression of force and endurance, for he had powerful bones, rather like those of camels. He wore a rich mantle of fine, dark cloth, with very wide sleeves, over a *guellabia* of black-striped yellow silk. He was not more than forty, and had calm, noble, and rather haughty features, and very soft brown eyes lengthened by kohl. They were like the eyes of these desert creatures which always seem to keep the melancholy of wide spaces and limitless horizons. His hands were white and delicately shaped, though not small, and they were covered with curious tattooings. His nails and palms were reddened with henna, and on his little finger he wore a silver ring in which was set a stone bigger than a hazel-nut. The blue tattoo marks on his cheeks indicated to which tribe he belonged. He was obviously a chief, whose riches consisted in innumerable flocks and herds on the mountains and plains. Gorgis adopted quite a different attitude to him, and his impatience changed into amiable smiles and words. I was introduced and obliged as a sign of honour to take the only chair.

The men were sent to kill a sheep, for our presence was the signal for a fête. Gorgis whipped off his coat, rolled up his shirt-sleeves, and declared that he would see to the cooking of it. He had become once more the handy sailor, ready to turn his hand to anything. While the sheep was being roasted whole before a heap of glowing wood, we discussed how best we could deliver my cargo.

The camels I had seen were most exceptional beasts,

trained to speed and endurance. Some of them were worth as much as five hundred pounds. These were racing dromedaries which could cover about seventy miles in a single night. They were castrated and trained never to utter a cry. This last quality was the most precious in the eyes of smugglers, and it was this which gave them their great value.

The camp where we were was a sort of caravanserai where the camels coming from the mountains laden with sheep and goat skins and smoked butter could halt, and where, on their return they could take loads of cloth, potteries, petroleum, sugar, and grain, in short, everything that could be needed by the nomads of the mountains. But this commerce was only a cover for less innocent traffickings, as was the case now. Omar was the chief of all the Bedouin tribes between the Red Sea and the Nile, north of Ras Gharib. Farther south, the country was under the domination of other chiefs. When some merchandise was landed on the coast, an agreement had to be made with the chief of the region, who in turn made agreements with his neighbours, for the safe transport of the goods to Cairo. What gave Omar his power and immense wealth was the fact that his territories touched Cairo, so that everything had finally to go through them, and nothing could be done without his consent. The goods were handed over to him at a given point on the coast, and for a fee which varied with the condition of business, the nature of the merchandise and the season, he undertook to transport them and hold them at the disposal of his customer wherever he wanted. He could even have them taken into Cairo or any other town in Egypt. Not, of course, in a single delivery—that would have been impossible—but little by little as the customer needed them.

Omar had hiding-places in the mountains, known to him alone, absolutely safe from discovery. On the dreary plateaux of those infernal mountains there were regions made inaccessible by the lack of water. In order to visit them it was necessary to carry a considerable provision of water, and also to make sure of having a supply for the return. In these deserted zones the Bedouins hid their merchandise. To reach them they chose the most rocky and torrid regions to cross, where there was not the slightest trace of either paths or water. At certain places they buried reserves of water and grain in the sand. After each expedition these places were changed, and to minimize the risk of treason, only the guide of the caravan knew where they were. In this way a light caravan could penetrate into those murderous deserts carrying only the consignment of goods. In these circumstances, what danger was there of unexpected pursuit after these swift camels rushing across this country of death? After a three- or four-hours' chase the pursuers would have to give up, for if the provision of water they carried at their saddle-bows gave out, it meant certain and horrible death. We discussed everything in great detail, and it was finally settled that I should deliver the goods to the caravan the following Friday, three days later, leaving just sufficient time for the camels to get to the coast.

Business being over, two Bedouins now carried in the sheep, spitted on a long stick. It was placed on two forked stands over an earthen dish filled with black wheaten pancakes to catch the gravy. I had luckily a good hefty pocket-knife; Gorgis had a magnificent cutlass at his girdle, worn on the right hip, sailor fashion. But poor Stavro searched through all his pockets, and finally produced a minute pearl-handled penknife. I had expected the gigantic brigand to draw from his belt a terrifying dagger at the least, and I could not repress a smile at sight of this dainty object in his colossal hand. Gorgis roared with laughter, and a charitable Bedouin handed Stavro his *djembia*, and we fell to.

I admired Gorgis, who had gone back to his sailor days. He held a huge bone in his hand, tearing the

flesh away with powerful teeth, and the big diamond
in his ring sent red and violet flashes between the grease
streaming down his fingers. I heartily enjoyed this
fashion of eating this hot juicy meat, beautifully cooked,
which we swallowed greedily without bread and practically without chewing. It is far and away the best way
to eat roast meat. The remains were taken out for the
servants and camel-drivers, who were sitting in a circle
outside in the shadow of the hut. They were all
relatives of Omar's. A boy of fourteen, handsome as
a god in his long, pale blue shirt, poured water on our
hands, then brought Omar's pipe. Stavro smoked with
him, Gorgis and I preferred cigarettes.

'You can see,' he said to me, 'how different these
Arabs are from those of the plains. These men are
still half savage and will remain so for long. I am not
very well up in such matters, but I believe they must
be of a different race, for they are as warlike, abstemious
and loyal as the fellahs are cowardly, treacherous, and
lazy. They hold human life very cheap, of course;
their own as well as that of others. They would find
it most natural to attack a caravan, pillage it, and
massacre those in charge. They would do it without
pity, and it would never enter their heads that they
were guilty of a criminal act. But on the contrary, if
you confide your goods to them, they will give their
lives to defend them, once they have passed their
word.'

'That is rather like the Arabs of Yemen and even
the pirate Zaranigs,' I replied. 'I shouldn't wonder if
these mountaineers come from the same race.'

'It's quite possible, for Omar has many relatives
round about Yenbo, and even much farther south.
There is much intermarrying between the people of
his tribe and those of the Nedj, Ouahabites, and
Chamars.'

'That is where my faithful Djebeli comes from,' put
in Stavro, who had been listening to us while he smoked
his narghile.

'You promised to tell me his story,' I said to Stavro; 'this seems a good moment for keeping your promise.'

'Oh, it's not exactly a story, it's a very ordinary incident, one of those obscure dramas played out with no other witness than the desert or the sea.'

CHAPTER XXXII

THE STORY OF DJEBELI

'BEFORE HE got the name of Djebeli, he was called
Moussa, and he earned his living fishing along with
his brother and his tiny son, the only child left him
by his wife, who had died away on the Arabian coast.
It was when he was nursing her for the small-pox of
which she died that he caught the disease and lost an
eye from it. Moussa and his brother were economical,
like all the Arabs of the Omran tribe, who are the
Scotsmen of Arabia, and had saved enough to buy a
fishing-boat, or rather to get one on credit. They came
to Suez, where there was a good sale for fish, and
worked hard a whole summer. Fish was plentiful, and
before winter they had paid off all their debts. These
two men were united by a great friendship and also
by their common love for the child they both adored.
Life seemed very good to them; they had all they
wanted. They resolved to continue fishing in the Gulf
of Suez for some time before going home.

'In order to understand what follows, you must bear
in mind that customs officers and coastguards make an
excellent living out of hashish smuggling. I speak of
the chiefs, who remain comfortably in their offices.
The others, the soldiers who patrol the coasts, or toss
on the seas, are just brutes, generally freed slaves, who
carry out orders without trying to understand them.
They can always be bribed with a few thalers, but it
is dangerous to try that.'

Gorgis nodded his head emphatically at this point.

'All the same, if one wants to make profits out of
the hashish smuggling, one must show zeal in the
service. So they arrange for the petty smugglers to
be captured. They are treated with merciless severity.
When twenty *okes* of hashish have been taken, all

the newspapers praise the vigilance of the chief of
police or customs of the place, and he is decorated
and promoted. When they run short of victims, some
poor devil is paid to act the part. It is not hard to
find some miserable creature who prefers the peace
of a prison to starving to death in the streets. So the
customs people give him a little hashish, which they
always keep in reserve for such occasions, and he goes
and gets himself captured at the place indicated
to him. So now you understand how important
the seizure of even a very small amount of hashish is
for the men who are charged with the suppression of
the smuggling. The quantity does not matter; that
there had been a capture is the main thing. The newspapers, who know their job here as elsewhere, spin it
out to the required importance.

'The coasts of the Gulf, the Asiatic as well as the
Egyptian, are patrolled daily by guards mounted on
swift camels. They go along the seashore to observe
if there are any suspicious marks in the sand. They
always go in pairs, and leave their posts at such hours
as to time themselves to meet their comrades from the
neighbouring post, fifty miles from theirs, about half-
way. There they tell each other what they have
noticed, then go on their way. Next day they repeat
the same performance in the contrary direction.

'At this time Gorgis and I were in touch with the
staff of certain steamers which threw us the merchandise
into the Bay of Suez. Some time before, we had lost
at sea a six-*oke* sack containing hashish. This happens
sometimes when the weather is bad and the night very
dark. I remember very well that on this occasion we
had to go away without picking up the sacks because
of a little steamer which was coming towards our boat.
It was a white steamer with very high masts, and we
were terrified by its strange appearance, but it was only
a pleasure yacht going south, which had steered towards
us simply in order to get a close view of a fishing-boat.
Probably it was the first time it had ever been in the

Red Sea, and the owner expected to see savages and strange beings. There was a most elegant company of passengers on board. The ladies in their light dresses, and the gentlemen with their admirals' caps laughed heartily as they watched our little boat dancing in their backwash.

'This little entertainment, these bursts of laughter, were to be the forerunners of a terrible drama. These people passed gaily on their way, little guessing that death was to result from their amusement, which had delayed us in picking up our sacks, so that we lost one. All night and next morning we searched for it in vain. Perhaps it had sunk to the bottom; anyhow, thinking it was lost, we went back to Suez. But it had floated.

'It must have stayed a long time on the surface of the water, carried hither and thither like the germ of a catastrophe. Some time after two coastguards from the post of Zafrana found it cast up by the sea. This packet had been exposed to sun and water for weeks, and its contents were completely spoiled. If they hadn't been, the two worthies would have got a friend to dispose of them, but they were worthless. But the sack had kept its shape, the name of the manufacturer was still legible and a vague odour indicated what it had contained. This was enough for the two honest coastguards. They dried the sack in the sun and hid it in the sand at a point where the fishermen often put in for shelter. Some days later they saw a *boutre* making for the shore, to avoid the storm which had aroused the sea to fury. It was the boat of Moussa and his brother. They anchored and almost immediately fell asleep, worn out with the night's hard work. The boy began to prepare their modest meal, over a handful of sticks set on top of a box of ashes. He sang happily to himself, full of the careless joy of all young things. The two soldiers saw from afar that here at last were victims. They came full speed on their camels to surprise them. The little boy saw them coming, and woke his father and uncle. Nobody likes having to do

with coastguards, it is so well known that they are
unscrupulous and capable of working much harm, so
the best thing to do is to avoid them whenever possible.
Moussa and his brother had no contraband on board
their vessel, but they had been away from Suez a long
time, and their papers were a little out of date. They
were afraid that the coastguards might create trouble
for them, so they decided to flee.

'Hastily they raised anchor and ran up the sail, for
the camels were rapidly coming nearer. In their hurry
they forgot to undo the reef point that held the sail
furled on the lateen yard. The boy, agile as a monkey,
swarmed up to repair the oversight. At this moment
a shot rang out and the child fell into the sea. One
of the coastguards had just fired and was gesticulating
to order the ship to put in again. Moussa threw
himself into the sea to save his child. His brother,
terror-stricken, crouched in the bottom of the boat.
Then the guards opened fire on this miserable drifting
boutre, trying to cut the halyard so as to bring down
the half-furled sail. Moussa swam along, carrying the
unconscious boy in his arms. He came close to the
boat on the side furthest from land, and his brother
leaned over to help him in. He seized the child and
laid him in the bottom of the *boutre*. Then, just as he
was stretching out a hand to help his brother, he fell,
his head shattered by a bullet.

'Moussa, mad with terror and rage, stood upright
in the stern, despite the bullets that whistled round
him. He raised his arms in token of submission, and
guided the ship towards the shore. The guards stopped
firing. Moussa did not act in this way out of obedience
to their orders, but his son was still breathing, and he
only thought of getting help.

'As soon as he touched land the two brutes threw
themselves upon him and bound his hands. They flung
him on the sand along with the still unconscious child.
The noise of the shots had been heard by the other
coastguards, who were now galloping up at full speed.

One of them was an officer, and he immediately assumed direction of the whole affair, as if he had been responsible for it. They told him that the occupants had been seen burying a suspicious-looking packet in the sand. They had tried to flee, so that the guards had been forced to fire, as the law permitted in such cases. The four soldiers agreed to adopt this version.

'The sack buried there some days before by the two guards was dug up, it was recognizable as hashish, and though Djebeli protested his innocence, pointing out in what a state the hashish was, it was no use. The law didn't say anything about the quality of the hashish. The evidence was there beside their boat, the corpse and the wounded child testified that there had been opposition to authority, it was a splendid and watertight affair.

'The unhappy Moussa begged that at least they would save his child; that was all he cared about. The bullet had gone right through his chest and was under the right shoulder-blade; he was gasping for air, a bloodstained foam on his lips. The soldiers threw him brutally beside his uncle, who was unmistakably dead. Half his brains had been blown away, and his eyes were starting from their sockets. They threw a coat over the two forms and a messenger was sent off post-haste to fetch the officer of the post, that he might give a legal aspect to this atrocious crime. The camels knelt down and the three guards drew out their water pipes and began smoking as if nothing had happened. Little by little the child's moans ceased. There was a rattle in his throat as the last vestiges of life fled, then silence. Moussa, kneeling there with bound hands, let his head fall on his knees and was still. He was not weeping; he gave himself up to his fate. He was condemned to two years' imprisonment; his *boutre* and everything he had were taken from him. The newspapers were loud in praise of the valiant coastguards, and the vigilance and initiative of their officers who, at the peril of their

lives, had upheld the law, and got the better of two
dangerous criminals.

'When Moussa got out of prison he sought me out.
All this happened ten years ago. I got him a job as
fireman on a ship bound for America; as his trial was
still fresh in people's minds, the police kept an eye on
him and he couldn't find work. Four years later he
was forgotten. He reappeared among the coolies
working at widening the canal. Nobody recognized
him, and he had taken the name of Djebeli. Even I
had to think before I could place him when one evening
he knocked at my door, saying he would like to work
for me. I realized that the two graves on the coast
between Cape Zafrana and the Ras Abu Diraj
bound him for ever to this country until God avenged
them.'

'And has God avenged them?' I asked.

'Who knows? Djebeli never speaks of them. Perhaps
he is waiting to find those who assassinated his brother
and son? Perhaps he has found them? There is no
use asking him, he will not say a word on this subject.'

'That is because he comes from the mountains of
Antar,' said Omar, who knew the story and had followed it in thought. 'It is a country where forgiveness
is unknown, and where an injury is never forgotten.
Djebeli, one night when I asked him about the death
of his son, told me this story instead of replying. There
is a legend that an old king of his country was taken
prisoner by Antar's soldiers. One of them put out his
eyes and took him for a slave. He accepted his destiny,
as all the Faithful must accept the will of God, and
did his menial tasks without complaint.

'When Antar came back from the war and learnt of
this cruelty, he ordered the soldier's hands to be cut
off, and he was driven forth to die in the desert. He
delivered the captive king, and took him into his own
household, where he was treated with every consideration. But the blind man did not know this, he thought
that Antar was the author of all his sufferings. For

twenty years he practised shooting with a bow and arrows; guided only by his keen sense of hearing, the slightest sound indicated to him where his target was. When at last he reached the point where he could silence the murmuring song in the turtle-dove's throat by a swift and silent arrow, he knew his hour had come and waited his chance.

'One night Antar was watching over his tribe and their flocks which were encamped in the middle of the mountains. The enemy was near, but dared not approach, so great was the prestige of the warrior chief. Then the blind old man heard him whom he considered as his assassin singing softly in the perfumed darkness. Guided by this song, a poisoned arrow flew through the still air, and found its mark.

' "You can take my life now, you who took the light from my eyes, for I am avenged. But hasten, for the subtle poison in this arrow, which I have saved for you for twenty years, will kill you in a quarter of an hour, and the enemy will be upon you, for they know I am to take vengeance this night," said the blind man.

' "May God forgive you, poor old man, twice blind. If I have still by God's grace fifteen minutes to live, I can employ them better than by punishing the mistake that has made you a criminal," replied Antar.

'So saying he sprang on his horse, and galloped off down the ravine, stopping at the entrance to the pass. He stood up straight in his stirrups with his back to the mountain, his lance thrust into the ground, and death surprised him in this warrior's attitude. The enemy, coming to take the camp by surprise, fled in confusion when they saw the grim figure of this motionless horseman rising into the night, and the dogs howled with terror.'

.   .   .   .   .

The afternoon was waning when we set out on our return journey. This time we took a path which led directly to the station, and the little train, crammed

with Arabs, took us back to Cairo. We finished the
evening, until the very late dinner hour, in a café,
which might almost be called a restaurant, for one
could eat a sufficient variety of hors-d'œuvres to consti-
tute a veritable meal. Gorgis, of course, knew the
landlord, who hovered round him with marked
deference. With his usual lavishness when he was in
public, he ordered a pound of caviare, a very special
caviare, it appeared, reserved solely for his consump-
tion. I looked at the people sitting near; not one of
them reminded me of the faces I had seen at Port Said.

'Here,' explained Gorgis, 'you won't see that horde
of down-and-outs, living by their wits, which can be
found in every seaport in the Orient. There, these
shady creatures batten on the sailors who come ashore.
They buy from the stewards or firemen of the liners
slim cakes of hashish in the form of soles, which are
hidden in their shoes, or some such shape.'

And Gorgis told me a lot of amusing stories, like the
one about the wandering minstrel who went and played
in the dining-saloons of the big liners, to excite the
pity of the passengers by his wooden leg and sightless
eyes. His wooden leg was most useful for hiding
hashish in, and his eyes were covered artificially by a
whitish film which could be removed at pleasure. He
overdid it in the end, by trying to use his violin too.
He dropped it one day when he was going down the
companion-way. Some one charitably picked it up for
him, and found it strangely heavy. He looked inside
it; it was full of hashish. This poor devil went and
fetched off the hashish for the lazy brutes lounging in
the cafés.

'There is nothing like that in Cairo. From all the
towns in the interior serious business men who act as
warehousemen for hashish come and buy wholesale
quantities, fifty or a hundred *okes*. The smaller fry
buy in their turn from them and furnish the fellahs in
the villages.'

'Is so much hashish smoked in Egypt as all that?'

'At least twenty to twenty-five tons a year, I should say.'

'But who smokes these enormous quantities?'

'The peasants and the workmen, the lower classes. The young gentlemen with the fez think it is too vulgar a drug and prefer cocaine, a poison which is making great strides in this country.'

'But how do you explain how all these fellahs and workmen look so healthy? It doesn't seem as if the drug hurt them at all.'

'Well, that depends. The workers, the men who work in the fields, and the coolies, for example, only use it to stimulate themselves and overcome their hereditary laziness. They are accustomed to it, like their ancestors for centuries before them, and it doesn't affect them.

'But those who lead an idle life, and use it to procure new sensations, quickly ruin their brains, and as often as not go mad.

'This pleasing result generally comes from the aphrodisiac action, helped along by the fact that Mohammedans are polygamous. A strong dose of hashish will prolong for hours an act which is naturally short, with the maximum expenditure of nervous energy. You can imagine the dire results. But these creatures are the exception, and I don't really think it matters if such seekers after unnatural pleasures destroy themselves.'

'Probably it was because of them that philanthropists took up the question and the Government banned hashish in Egypt?'

'If it was, then these contemptible degenerates have been of some use, for its prohibition is what sent up the price. Perhaps right at the start a few old ladies or clergymen protested in the name of morality, but once hashish was prohibited, the prices soared to such an extent that the Government saw what profits could be indirectly made by them.'

'But how can you struggle against this army of spies,

customs officers and police, without greasing their palms?' I asked.

'Because they are imbeciles, cowards and incompetents. Among the chiefs there are a few clever men, but they are not Egyptians, they are English. They are rare, I grant you, but they do exist; but what can they do with all those boobs who come and enlist because they are unable to earn their bread unassisted? The majority of them are cowards, and might well have finished at the business end of a noose if the Government hadn't employed them for this low police work.'

'All the same, all policemen and customs officers aren't fools.'

'Oh, you, with your European ideas! Perhaps that is so in your country, but here the police are the most corrupt body imaginable. I'm not fond of the English any more than you are, but if they didn't rule Egypt with a firm hand, it would be the most barbarous and cut-throat country that ever pretended to be civilized. All the people who are diseased, suspected, under a cloud, more or less kicked out of their own country, come and settle here. First they live as best they can by nameless occupations; or this is a country where all the vices flourish open and unashamed, and such people can always make a livelihood. And once they have a really ignoble reputation in their particular line of filth, they can always get into the secret police. Most of them are Italians, Greeks, Turks, or Maltese, generally expelled from their own countries or deserters. They accept very small wages, counting on their practical common sense to augment their earnings. These men are ready for anything. Then one fine day they appear in the official world, in a smart uniform and glittering tarboosh, and their brilliant career begins. You can imagine that one would have to be insane to trust these beauties. If you are not betrayed, and you never are when you work alone, you take no risks. This fine police force that you see parading when the big liners come in is good for nothing but tormenting the unlucky tourists arriving in Egypt about their passports.'

I thought privately that Gorgis was exaggerating. I still had some illusions. I was to learn some years later that the picture he painted was only part of the reality. I shall recount that stupefying story another time.

Stavro said good-bye to us. I realized that he did not like going to Gorgis' house, the luxury of which upset him, and Gorgis on his side did not try to persuade him to stay.

'Really,' he said to me, 'Stavro is too picturesque-looking. Everybody turns and stares at this brigand who looks as if he had escaped from the screen of a picture-house.'

'That's true,' I admitted; 'he is a bit conspicuous, but he must be most useful to you in Suez.'

'Of course he's useful to me, but his presence often weighs on me. He never risks a cent in any deal either; I have to stand all the racket, including his share. So if anything goes wrong, he does not lose anything. Watch him taking money out of his purse, he never fails to make an involuntary motion to hide what he is doing.'

'Yes,' I replied, 'I had noticed that and it amused me. I've seen the peasants at home make the same gesture on the fair grounds. It's very atavistic, this fear of pick-pockets.'

'And another thing,' went on Gorgis, 'he simply can't resist having little deals on the side, to make a few pounds unknown to me. I had a most violent argument with him about those two *okes* that you lost. In the hope of finding them without saying anything to you, he had the whole coast searched, risking drawing attention to it just when it was so important not to. Don't ever confide anything in him, and never do business with him without telling me. What else can you expect? He is a peasant, as you say, cunning and suspicious. You must just accept him as he is. Apart

from those little manias, he is a very good fellow, and
I can rely on him absolutely. All the Arabs of Suez
are in his power. Thanks to this, he always knows
what is going on in the customs offices, and every
movement of the police.'

'You say he searched for the two *okes* I had lost, but
did he tell you he hunted for my hiding-place as well?'

'What makes you think he did that?'

So I told him what Abdi had seen, the night he was
coming back along the shore on foot.

'You are right to tell me about this. Every detail has
its importance. We must walk warily; I shall warn
Omar this very evening.'

At last I was on the platform of Cairo station, waiting
for a train to take me back to Suez. I was impatient
to get back to my *boutre*, first to see that everything was
all right, for one never knows what may happen, and
secondly, to get out of this business atmosphere, where
I had to act all the time in order to appear at ease, in
which I could never be natural for one second. I met
Stavro in the train, and he immediately began to talk
about Gorgis. I praised him warmly, saying I had
found him a very fine fellow, and he couldn't resist
running him down a little.

'It's a blessing I am there to arrange everything,' he
said, 'for I am the one who discusses business with the
Bedouins. I know how to manage them; and when
somebody has to go out and be tossed about in the Gulf,
it's always me. And yet, though I'm the one to take
the risks, Gorgis puts most of the profits in his pocket.
He is the big business man, established and respected,
while I am looked on as a low smuggler. And when we
are in the street together, I have to walk ten yards
behind so as not to compromise him.'

'But after all,' I objected, 'it is he who advances all
the money.'

'Oh, he told you that, too, did he? Don't you
believe it; you can bet your bottom dollar that not one
sou comes out of his little pile. The money he gave

you came out of the sum paid on account by his customers in view of the arrival of your merchandise.
If anything went wrong, which God forbid, he would
tell these people that all was lost, that it was a misfortune for which he was in no way responsible, and
he wouldn't refund their money for a long time,
perhaps never.'

What Stavro had just told me made me see how
skilfully these men managed to protect themselves
against the risks of their trade, and how very badly
protected I was against the risks of mine.

Stavro went on grumbling about his partner. To
listen to them you would have thought that they
endured each other with great difficulty, each one
weighed down by a debt of gratitude, each one claiming
to act generously by the other who was very mean.
And yet they could not move a step without each other.
At the first sign of trouble, they rushed to each other's
houses in order to calm their fears, and Stavro and
Gorgis would have died rather than betray each other.
Yet as soon as they were separated, neither could resist
running the other down. It was just their little way,
and really meant nothing.

CHAPTER XXXIII

THE LANDING BY NIGHT

AT LAST I set eyes on the *Fat-el-Rahman,* peacefully riding at anchor. Nothing untoward had occurred during my absence. It had been agreed in Cairo that I should take my cargo to a point on the coast which would be indicated to me by one of Omar's men. He would be there waiting for me when I arrived, and would embark with me. I wondered how I could go out to sea without attracting attention. The simplest thing to do was to pretend to be going for a sail in the roads. The curiosity aroused by my *boutre* had already died away, and I hoped that my short absence would pass unnoticed. Just to be on the safe side I went to see Spiro and told him I meant to ask for permission to fish for mother-of-pearl in the Gulf. He telephoned to his 'intimate friend', the commander of the coastguards, to ask what I should do.

'Go and see him; he is expecting you at Port Tewfik. He is a charming man,' said little Spiro.

So here I was at the door of the coastguards' barracks, between two cannon dating from the time of the Khedive Mohamed Ali. I gave my card to an orderly. At once a young Egyptian officer came out of the yellow building at the end of the courtyard, and took me to the commander, who was a fat and florid creature, fairish, badly shaved, but very neat. His fez made him look like a Turk, but he was a Maltese, and spoke Italian fairly well.

'I was much interested in your idea,' he said. 'I should be delighted to have your vessel going backwards and forwards along the coast, for you could tell us many things that escape us in spite of all our vigilance.'

I wondered if he was going to ask me to keep my eyes open for hashish smugglers.   .

'Yes,' I replied, 'I have heard that a certain amount of smuggling goes on. But tell me all about it, so that I can be useful to you in the matter.'

'What interests me is the gun-running.'

'What, that goes on here? And who buy the arms?'

'Oh, you've no idea how eager the Bedouins always are to get arms. There are always agitators stirring up rebellions in Upper Egypt against the English.'

'And is there hashish smuggling too?'

At the word 'hashish,' the commander started as if I had said something obscene. He looked involuntarily at the door to see if it were shut. Then he forced a smile.

'Certainly there is, but we are not customs officers. Besides, it doesn't amount to a row of beans here. At Alexandria and Port Said it's a different story. But what is really grave here is the traffic in arms.'

He hastened to change the conversation, and we spoke of fishing and the temperature, as one always must if one has come up from Djibouti. I noticed that this gallant soldier had rather vague notions of geography. He placed Djibouti in Madagascar, opposite the mouth of the Congo! My question about hashish had shaken him a bit. No doubt this was too delicate a matter to be discussed with a stranger.

Of course I displayed the pearls I was supposed to have found in the Gulf, and presented him with one of them. It was agreed that I should make a written demand for permission to fish for mother-of-pearl. He would give it his warm support, and he did not think it would be refused. I was pretty sure, however, that the English, who would have to be consulted, would find some pretext for not granting my request.

.   .   .   .   .

The day before that fixed for my expedition, Djebeli brought a basket of vegetables as an excuse for coming

to see me. Omar's Bedouin had arrived from
Cairo; he was at Stavro's and they expected me that
evening.

At nine o'clock I was knocking at the little door.
Stavro looked worried. He had been warned that the
coastguards had been doubled, that is to say, that there
was a night patrol as well as a day one.

'Has something leaked out? Are their suspicions
aroused?' I asked.

'I don't think it is for your benefit. For some time
the authorities have been dreading a rising in Upper
Egypt, and they are on the look-out for gun-runners.
Djebeli is on the watch, and will find out if there will
be a patrol to-morrow night. You must go to the point
of Ras-el-Adabieh, under the mountains of Ataqa,
where he will be waiting for you, and will tell you
what to do next. The Bedouin sent by Omar will be
with him. He knows where you must put in to deliver
the goods. Look, here he is, so that you will be able
to recognize him.'

He advanced towards a form huddled in a corner of
the room, and said:

'Come on, Ahmed, you've slept long enough. Come
here. It's terrible,' he added, 'the way these people
sleep when they have nothing to do. They curl up
and drowse like hibernating dormice.'

A very dark-skinned Arab with a sunburnt face came
out of the corner where he had been lying, wrapped in
his *burnous*. He was dressed in the thick woollen
stuffs worn by the mountaineers, because of the chilli-
ness of the nights. He was very dirty, and smelt
strongly of the stable, as do all those who live constantly among camels. He kept scratching himself,
with so eloquent a gesture that when he touched
my hand in greeting I began to scratch myself too,
for I felt that his invisible vermin had invaded my
garments.

I listened attentively to all the instructions about
how the goods must be packed before they were landed,

then I said good night to the black-robed women, who would no doubt pray for my success before the icon. As I went out, I noticed that a propitiatory candle of yellow wax was already burning. I stopped on the threshold, for it had just struck me that if there was any muddle and my guide didn't manage to turn up the next day at the appointed hour at the point of Ras-el-Adabieh, all our plans would come to nothing. It would be wiser for him to accompany me at once on board the *Fat-el-Rahman.* Stavro quite agreed. There was no danger, for it was late and very dark. Besides, everybody was accustomed now to seeing my sailors coming and going, so I could embark him without attracting any attention. We took the precaution to remove his vast *burnous*, which might have attracted the notice of the sentinels on the quay, and he walked in front of me, lightly clad like the rest of my men. The sentinels took not the slightest notice of him. It was a triumph to have got him on board so unobtrusively, for there were no Bedouins at Suez, and it would have been remarked if one of them had been seen going on board my *boutre.*

Spiro advised me to go and see the assistant harbour-master before I left. He was an Arab, and another 'intimate friend'. In addition to his administrative functions, he did coasting for the Messageries with a large *boutre.* The agent of the Messageries Maritimes at Suez only had to do with arranging passages on the liners. He never had to arrange for important cargoes. So active and ambitious agents would not have liked this post. No coaling, no taking on of firemen, no provisioning; it was really more or less an honorary post, something like a consulship, an easy but not very remunerative, situation. Naturally, only a man who was incapable of the little traffickings in which his colleagues of the other posts indulged would want such a post. Only a disinterested and honourable man who wanted to wind up peacefully an unblemished career would be found there, and such indeed was

Monsieur Le Coufflet, who is probably there to this day.

The consul had his Spiro and Monsieur Le Coufflet had his Demartino. He did everything, and seemed to run the whole agency. He was treated as the son of the house, one might say, for everybody in this agency had an air of belonging to the same united family. The office with its old-fashioned desks never saw a stranger. Who could have guessed that the Messageries had an agent in Old Suez? The native staff had been born on the premises and had succeeded their fathers, and their children would take their places when they died. Even the old tree in the courtyard seemed to be venerated as an ancestor, and though the branches had pushed their way right against the windows, nobody would have dreamed of pruning them.

The old tugboat, the *Helen*, had an aristocratic air, with her high, old-fashioned chimney. She wended her way sedately among the swift launches which crossed the roads in all directions, seeming to protest against the insolent tumult and feverishness of this twentieth century by her dignified leisureliness.

Monsieur Le Coufflet received me cordially. When I had explained what I wanted, he summoned the assistant harbour-master, whose *boutre* did the coasting of the rare cargoes confided to the Messageries here by eccentric traders. Introduced by Monsieur Le Coufflet and recommended by Spiro, I was able to come to an understanding with this Arab in no time. He was so fat and flabby that one felt vaguely uneasy if obliged to remain in his immediate vicinity. His belt had a helpless air as if it really couldn't guarantee to control these vast billows of fat much longer. I couldn't help thinking of the hoops of my water-barrels, which had burst during the voyage. Demartino spoke the local Arabic much better than I, so he discussed the matter with the harbour-master and it was agreed that for two thalers I could go out for a short time from the harbour without any one even noticing. The harbour-master was an Englishman, but all his faculties were absorbed by whisky-drinking, which left him just enough leisure to sign papers presented to him without bothering about their contents. His assistant attended to all the ordinary routine affairs. This had been an established custom for long, and the English are very conservative, so there was no reason to fear any sudden change.

After the two days I had just spent in Cairo, I felt delightfully soothed by the atmosphere of this agency of the Messageries Maritimes. There was an old-fashioned charm in the antique furniture, and something of the past seemed to linger within these walls, something of the days when the Chinese mail-packet spread billowing sails to the monsoon in the Indian Ocean. Then, too, I felt at home with Monsieur Le Coufflet; there was no longer any need to wear a mask. I was sorry to return to Port Tewfik, that modern town of Thomas Cook and his fellows. My *boutre*, which would soon take me away from all that, seemed a refuge.

I set sail discreetly in the afternoon. Only the Harbour and Lighthouse Service could have questioned my departure, and I knew that the fat Arab would make that all right. The pretext I had given was a fishing expedition to pass the time, for I was supposed to be waiting for the Admiralty's reply to my application for a concession. I therefore made first of all for the reefs near the Mountains of Ataqa. As soon as twilight fell I was far enough off to be invisible from the coast. My Bedouin was slumbering in the foot of the hold, but as soon as we got outside, though there was very little swell, he became violently sick. This did not seem to suit his vermin, which spread all over the boat. My men did not seem to realize at first why they wanted to scratch, but when they did they shook all their possessions violently in the wind.

As soon as the sun had disappeared behind the

mountains we crowded on sail and made for the south.
I stopped the *boutre* opposite the point of Ras-el-
Adabieh and sent the *pirogue* ashore to parley with
Djebeli. He was crouching on the beach, as motion-
less as a rock.

'Go away,' he said; 'a patrol coming from Suez is
about due, and they must not see your ship.'

'How many men?'

'Two, no doubt, but that is enough. Even if they
happened on us by accident they wouldn't prevent us
from doing what we have to do, for they know that the
Bedouins are armed and they have no desire to be
killed. They would take to their heels, but the frontier
guards would be alarmed, and the police in Cairo
would know in less than an hour, so that for at least a
month we shouldn't be able to budge. Come, be
quick, I'm coming on board with you.

Once more we were at sea. Djebeli had relapsed into
his usual taciturnity, and sat smoking Abdi's pipe.
He indicated exactly what direction I must take in order
to get to the meeting-place. About midnight, a chain
of hills began to stand out against the sombre background of the high plateaux. They seemed to be
fairly near the coast. It was there that the caravan
was waiting for us. I anchored in sixty feet of water.
According to the chart that meant I was about a mile
from shore. That was far enough to ensure invisibility
from land. Ali Omar, Djebeli, the Bedouin and I
went on ahead of the others. Everything before us
looked dark. It is always easier to see things on the
water, especially if the watcher is low down. Djebeli
stopped the *pirogue* as soon as the paddle touched
bottom.

'Stay there,' he said; 'I shall go on alone. If you
hear voices, go away, but if, on the contrary, you see
the glow of a cigarette, come towards it.'

'Have you matches?'

'No, but I have a flint in my pocket.'

The 'flint' was a piece of camel-dropping, which he

had lit before leaving home. As he had been behind me I had not smelt this natural wick. The water reached his waist; I saw him go slowly into the darkness, his clothes in a bundle on his shoulder. Only a faint line of phosphorescence showed where he had passed, but now I smelt the fire he carried with him in his turban. Then he seemed to begin to make as much noise as possible as he walked in the water. He spat, cleared his throat, churned up the water like a man who was performing his ablutions without any attempt at concealment. I understood that he did this on approaching land, so as to attract the attention of a possible sentinel, who would call out when he heard the noise. This was the best way of finding out if danger lurked in these mysterious shadows.

Then silence fell. He had probably left the water. We remained motionless and silent while the minutes dragged by. From time to time we could hear the cry of a sea-bird echoing among the rocks or the swish of the water at the passage of the little coast sharks, but on shore there was profound silence. This continued so long that I was afraid I had missed the glow of the lighted cigarette, but at last we perceived on our right the intermittent blinking of the little red eye.

So the way was clear. We advanced fearlessly, and found Djebeli waiting at the edge of the water. He bade us hasten and walk exactly in his footprints over the sand. Thus it would seem that only one man had passed this way. Anyhow the strip of sand was very narrow; almost immediately we found ourselves walking on hard soil. We crossed under the telegraph wires which skirted the coast from the entrance of the Gulf, the poles studding the path along which came the patrols.

'They have passed,' said Djebeli. 'I saw the traces, and I was lucky enough to find these camel-droppings. They are still warm, which proves that they passed about half an hour ago. The guide must go and announce our arrival without losing a moment, so that we can get everything done before the patrol comes back.'

The Bedouin, thankful to be back on dry land, had already vanished in the direction of the hills. Djebeli sat down in the hollow of a rock from where he could see without being seen. From here he could signal to us with his everlasting cigarette if the way was clear. I noticed how he did it. He enclosed the cigarette with his hand so that the light could only be seen from one direction, and the incandescent glow was visible at night from a considerable distance.

We went back to the *boutre* to fetch our merchandise. Half an hour later the first load of bundles arrived, watched over by the little red point of fire. We tried as far as possible to walk in the same prints or at least to reduce as much as possible the width of the trampled belt of sand. There were fourteen bundles attached in twos in such a way that if necessary they could be thrown over a saddle without a second being lost. They were shaped so that they could be placed in two openings hollowed out in the stuffing of the saddle. The whole crew had swum ashore, for the *pirogue* was heavily laden with the goods. Silently each man seized his double bundle, weighing nearly a hundredweight, and ran off in Indian file. The last one had just crossed the path with the telegraph poles; the worst danger was now past. We were swallowed up by the darkness, the bushes, and the rocks. Firan had rowed the *pirogue* about three cables' lengths out and was waiting for us. If any one did pass along the path he would see nothing.

As soon as we had got a safe distance from this dangerous path we laid down our bundles and waited for the return of the Bedouin who had gone to tell the camel-drivers. Time passed and he did not come back. I began to be anxious.

'Don't worry,' said Djebeli; 'the camels are often at

a considerable distance and our messenger may not be back for some time yet. We have no time to lose; it would be better to fetch the rest of the bundles, for the great thing is to get them across the path. Once they are here the risk is very slight, and we can wait calmly for the camel-drivers.'

So we set off to fetch the second and last part of the cargo. Only one man went with the cabin-boy on board; the rest of us waited on the beach. Djebeli was with us. I calculated that the *pirogue* would be back in about a quarter of an hour. That would be the critical moment, for what a disaster if it reached the shore just as the patrol came back. I waited, strung up to a high pitch of nervous tension. Every minute I thought I could see the lofty silhouette of a man on a racing-camel. The very telegraph poles became threatening. I was eaten up with impatience for the return of this *pirogue* which seemed to be so long in coming. Djebeli was crouching near me. He had just lit a fresh cigarette and was drawing long whiffs between his cupped hands.

We were right at the edge of the water, sheltered from indiscreet eyes by a small dune covered with bushes. The path lay thirty feet behind us, guarded by two men I had posted one on each side of us. In this way each sentinel had only one direction to guard. They were to throw a pebble towards our bushes if they saw the slightest shadow. This sound would be enough to warn us while it could not be heard by any one approaching. So we had only to keep watch on the sea before us, wait for the *pirogue* to arrive, and listen.

Ali noticed a black speck on the water. It grew bigger; it was the laden *pirogue*. Through my glasses I could make out the heap of bundles. At last we could get on. Just as we were about to spring up to go and meet it, the sharp sound of a rolling stone froze us into immobility. A second pebble followed: probably the sentinel had been afraid we should not hear the first.

Djebeli instantly put out his cigarette, and we waited, holding our breath. The accursed *pirogue* seemed to fill the whole horizon to the exclusion of everything else. The signal which was to guide her had vanished, but would the men understand what had happened? She came on, slowly and noiselessly, but undoubtedly approaching. Then a dull, rhythmic sound beat upon the air, and we heard the stones rolling under the swift gallop of two racing-camels. The soldiers reined in their mounts to a foot-pace. I could plainly make out the two men through my night glasses, and even distinguish the barrels of the rifles slung across their saddles.

The *pirogue* now seemed to have stopped. They had realized the danger. But instead of remaining in the same position she veered round and presented her broadside to the land. This time she was clearly visible; we were lost. The two camels passed a bare fifteen yards behind us. I heard the soldiers clicking their tongues to encourage their camels, which started to trot. The *pirogue* continued to swing round until she was just a vague speck in the night. She had taken up a position at right angles to the shore. The meharists had now passed us. They trotted off, and in a few seconds the sounds of drumming hoofs died away, and there was silence again.

'We certainly are lucky,' I said to Djebeli; 'it's a miracle they did not see the *pirogue*.'

'*Nocib!*' replied Djebeli, 'but I think they did see it, only they were afraid they were surrounded by armed men hidden in the bushes and they preferred to trot off as quickly as they could. When the frontier guards are in detached pairs they are not very dangerous. But we'll have to hurry, for they will give the alarm at the first post which has a telephone, and before morning there will be a whole army here. It's rather a nuisance.'

While he was speaking he searched for fire to relight his cigarette, but he hadn't any more and my matches were damp. Those stupid details can sometimes start the most tragic and far-reaching dramas. Somebody has called these infinitesimal beginnings of great convulsions 'the conjuration of imponderables'. I should be obliged to call the *pirogue*. It was most imprudent, but there was nothing else to be done. Making a megaphone of my hands I stooped down and sent a call softly over the water. By this means those who are near the surface of the water can hear at great distances. Perhaps the vibrations are transmitted by the mass of water, or the elasticity of the surface; the superficial tension acts as a membrane. But at this moment I was far from indulging in speculations about acoustics; I contented myself with doing as I had seen fishermen do.

But the *pirogue* did not seem to hear, so, throwing prudence to the wind, I shouted. Let come what might. At last I heard the dip of the paddles, and the *pirogue* grounded on the beach. We threw ourselves feverishly on the bundles and carried them off instantly in a sort of frenzy, as if avenging ourselves on them for the anxiety they had made us endure for three-quarters of an hour.

At last everything was gathered in a sort of little ravine at the foot of these hills which had served us as guides. Still our Bedouin had not come back. The dawn was near, the morning star had just risen out of the sea and was rapidly climbing the sky. How quickly it seemed to go up to-day. I thought of the stormy nights when I had sighed after its appearance and when it had seemed to linger on purpose. But now when it was a few degrees higher the sky would begin to pale.

Djebeli was worried too. He said nothing, but I could follow his thoughts. This night patrol, the distance at which the camels had remained, all that was not reassuring. If anything happened here our merchandise was spread out in full view and there was no chance of hiding it in this rocky ground. In less than an hour we should be forced to beat a retreat, abandoning everything.

I cursed Gorgis and Stavro who had so lightly led me into this scrape. If I had been in their place I should rather have died than go back on my word. And I thought of Gorgis' palace with its pink marble staircase and his ostentatious spending. What did he risk? His customers' money, that was all. No doubt he was sleeping at this moment and snoring like a brute. All Stavro did was to burn candles and dream dreams. Nice mess I had got myself into, thinking I was plunging into a romantic adventure. I had wanted to play at smuggling and act for my own benefit. Up to the present I had adventured alone, counting only on myself, but now I had to depend on others. That was where I had made the mistake and I was to pay dearly for it. But it served me right. I was well punished for having neglected the Arab proverb which says: 'Think always that everybody depends on thee, but do thou depend only on thyself.' When one forgot this proverb one raved of ingratitude, injustice, persecution, and so on, and one became morose and soured. I tried to whip up my courage by such reasoning to give me the strength to go through with this disastrous abandon without complete despair.

Just at that moment, when I had resigned myself to the worst, shadows suddenly and silently began to flit between the rocks round us. They undulated and crouched. I could see the gleam of rifle barrels. Then they stood abruptly upright. One of them came forward; it was our Bedouin guide. A score of others advanced as soon as he had recognized us. All my philosophy was forgotten; only one thing existed in the world; that was the necessity of loading our merchandise on the camels at lightning speed.

Without a word each Arab seized a double bundle and vanished into the ravine. Djebeli held a low conversation with four hefty fellows armed with Remingtons. His first words had been to ask for matches, for he could not remain a single hour without smoking. I admired his imperturbable calm; he seemed to be a blasé spectator of all this feverish activity. This strange being never showed the slightest emotion. I had to ask him to interpret for me, for I could not understand a word of the dialect of these mountaineers. They had been forced to leave the camels six miles away because all the patrols had been doubled the last three days, and the presence of this herd of camels would have aroused suspicion. Nobody knew yet the reason for this extra vigilance.

The leader of the caravan had thought it would be more prudent to put the affair off until another day, and had sent a man to warn us that he would not be there. Our Bedouin had happened to meet him halfway, and had explained that as all the cargo had already been landed there could be no question of putting off till next day, for if we did we should lose everything. Thanks to this chance meeting, which was almost miraculous when one reflects that it was very dark and that neither man followed any definite path, the camel-drivers had come themselves to transport the bundles while the camels advanced slowly to meet them. When they had all disappeared with their loads, the four armed Arabs who had been the advance guard now closed the rear.

When I saw these grimly determined men I realized that their way of earning their living is a most dangerous one. Once they had started on an expedition human life was cheap indeed in their eyes; they became primitives ready to kill an adversary without the slightest hesitation or scruple. That is what happened to us in the war, though we were alleged to be civilized and had been brought up to venerate human life. After a little training we massacred men who had done us no harm, with as little hesitation as we might have shot a pheasant before the war. I also realized that the job of frontier guard was no sinecure when they went out after these desperate men, and I quite understood the haste with which the two soldiers of the patrol had spurred on their mounts when they saw on the sea what they had taken for a boat.

CHAPTER XXXIV

FOOTPRINTS IN THE SAND

WORDS CANNOT describe our lightness of heart as we made our way back to the sea; it was almost worth all the worry to have such a glorious feeling. The most urgent thing to do was to efface the marks of our bare feet in the sand. I realized that we should never manage to restore its virginal appearance to the trampled sand, but on the contrary, any attempt would simply point to a guilty conscience. If an innocent fisherman had landed there he would never think of trying to efface his footprints. So I stopped my men levelling the sand, and sent them to pick up driftwood. I was lucky enough to find some fairly big branches, and I set up three stones to make a primitive hearth, as the fishermen do. Thanks to the matches Djebeli had luckily thought of asking, I contrived to light a fire in the shelter of a rock. I piled up the wood so as to get as much ash as possible. If a patrol came to inspect the beach next day this fire would explain the footprints. Since the camels had remained several miles inland, there were no suspicious traces to upset the theory that a peaceful fisherman had been here in the night.

We quickly entered the water to look for the *pirogue*, which we had taken the precaution to sink. Only her two tips stood above the surface like pebbles. If we hadn't known she was there we should never have seen her. In a few seconds she was afloat, still half full of water. We climbed aboard, half of us paddling and the rest baling out. At last we reached the *Fat-el-Rahman*, whose mast stood out against the already paling sky. We unfurled the sail which we had left rolled round the lateen yard so that we could be off at very short notice. When finally dawn flamed in the sky we were two or three miles from land.

The hills we had just left, these black cones dimly seen through the darkness, these gloomy ravines where we had lived such anxious hours, all this stretch of country which our terrors had peopled with hostile shadows—all this became suddenly rosy and smiling in the glory of the rising sun, and when the big red sun appeared over the purple plateaux of Asia, spreading a shining veil over all nature, the anguish vanished from our thoughts as if it had never been, leaving us joyous and care-free.

Djebeli had decided to remain ashore, first because his presence on the *boutre* was superfluous and even dangerous if it were known, but also because he wanted to be at Suez as rapidly as possible, to find out, from one of his numerous friends in native circles, why the patrols had been doubled.

The wind blew from the north as always in this gulf. We had to tack, but I had never so enjoyed a tedious piece of navigation. Now we were really free from all care. I didn't care if misfortune did overtake the caravan; I should have sacrificed the rest of my money with a light heart; the fact of having succeeded was reward enough, and the sum I had already received was nearly double the small capital with which I had set out. Instead of going back and anchoring in the roads I went on to the little harbour at Old Suez, at the end of the tortuous channel that wound across the lagoons to the left of the canal. The tide was rising and bore us in rapidly. The agency of the Messageries Maritimes was on the quay of this old harbour, to which nowadays only an occasional *boutre* came. The *Helen*, the only steamer which ever deigned to put in here, was drowsing with banked fires opposite the entrance.

There we were within the customs' waters, and when the customs officer who was on duty perceived us he came on board and had a conscientious rummage. I was delighted to have him poke his nose into every corner. I could not wait till evening before seeing Stavro. The sooner I told him about the night's adventures the better; he was the only man who could draw a plausible conclusion from these happenings. He was at home, for he had seen my *boutre* and was expecting a visit from me.

'You have had unheard-of luck,' he said to me. 'I spent a ghastly night for I thought all was up with you. I had sent a man to warn you of the danger and tell you not to go, but you had already set sail and I couldn't lay hands on Djebeli. A fisherman has been arrested with your two *okes* of hashish in his possession. To save himself he invented a long story about a caravan coming from Syria, and if you had been captured on the Asiatic coast your goose was cooked.

'For my part, I had some of my agents report that they had seen a herd of camels beside Ras Sudr. This fixed the attention of the police on this shore of the gulf, but once the police is alarmed it is like setting fire to a heap of straw; everything burns. Encouraged by the hope of making a profitable capture the frontier guards on the African coast also showed abnormal zeal, and that was why I feared for you.'

At this moment there came a knock at the door. Stavro's face became the colour of paper. I was surprised to see how jumpy this colossal creature was. We held our breath, waiting for the visitor to knock again, but the minutes passed without anything happening; so it was one of the band.

The sister-in-law went and opened the door. It was Djebeli. Stavro's hands were trembling slightly and beads of perspiration stood on his brow. His eyes were two points of interrogation. Djebeli saluted, unruffled as ever.

'Well, what is it? Speak, for heaven's sake.'

'Everything's all right, at least things might have been much worse.'

'So there is something?'

'Yes, the *pirogue* was seen yesterday, but the guards did not recognize it. They called it a *boutre*, probably to excuse their flight. This morning, an officer and twenty men went to examine the spot where the alleged *boutre* had been seen.'

Djebeli stopped and searched in his pockets for a cigarette.

'Well then? Go on, for heaven's sake,' implored Stavro, white as a sheet.

Djebeli cast him an ironic glance from his solitary eye, which seemed to laugh in the reflection of the candle at whose flame he was lighting his cigarette. Stavro clenched his fists as if he could hardly refrain from striking him.

'Well,' continued Djebeli tranquilly, 'they found the hearth. Though the ashes were cold, it was obvious that there had been a fire there only the previous night. This detail put the guards out of countenance. They were immediately asked how it was they had not noticed this fire. The details they had invented to justify their cowardly flight seemed ridiculous. This cooking in the open air, those footprints innocently left on the sand, not the slightest trace of camels, everything showed that the nocturnal visitors had been merely fishermen who had landed there to warm themselves and heat their supper while waiting till it should be time to lift their lines. The officer was furious, and condemned the guards to a week's imprisonment to teach them to run away from fishermen.'

As Djebeli spoke, Stavro's face cleared; he seemed to be breathing in new life. The portrait of the old fighter hanging on the wall above his rifle seemed to look down pityingly on this colossal son of his, who hid such a timorous soul in his huge body. Fire brings forth ashes, as the Arabs say. Stavro was quite reassured now and became his normal self. He reassumed his imposing air and his grey eyes had once more their eagle gleam. He escorted me to the door, rubbing his hands together gleefully. We made an appointment for the morrow in Cairo, when I should receive the rest of my money, if all went well.

CHAPTER XXXV

THE JEWS

I WAS NOW at ease and could leave my *boutre* without being haunted by fears of disaster. The same evening I set out for Alexandria. I wanted to see Jacques Schouchana (see *Secrets of the Red Sea*) and if possible sell him the pearls I had left. Last time I had seen him at Massawa he had given me his brothers' address.

When I reached Alexandria I took one of these old horse-cabs at the station, and drove to it. It was a very fine jeweller's shop in the Rue Sesostris, in the richest part of the town. I was received with great cordiality, after the Jewish fashion. Jacques had spoken about me, and immediately they called me Mr. Henri and treated me as an old friend.

'Yes, Jacques is here. He arrived from Massawa ten days ago. He will be here presently, but it is only nine o'clock yet; that's a little early for him. Did you bring any pearls?'

They lost no time in getting down to brass tacks. I showed all I had left. They made disparaging faces and began bargaining discreetly, as was seemly with a friend.

'But I'm not at all anxious to sell them,' I said; 'I'm simply showing you them in order to have your opinion about them.'

'You're wrong, upon my word, you're wrong. Look what Jacques brought with him.'

And he opened a safe and showed me some magnificent pearls. Naturally mine looked very measly by contrast.

'Well,' went on the brother, 'what do you think he paid for these?'

And he named a ridiculously small sum. I was completely crushed.

249

'Pearls are getting cheaper every day,' he went on after a moment's silence; 'diamonds are what are in demand. Look, I have a splendid stone here. I got it cheap—it was left as security for a loan. You ought to take it and get rid of your pearls, that would be a good spec. for you.'

I felt as a mutton-bone overrun by ants must feel, that I should be cleaned to the last fragment of meat. Luckily, Jacques arrived. A messenger had gone to tell him I was here. He had got up in my honour and greeted me affectionately, saying 'thou' to show what an old friend he was. I was very pleased to see him again, for he was a frank, loyal, and good fellow, honest as the day, and he recalled the good old days when I had started pearl fishing. And then we had an inexhaustible subject of conversation in the death of Saïd Ali, for at this time I had not yet solved that mystery. (See *Secrets of the Red Sea*.) I could not think of lying to him, so told him frankly what had brought me to Egypt. He looked absolutely terrified; his eyes started out of his head.

'Four hundred *okes*? But that is an enormous quantity. How much did you get the *oke*?'

'Three pounds.'

'What, you have been robbed. Hashish is worth more than thirty pounds just now. Ah, if you had only come to me; you must have fallen into most unscrupulous hands.'

I explained that in the deal I had made all the risks of smuggling had been eliminated as well as all the tiresome formalities and heavy dues of the customs.

'But there's no danger whatever,' he exclaimed; 'at least for those who are not under suspicion, for those who have a genuine profession, as I do, and a clean reputation.'

'What, Jacques, you would have dared?'

'Oh, you don't know me. I look like a softy; you are always poking fun at my ties and my perfumes, but

I'm bold enough, yes, yes, you needn't laugh, I'm bold enough.'

'I'm sure you are, Jacques,' I answered, smiling, 'but have you ever tried to bring hashish into Egypt?'

'No, never, but nothing could be simpler. I can go anywhere with my suit-case in my hand without any one thinking of asking what it contains.'

'Yes, but—the customs?'

'Oh, at Suez you can land easily outside the customs limits. I should be there with my valise, and there you are. Just think, thirty pounds; what a marvellous deal!'

I was greatly astonished to see that this soft-living, rather timorous Jew had a taste for adventure and risk. But he did not realize what such an adventure involved. He saw himself as a cinema hero. And I'm sure if I had had hashish there he would have run all over Egypt with his suitcase, so taken up with his romantic role that he would probably have done wonders. I smiled at the thought, but all the same I had often made use of the same expedient to spur on my failing courage. One can face danger more bravely if one imagines an audience hangs breathless on one's every movement. Sancho and Don Quixote, all the time. So I needn't have laughed at Jacques.

'Everybody in Egypt dreams of making money by smuggling hashish,' went on Jacques.

'Yes, but there's a dangerous precipice between dream and reality.'

I listened with amusement while he expounded his ideas on how to smuggle hashish. After all, why not leave him his illusions? They did not harm anybody. We decided to go out for a walk.

'Where shall we go?' asked Jacques.

'First of all I must buy some clothes; I'm rather a scarecrow in this khaki suit.'

'I know the very thing for you. We'll go to my brother Abraham's. He has a ready-made clothes shop.'

So we went to this other brother's. He was of the same type, but older, and pallid with living in the darkness of his shop. He declared that he could do nothing for me in this shop, as here he had only very cheap articles which, alas, were often sold at a loss. And he sighed despairingly.

'Come with me,' he added briskly; 'I'll soon get you what you want.'

He put on his hat and we set off across a veritable ghetto. We stopped for a moment at his other shop where he sold second-hand clothes. Gorgeous uniforms, evening clothes, fur-lined overcoats, hung side by side, and from among them crept out the manager, a little round-backed Jew with damp hands. Abraham said a few words to him and we went on our way.

At last we reached our destination, a third shop belonging to Abraham. There were only Jews in this quarter; every street was full of them, and every single one seemed to know Abraham. We had to go into several shops, shake hands, ask the family news, have a coffee, and so on. Naturally, since Jacques said 'thou' to me and Abraham treated me as an old friend, everybody thought I was a Jew too, and this allowed me to see the little Jewish shop-keepers in their true colours. Anyhow, I had always had a secret sympathy for this race, eternally oppressed, docile and meek, who are called cowards because they have often the courage to appear to be afraid. From this inside view I was now getting I saw that this humble appearance often covered an unbelievable tenacity and ferocity when it was a question of money.

The moneylender would patiently bring about the ruin of a debtor until it was safe for him to pounce. He would take the jewels off a corpse to pay himself for an unsettled debt. He would steal from the orphan if he legally could. And all this with the calm implacability of an automaton. Yet the same Jew would work himself to death to educate his children, follow the most humiliating occupations in order to keep his old parents, or even distant relatives, and he would be most charitable to a fellow-Jew in distress. In them slumbers a mysticism old as the race and changeless as time. When by some chance their fierce commercial instinct is deviated from its ordinary aim, then this mysticism comes to the surface and accomplishes wonderful things. This Jewish humility, this resignation of a persecuted race, would appear to be a sort of hoarding of the genius of the race so that it can be used for these sublime exceptions, for prophets and great revolutionaries.

CHAPTER XXXVI

HOW HISTORY IS WRITTEN

JACQUES CAME to the station to see me off. We spoke of Massawa, and always the conversation came back to the shipwreck in which Zanni had disappeared, the strange death of old Saïd Ali, and the miraculous saving of his treasures.

'Ah, all years aren't the same,' sighed Jacques. 'I have just spent two absolutely wasted months shut up in Massawa. I couldn't go to the Dahlak Islands as I generally do; simply couldn't get a permit. So all the Arab brokers, free to go where they liked, snapped up wonderful bargains under my nose.'

'But why couldn't you get a permit? You never had any trouble in previous years. The governor is generally very obliging towards foreigners.'

'It wasn't his fault; indeed he was very sorry he had to refuse me. It is a new military regulation. It appears that there was an attempt at a Turkish invasion of Eritrea at Takalaï, a place on the coast a little to the north of Massawa. The colony was under arms, two battle cruisers were sent from Italy, and a regiment with artillery was stationed at Takalaï since it was acknowledged that this was a vulnerable point.'

'At Takalaï, did you say? What was the date of this alleged invasion?'

'It happened a little over a month ago, but thanks to the courage shown by the native soldiers it didn't succeed. A corporal nearly captured a disguised Turkish officer, who was probably Saïd Pasha himself. A rope-soled sandal was found, and the secret police discovered that the general is in the habit of wearing this rather unusual type of footwear when he is not in uniform. It was the same size as he wears, too. If this attempt had succeeded, Massawa would have been surprised and surrounded and all communications cut off.'

But I had subsided in a gale of inextinguishable laughter.

'Stop, stop, Jacques,' I cried; 'I was Saïd Pasha, and this famous sandal was one of my Catalan espadrilles. As for the Turkish squadron, it was simply my *boutre*.'

Jacques looked at me with dilated eyes; I could see he thought I had gone suddenly mad. I should have to explain the affair in detail, as otherwise he would never be able to reconcile what I had stated with these wild fictions of the Italian imagination, so I told him the story the reader already knows.

'All the same,' I said, 'I sent a letter from Kosseir to the Governor of Asmara, to let him know of the behaviour of this native, who had declared himself an askari of the Government, but who had no uniform to prove it, and that for this reason I had refused to obey his insolent orders. I'm surprised that that did not settle the whole affair.'

'Probably your letter arrived after my departure, and I knew nothing about it. But you were wrong to write; the affair has become very serious now, and has been mentioned in the newspapers. Take my advice and don't go back to Massawa, since you are to blame for this panic. I believe the Italians would show more indulgence now towards some one who really had tried to take their colony by force, than towards some one who came and said they had been tilting at windmills.'

'On the contrary,' I replied, 'I shall stop there. I have nothing on my conscience, after all, and if the Italians have made fools of themselves it's not my fault. Besides, all this is only supposition, and I think you take a very pessimistic view, considering how kind and obliging the authorities at Massawa have always shown themselves towards strangers. No, I really have no reason for avoiding the place, especially after writing that letter.'

'You are absolutely crazy. They will make you pay

for the whole ridiculous business. They are quite capable of having you shot just to teach you to make jokes at their expense and have the whole world laughing at their Government.'

'No, Jacques, you are letting your imagination run away with you. That would cover the army with shame without making it a whit less ridiculous. I think they will rather ask me to keep my mouth shut, for I'm sure my letter was kept secret.'

I left Jacques all upset, and he said good-bye to me with tears in his eyes, convinced he would never see me again.

CHAPTER XXXVII

A PAIR OF POLTROONS

I REACHED CAIRO at midnight. Gorgis was not on the platform waiting for me, but I thought this of no importance, since I knew his address. I went out of the station, but hardly had I given up my ticket when a young man put his hand on my shoulder. He had all the appearance and gestures of a plain-clothes policeman. He read this thought in my eyes, and smiled as he said:

'I came to meet you off the seven o'clock train; you were expected to dinner.'

These words reassured me, but all the same I remained on my guard, and to show this young man how cautious I was I said:

'But who are you? I don't have the pleasure of your acquaintance.'

'I am in the employment of Gorgis,' he answered, still smiling. 'He could not come to meet you, so told me to take you to your hotel. Stavro arrived at noon. We have had news from Omar; everything went off very well. But it is injudicious to go straight to his apartment, and that's why I came to meet you.'

This explanation showed me that this young man knew all about my affairs, and my distrust vanished. He amiably took hold of my suit-case, and said he knew me already, having seen me in the funeral undertaker's establishment. He was a young man of about twenty-six, dressed quietly; indeed, it was obvious that he tried to be as little noticeable as possible. Every item of his dress had been chosen so that the general effect should be absolutely ordinary and without originality, so that in any kind of crowd he would have passed unremarked. That was what had made me think he belonged to the police, for such individuals, invisible

257

in a crowd, have something odd about them when seen
alone and out of their usual surroundings, something
which causes them to be classed among those functionaries who are called in French slang 'saucepans'.
This youth's face, too, was unremarkable, a face one
would forget, a sort of average of all the faces of a
crowd. He spoke all European and Oriental languages.
He knew all the secret police of Cairo, Port Said, and
Alexandria, and pointed out several of them to me as
we went along. The carriage with the silent coachman
which I had already seen was waiting for us outside
the station, and took me to the hotel where I had already
stayed. The landlord welcomed me with a knowing
air. Stavro was there too, it seemed, but he was asleep,
for I heard snores coming from under his door.

Next morning the young man who had met me at
the station called for us and took us to the funeral
undertaker's shop. Gorgis was there sitting behind his
desk. He looked grey and worried, and his features
were drawn as if he had slept badly.

'So everything went off all right, it seems?' I asked.

'Great God, I hope so,' he replied in Italian, 'but I
have been waiting for Omar for an hour; he was to
come and confirm the news. He should have been here
long ago. Last night he came to see me at ten o'clock
to tell me of some uneasiness due to the movements
of the police, of which Michael had informed him.'
Michael was the young man I had taken for a detective
the night before. He had discreetly left us alone, and
was busy scratching spots of paint off the shop windows.
A boy wearing a long Egyptian *gandoura* placed cups
of Turkish coffee on one of the luxurious coffins laid
out for show in the entrance. I was not quite accustomed to this furniture yet.

'No, no,' said Gorgis, 'not there, I beg you. You
will make stains; take the table over there and put the
cups on it.'

While the boy was carrying out this order, Gorgis
went up to one of those glittering coffins, opened it

carelessly, chatting the while, and took out of it a tray
on which were caviar, rolls of fresh butter, toast, and
lemons. When this tray appeared, a superb Angora
cat which had been lying on a window-sill, rose, mewed,
arched her back, and sprang lightly to the ground, then
went, purring, to rub herself against her master's legs.

'Ha, ha, brigand; that's what you were waiting for,'
said Gorgis, stroking the cat; 'if I hadn't put it where
you couldn't get at it, you would have lunched before
me, as you did yesterday. Come, captain,' he added
to me, 'let us lunch. I was waiting for your arrival to
taste this caviare which arrived yesterday from the Sea
of Azov. It is a special fresh caviare which the captain
of a Russian steamer brings me every month.'

I need no second bidding to taste such delicacies.
Gorgis helped me as if he were ladling out porridge,
and advised me to eat it like that by the spoonful
without bread. It was pitiful, he said, to see people
making mean little sandwiches when they ate caviare.
He always ate at least a pound, so that he really got
the taste of the stuff, and then it looked rich and
impressive to do so. He gave a pleased smile when he
saw how taken aback I was at this gastronomic extrava-
gance. But suddenly he grew grave; Stavro had just
come in. He had left me at our hotel door to go and
see what he could find out.

He had a sinister air, and when Gorgis invited him
to join us, he replied in hollow tones:

'No, thank you, I'm not like you, I'm not light-
hearted enough to eat this morning.'

And with a weary gesture he put down his enormous
hat on a coffin and heaved a profound sigh. Gorgis
felt his throat tightening with apprehension, the
mouthful of caviare he had just smilingly carried to
his lips refused to go down. While Stavro was speaking
his face had become greenish and his features all
twisted. In a few seconds he had aged ten years. The
giant let himself fall heavily into a chair and explained
that an order had been given that no ship was to leave

the roads of Suez. Nobody knew the reason for this. Perhaps at this very hour Omar was already in prison. And if he were cleverly cross-examined and harassed with questions, goodness knew what he might not let out.

As he said these words, which fell on the air like a passing-bell's tolling, Stavro shot a secret glance and almost imperceptible wink at me. Michael continued to scrape paint, and his face bore a look of suppressed laughter. I realized that Stavro was pulling Gorgis' leg. He was taking a malicious pleasure in terrifying his wealthy partner and showing me what a coward he was when any danger threatened. Perhaps, too, he wanted to make me forget that he himself had acted just like Gorgis the day before, when Djebeli had stopped his narrative to light his cigarette at the candle burning before the icon.

In the twenty years these two men had worked together they had constantly staged these little comedies. Each time the other fell into the trap, and his partner felt very brave and superior. Stavro took a special delight in his victim's distress because of my presence.

A tall shadow crossed the threshold; it was Omar. He came in wrapped in his black cloth mantle, smiling, calm, and majestic as usual. As he passed in front of a neighbouring café he had motioned to the waiter to bring him a water pipe. He replaced his coral-beaded Mohammedan rosary in his silk girdle, saluted us and sat down, stretching out his beautiful hand immediately for his beloved pipe. Once he had got it going, he listened to Gorgis' anguished questions. His smile did not fade, he declared that Stavro's fears surprised him very much. A Bedouin had arrived during the night to tell him that the caravan had safely arrived at its destination. Certainly there had been a police alarm, but it had nothing to do with hashish. Gorgis mopped his streaming forehead, and began taking long breaths like a diver who had come up to the surface. His habitual air of self-possession returned, and he darted

a scornful glance at Stavro, the coward, who looked
meekly at the floor as if overcome with confusion, but
hid a smile under his heavy moustache.

The accounts had been prepared, and Gorgis handed
me a thick roll of bank-notes. I seated myself at his
big desk and counted them. Business was now over;
my venture had succeeded. I must now be thinking
of getting home, and decided to employ these last few
hours in making a few necessary purchases. Gorgis
lent me the faithful Michael as guide. This young man
spoke French very fluently, and we had taken to each
other at once.

'Did you notice,' he said laughing, 'how these two
cowards spend their time frightening each other? It's
always the same. If it weren't for me goodness knows
what awful bloomers they would have made owing to
their ridiculous terror at every shadow.'

'Have you known Gorgis long?' I asked.

'He brought me up, in a way, and now he takes
advantage of the fact to exploit me. What do you think
he pays me? Ten pounds a month and a small present
of forty or fifty pounds occasionally when he has put
through a deal on which he makes ten thousand.'

'Why do you stay, then?'

'Yes, I know I am a fool to stay, but where could I
go if I left him? I have no trade; all I have been taught
is to serve Gorgis' interests. I've never had time to
think of myself. Besides, my mother and sister are
dependent on me, and I can't expose them to the risk
of want if I didn't manage to get work elsewhere.
Anyhow, Gorgis is not a bad fellow—at heart he is fair
enough. And he has a very commanding personality.
If ever I open my mouth to grumble, he quells me
with one look. He is very good at making slaves of
people.'

He was a curious fellow, this young Hungarian;
intelligent, active, remarkably gifted as are so many
slaves, but without will-power; bound to his master
by a very complex sentiment, into which entered fear,

gratitude, some affection, and the bitter regret of his wasted life. The whole mixture gave a blind devotion.

This was Gorgis' great power. This ex-sailor, illiterate though he was, had this faculty of binding men to his service. They criticized him, they realized his faults and suffered from his egotism, but an indefinable charm caused them to love him without knowing why. Stavro felt like this about him, and I'm not sure that I didn't myself.

CHAPTER XXXVIII
THE MYSTERIOUS DRUG

I WANTED TO play my role of tourist conscientiously, so I went to see the Pyramids. What a disappointment they were to me; I thought that the majesty of the desert completely overwhelmed them. The only thing one might possibly admire is the stupendous human effort it must have been to build them, and this sort of admiration demands the mentality of a German tourist. The smallest hill which rises in the solitude of the desert is more grandiose than those geometrical volumes surrounded by cafés, photographers' booths, and imitation caravans, with black-coated clergymen perched on camels. The sphinx is lamentable. Nose in air and mouth wide open, it seems to be listening to the droning of the guide. A *Herr Doktor* from some obscure university north of the fiftieth parallel was writing postcards to his students on the monster's paw, while his family opened tins of sardines, dreaming dutifully of the forty centuries which contemplated them.

I fled in disgust, as if I had been present at some sacrilegious act, and suddenly I was homesick, terribly homesick for the real desert. I longed feverishly to be back on the deck of my ship, to be pacing those few square feet of wooden planks, which were sometimes burning and sometimes streaming with spray, but which were to me the magic carpet of the Arab legend, which had transported me to enchanted countries which never change, where I had tasted the joy of believing that time and death did not exist. They represented the sea, the wind, the virgin sand of the desert, the infinity of far-off skies in which wheel the numberless hosts of the stars. And nothing between me and all those things, nothing to diminish their grandeur and interrupt the dream in which I become one with them.

With my mind full of such visions, I got into the train for Suez. It was full of tobacco smoke, lit by pallid lamps, and full of unknown people with dreary faces, who read newspapers, played cards, discussed the market prices, or slept stupidly with open mouths. I took refuge in the corridor and thrust my head out into the darkness. The clamour of insects rose from the warm sand, into the calm air. But the blind rush of the train destroyed the serenity of the tropical night, raising a whistling wind which sang past my ears. The plumes of smoke from the engine, the clouds of dust we stirred up on our passage, and the lofty palms which rose between the dunes flitted across the sky like mad ghosts. At last we reached Suez. Soon I saw my *boutre* lying asleep in the roads. A familiar voice replied to my hail and the *pirogue* came towards me. I made prodigious efforts to get off next day. The consul informed me that the English could not allow me to fish for mother-of-pearl in the Gulf, alleging that some investigation must be made. All right, I wouldn't fish for mother-of-pearl. At six o'clock everything was ready at last. I had said good-bye to the consul, to Spiro, and to the agent of the Messageries Maritimes. I had my sailing papers in my pocket.

I had still time to take farewell of Stavro. I had to accept a last dinner in the room of the bark, the icon and the old rifle of the warrior chief. This time there was no reason to fight shy of the Samian wine, and its warmth lent an agreeable cordiality to this final *tête-à-tête*.

'When will you be back, that's the important question?' asked Stavro.

'Heaven alone can tell, since Gorgis informs me that the new Greek Government are banning the cultivation of hemp.'

'Yes, I know; it will probably be enforced, since it is the English who have brought about this decision. This law will ruin a considerable number of people in spite of the indemnities paid, and I'm afraid will lead to trouble. It's a sure thing that it isn't the Greek Government which is paying these indemnities. It is too poor in the first place, and, like all governments, most unwilling to shell out money.'

'That's a funny thing,' I replied. 'If the English are sowing drachmae in Greece, it is probably in order to reap pounds sterling elsewhere. They have probably some interest in preventing your country from producing hashish. The question of morality is only the classic excuse, most valuable as an argument, since it is unanswerable. These high principles did not prevent the English from methodically poisoning a magnificent race, the Red Indians, with alcohol, in order to seize their country. The same clergymen who are to-day declaiming in America against the sale of intoxicating liquor, lavished the deadly fire-water on the natives, accompanied, it is true, by Bibles and sermons. Their bodies were killed in the name of the Great Nation, but their souls were saved in the name of the Lord, so John Citizen's conscience was clear. I'm only mentioning all this to indicate the importance which must be given to philanthropic movements on the part of governments. Anyhow, I don't blame the English for killing the Red Indians as they did. Since they had to be killed, it was preferable to do it painlessly by selling death by the glass. You see how natural it is to suspect that the English have a commercial interest in stopping the Greeks from growing hemp. Hashish must exist in one of their colonies.'

'You open my eyes,' said Stavro; 'two or three times already my native agents have sent me samples of hashish they had bought from the crews of English ships.'

'Where had the ships come from?'

'From Bombay. I have been told that this product, which is much dearer than Greek hashish, is sold in India in special shops which have a licence.'

'Something like our monopoly of opium in Indo-China, very likely,' I replied. 'On the pretext of not depriving the native population of the opium to which they have been accustomed for centuries, we sell them the poison at a hundred times its value.'

'You may be right, for the sepoys in the barracks at Ismaïla smoke a sort of hashish which is regularly distributed to them every week. It would be interesting to study the question. You should go and find out, since you are on the way to India.'

'We'll see about that later on. Meantime, I'd be glad if you will keep me posted in any information you may get on the subject.'

To tell the truth, I wasn't over keen to mix myself up again in this business. To be successful in it, I was obliged to rub shoulders with people whose mentality was too different from mine, people who only thought of gain. It had been interesting to discover these circles, but now it held nothing new for me, so why recommence? This is how my thoughts ran, and what a greenhorn I was. I had not seen the hundredth part of all this underhand trafficking; I still had practically everything to learn about the stupendous secret organizations which controlled the smuggling of the drug in Egypt. Besides, though I did not know it, I had been sucked into the whirlpool. After the dangerous play and emotions of this struggle, it was going to be very difficult to settle down to humdrum coasting. To do this one has to be a wise old philosopher who has seen through the vanity of everything, but at this moment I was only thirty-eight.

CHAPTER XXXIX

WRECKAGE

THIS TIME it was good-bye to Suez and its customs officers and frontier guards. It was good-bye also to the terrible north wind which had eternally barred my route. It now became the kindest of following winds before which my *boutre* slid gaily along over the foaming water. Already the mountain of Ataka had faded into the darkness, and only the reflection of the lights of Suez was visible in the sky, every moment growing fainter and being replaced by the stars. The sea sang and chuckled under the stem which cut through the dancing water, seeming to bear me along in a crazy dance of joy. I listened to it with great happiness, and I am sure my men felt the same sentiment, although they could not analyse it, for not one of them thought of going to sleep; all in silence watched the sea and the stars wheeling in the sky.

But nothing endures, especially for the sailor who dares to rejoice in fine weather. The *boutre* began to pitch heavily, throwing up billows of foam, on the long southern swell which attacked her on the prow. It churned up the waves which bore us along into breakers which were sinister heralds of the bad weather into which we were running. Then the north wind slackened, blew fitfully, with less and less force, and died away. The silent swell passed under us in a dead calm, but the wind which had formed it was not long in arriving. The sails shook; we had to hoist home the sheet so as not to go too much off our route; a few preliminary gusts, then the south-east wind ·settled down to blow with all the violence the swell had led us to fear.

I had our mainsail changed for a smaller one, in view of bad weather, and it was not long in coming, for the wind was rapidly increasing to a gale. In my outward voyage I should gladly have sold my soul to the devil for forty-eight hours of this wind, but the wind had blown persistently from the north, and now that a north wind would suit me it blew from the opposite direction. It really did not matter very much, for my mission was over, and this weather was most exceptional in these parts, and could not last more than a day or two. But if the south-east winds are rare in the Gulf of Suez, when they do blow it is with the violence of a tempest. In less than an hour there was a raging sea, with huge, choppy waves. Luckily, less than twenty-four hours had passed since our departure when the storm struck us, and the sun was still shining in a clear sky. I had no illusions as to what the coming night would be, however; I knew that the tempest would be extremely violent. It was no good lying-to; I preferred to go and seek the shelter of the coast, behind Ras Abu Diraj. A single tack brought me to it.

It was a desolate and arid district, a luminous symphony of golden tones, but deprived of its only grandeur, that of solitude, by the telegraph wires which ran along the coast. This completely broke the spell, and I saw nothing but a monotonous and soulless country, which might have been carved out of concrete. The narrow beach which separated the sea from the rocky desert was edged with strange vegetation. Through my glasses I could make out heaps of the most varied flotsam and jetsam. What a find for us, since we were forced to remain there in idleness waiting for the turn of the wind. We were all on fire to go and examine these wonders more closely. The currents of the Gulf, helped by the north wind, seemed to have thrown up here everything that would float on water.

On the edge of the desert, in front of those arid mountains with their waterless ravines, in this dried-up world so indifferent to life, these poor relics might have stood for the sad image of the fate in store for